EARLY PRAISE FOR *NO LIMITS BUT THE SKY*

"You can't spend absolutely every day in the mountains (at least at my age). So for the days when you sit by the fire, you need this book—especially if you have a spot in your heart reserved for the peaks of the great Northeast!"

—Bill McKibben, author of *Wandering Home*

"*No Limits But the Sky* is a treasure. This collection of stories from over a century of mountain adventures captures the richness of the climbing life and the wild and varied lineage of all who wander out into the hills."

—Sarah Garlick, climber and award-winning science and nature writer

"*No Limits But the Sky* takes the reader on a trek through more than a century of *Appalachia*, with authors ranging from world-renowned to little-known. All share a passion for mountains and an unquenchable thirst for adventure. Locales vary from mighty K2 to modest Mount Crescent—the scale of the peaks varies, but the spirit of the authors is invariably high."

—Peter Crane, Curator, Mount Washington Observatory

"If you share my passion for mountain adventure, *No Limits But the Sky* is a must-read. This is mountain writing at its absolute best."

—Mark Synnott, AMGA-certified mountain guide,
founder of Synnott Mountain Guides,
author of *Baffin Island: Climbing, Trekking, and Skiing*

No Limits But the Sky

NO LIMITS
BUT THE SKY

The Best Mountaineering Stories
From *Appalachia* Journal

EDITED BY CHRISTINE WOODSIDE
Foreword by Michael Wejchert and David Roberts

Appalachian Mountain Club Books
Boston, Massachusetts

AMC is a nonprofit organization, and sales of AMC Books fund our mission of protecting the Northeast outdoors. If you appreciate our efforts and would like to become a member or make a donation to AMC, visit outdoors.org, call 800-372-1758, or contact us at Appalachian Mountain Club, 5 Joy Street, Boston, MA 02108.

outdoors.org/publications/books

Front cover photograph © Jerry and Marcy Monkman, EcoPhotography.com
Cover design by Matthew Simmons, myselfincluded.com
Contains text adapted and abridged from articles previously published in *Appalachia* journal.
Detailed text and image credits may be found on page 251.

Library of Congress Cataloging-in-Publication Data
No limits but the sky : the best mountaineering stories from Appalachia journal / edited by Christine Woodside.
     pages cm
  ISBN 978-1-62842-021-0 (paperback) -- ISBN 1-62842-021-9 (paperback) 1.
Mountaineering--Anecdotes. 2. Mountaineers--Biography. 3. Mountaineering expeditions.
I. Woodside, Christine, 1959- editor of compilation. II. Appalachia (Appalachian Mountain Club : 1876)
  GV199.82.N6 2014
  796.522--dc23
                     2014017703

The paper used in this publication meets the minimum requirements of the American National Standard for Information Sciences-Permanence of Paper for Printed Library Materials, ANSI Z39.48-1984. ∞

Interior pages contain 30% post-consumer recycled fiber.
Cover contains 10% post-consumer recycled fiber.
Printed in the United States of America, using vegetable-based inks.

10 9 8 7 6 5 4 3 2 1   14 15 16 17 18 19

FSC
www.fsc.org
MIX
Paper from
responsible sources
FSC® C005010

CONTENTS

FOREWORD

Michael Wejchert and David Roberts

ONE OF THE JOYS OF *APPALACHIA* RESIDES IN ITS VARIETY. Nestled beside homely pieces about modest excursions in the White Mountains of New Hampshire are articles that narrate cutting-edge mountaineering deeds from around the globe. Alpine giants such as Fritz Wiessner and Bradford Washburn must be content to be wedged between lesser-known authors and less important accomplishments.

In a sense, given the longevity of *Appalachia* as a record of mountain adventure—the semiannual publication is 53 years older than the *American Alpine Journal*—this anthology serves to remind us of a more innocent age when Tuckerman Ravine still felt like wilderness and climbing Mount Adams in winter could be regarded as a heroic feat. In Great Britain, the early issues of *Peaks, Passes, and Glaciers* (the forerunner of the august *Alpine Journal*) abounded in equally unassuming pieces about equally modest excursions in the Alps.

Appalachia never intended to be the official record of breakthrough climbs, even in the Northeast. A landmark deed such as the solo first ascent of the Black Dike on Cannon Mountain by John Bouchard in 1971 went uncelebrated in its pages until it appeared in a retrospective many years later.[1]

---

[1] John Bouchard's ascent at age nineteen, using wooden ice axes, remains a very important milestone in the White Mountains. Apart from Jimmy Marshall and Robin Smith's climbs in Scotland, we cannot think of any ice climb in the world more difficult at the time. The story of his development into one of America's best alpinists was Arthurian: Bouchard was so young, dismissed by most of the famous ice climbers of his day as a liar (until he repeated the climb with Rick Wilcox, John Bragg, and Henry Barber). Laura Waterman was the first woman to climb the Black Dike, in 1975.—Editor

Throughout its history, instead, *Appalachia* has striven to define merit not in the mountaineering accomplishments of its writers but in the stories themselves. In that respect it has been successful, and the pieces in *No Limits But the Sky* have been chosen according to that criterion. How, at first glance, is hiking the Four Thousand Footers comparable to Wiessner's tragic retreat on K2? How can sitting out a storm in a stone hut during autumn on Mount Washington stand shoulder-to-shoulder with an all-out gale on Alaska's unclimbed Mount Crillon in potentially lethal conditions?

The authors in this compilation seem to understand this. George Whipple laments, in 1905, that Mount Washington's Great Gulf doesn't hold a candle to the Alps, nor can he be ranked with legendary climbers such as Edward Whymper. Eighty-five years later, Doug Mayer admits that his crawl down Mount Madison's Valley Way after breaking a leg pales next to epics like the one recounted in Joe Simpson's *Touching the Void.* So what is it, then, that brings this miscellany of pieces together in *No Limits But the Sky*?

Are deaths on Mount Washington or Katahdin less tragic than those on K2 or in the Canadian Rockies? Is the relief at finding shelter from a storm any less great at 4,000 feet than at 26,000? This anthology offers a generous sampling of all that mountains have to offer, from a simple hike in Franconia Notch to an alpine-style first ascent in the Himalaya.

One of the reassuring aspects of the accounts in *No Limits But the Sky* is the familial ties many pieces share. Jack Durrance, one of the key players in Fritz Wiessner's treatise on the 1939 K2 expedition, had pioneered the route on Devils Tower that Jan Conn and Jane Showacre quickly dispatched on the first all-female ascent (a feat as important for American women's climbing, arguably, as *Appalachia* editor Miriam Underhill's early ascents in the White Mountains and the Alps or Lynn Hill's incredible free ascent of Yosemite's Nose route).

In this anthology, the reader follows the evolutionary changes in American mountain climbing itself. It's a stretch to assume that Paul Simpson McElroy's nationalistic attempt on Kilimanjaro in 1932 lies in the same league as Todd Swain's near-miss on the Sword in southern Patagonia in 1988. Dorothy May Gardner's genial 1943 ramble on the San Francisco Peaks in Arizona can hardly compete with the solo Alaska exploits of the "Japanese Caribou," Masatoshi Kuriaki.

But ultimately what *No Limits But the Sky* conjures up is the ambience of the mountains. Perhaps what all the writers in the anthology could agree on

Wearing hats and suit jackets, roped climbers forged across a crevasse, probably in the Alps around 1920.

is the importance of feeling the sun and wind on one's face, the relief after a long day's outing completed, the joy of a summit, the agony over a lost friend. These, after all, far outweigh the names, heights, and locations of the piles of rock and snow on which we climb. In our purest moments, we forget the significance of our climbs and simply push onward, only *climbing*, no matter what form it takes. This collection of articles from the past 137 years invokes, in the end, the range of moods and experiences that the great British Everest veteran Frank Smythe, in a deliberate understatement, called "the Spirit of the Hills."

In 2014, MICHAEL WEJCHERT's essay, "*Epigoni,* Revisited," about an attempt on Mount Deborah, won the Waterman Fund essay contest that *Appalachia* cosponsors. He works on the Appalachian Mountain Club's construction crew and as a climbing guide for International Mountain Climbing School in North Conway, New Hampshire. Both jobs keep him outside all day and well equipped to take annual trips to Alaska and South America, where he attempts to climb remote mountains with varying degrees of success.

DAVID ROBERTS of Watertown, Massachusetts, has pioneered climbing routes in North America since the 1960s. He won the Prix Méditerranée and the grand prize at the Banff Mountain Book Festival. He is the author or co-author of *No Shortcuts to the Top, Finding Everett Reuss, K2, Mountain of My Fear,* and *Deborah: A Wilderness Narrative.* Roberts's first ascents include the Wickersham Wall on Mount McKinley, the West Rib of Mount Huntington, climbing in the Western Brooks Range and the Kichatna Spires, and the East Face of Mount Dickey.

INTRODUCTION: MOMENTS OF DECISION

Christine Woodside

*T*HE FIRST MEMBERS OF THE APPALACHIAN MOUNTAIN Club were professors and lawyers. They analyzed their adventures from day one, meeting in Boston to read their papers. They recounted miles they covered, gear they chose, and the weather they faced. In telling those stories they also considered the emotional profits those joys and trials carried. And almost the second thing those early AMC members did was to publish a journal with these stories in them. The phrase on *Appalachia*'s title page, "America's Longest-Running Journal of Mountaineering & Conservation," dates to 1876, although we did not use that slogan until 1978, when we began to appreciate its longevity.

If the club were to survey today's *Appalachia* readers, it might find that a minority climb cliffs or unnamed routes with ropes and carabiners. Most of their shoe soles maintain contact with rock. But they'd also find that most of them love big adventure and lap up stories of first ascents and stormy scrambles because those trials are relevant to even the smallest of their own adventures. Even a ten-year-old boy counting toads as he gallops two miles pushes himself. A mountain climb's difficulty measures as large as the limits of its particular climber.

Most great mountain narratives come from the armchair. After the fact. They might start with the report of record, just saying where the participants went and what they did, for the history books. When it was both the journal of AMC and the official organ of the American Alpine Club, *Appalachia* used to print those kinds of reports. But in 1929, when the AAC formed its own journal, *Appalachia* found itself freed of the responsibilities of publishing complete high-altitude records. The change seemed a loss at the time, but in retrospect, this was *good*. It made the journal—like the reflective and insightful pieces of which it was now composed—more introspective and philosophical about what exploration means. It made our journal more literary.

We call this anthology *No Limits But the Sky* after an oft-quoted phrase by Miguel de Cervantes Saavedra (1547–1616) in Chapter 3 of *Don Quixote*. The Spanish reads, "*Tenia por limite el cielo.*" Cervantes's proverbial ideas in various English translations form such a solid foundation (Shakespeare sometimes copied him) that we freely admit to the possibility that we have found our own meaning in this line. But we do so with great respect for a writer who in the early seventeenth century outlined a physical quest in a way that still speaks to us in the early twenty-first century.

In the dichotomy our journal embodies—that is, most of our readers are not technical climbers, but all of them think and care deeply about big adventure—lies the beauty, we think, of our mountaineering writing.

———————————

In the 25 essays here, you will find a mixture of technical understanding, emotion, and the sense of humor that carry trekkers through difficult and sometimes life-threatening predicaments. Even in the late 1800s, our writers made deeper points within the action. Every haul over wet rock, and every ford through a melting torrent, rode on crucial decisions they made. Should they turn back? Should they go on ahead? They weighed practicalities—weather, fatigue, approaching darkness, food or lack thereof, and even society's disdain—against their addiction to getting somewhere. Because they puzzled over these decisions, and then wrote about them, they held up for examination their obsessions with exploring the high country. Clearly, something had a grip on them. We readers feel it, too, and wonder what it is about the mountains that has pushed us headlong into our deepest doubts and fears and why overcoming those doubts and fears matters so much. Maybe we'll never have that answer, but we do know it is an important question we who love adventure share.

In the first essay, published in 1877, a couple realize they have run short on time during their late-afternoon slog over exploding spring streams to look at snow arches in Huntington Ravine. The choices are to descend through

Charles E. Fay, with long beard and cup and seated atop Canada's snowy Mount Gordon, edited *Appalachia* for forty years. He established the tone that grew from an intellectual's zeal for adventure. He expanded the club's and the journal's focus when he pushed for expeditions to Colorado and the Canadian Rockies.

the woods and get stuck in the dark, or to climb through a brewing storm to the exposed summit of Mount Washington, where the Tip-Top House, a hotel, was then operating. "At last he broke the silence," wrote M. F. Whitman. "'To return is impossible; our only hope is to reach the top. Are you equal to it?' With no conception of the further difficulties before us, but reading the necessity from the tone and look of my companion, I answered, 'I think I am,' and without delay we started." This scramble up the Rock Pile was novel just for the fact that they had done it at all—because so few had at the time—but also for the decisions made and the style with which this brush with catastrophe is told. Of course, because we are reading the story, we realize that they didn't die—but we know that they're in for some hell.

As too many well know, the choices made don't always play into the cause or effect of accidents in the wilderness. In "The Casualty on Mount Lefroy," first published in 1896, Charles E. Fay wrote what might have been among the first of the genre of climbing accident elegies. Philip Stanley Abbot, who

In the late 1800s women, like men, climbed in their everyday clothing. Here, a woman traverses a plateau, probably in the Alps.

also had written jauntily of his climbing exploits in the journal's pages, fell to his death that year after attempting a tricky technical climb on a 75-foot cliff near the top of Mount Lefroy in the Canadian Rockies. Fay's utter sadness at Abbot's death, but conviction that his fall was due to fate and not any serious mistake on Abbot's part, poured onto the pages in his piece: "Caution governed every movement, indeed as it always did when Abbot was at the fore."

Fay's mark on the journal is visible in more than this single article: as *Appalachia*'s longest-tenured and possibly most important editor, Fay was involved from the very beginning and edited the journal from its second volume in 1879 until 1919. He established a format that in many ways remains unchanged. I credit Fay for the voice most of our writers share, one that comes from a zeal for climbing. He took many trips to remote and unclimbed areas, wrote about many of them, and philosophized about the value of adventure in the industrializing world. But Fay had not himself been a technical climber when he started editing the journal. He began as "a spry and enduring walker with his beard looking much like Balanchine made up as Don Quixote," wrote longtime Alpina department editor Jeffery Parrette (in his two-part essay, "Appalachia as a Mountaineering Journal").[2] Fay climbed often in the journal's "home range," New Hampshire's White Mountains, but he later pushed for expeditions to Colorado and the Canadian Rockies, expanding the journal's focus along with that of the club's members.

This broader horizon and a far more dispassionate grasp of climbing's multifaceted risks showed in an essay more than a century later. Jonathan Waterman described the risks of the terrain and of climbing with mere acquaintances on the formidable Thelay Sagar in the late 1970s: "We were probably the most diverse lot of mountaineers ever assembled in India. . . . The ice, though moderately angled, made us feel like we were climbing vertical waterfalls, 60-pound loads slowing us beneath seracs that could roar down the couloir and engulf us. There was no escape from the game we were playing, no refuge in daydreaming, no rests anywhere."

We all know the feeling that washes over us when we've gotten into the mountains a little too deep and begin shuffling through the files of our logy brains searching for the reason we went at all. Brad Washburn addressed that riddle in his 1934 story ("The Attack on Crillon"). "The immediate reaction to our desperate struggles, in 1932, with Mount Crillon and its August storms was that none of us ever wanted to see Alaska again as long as he lived," he wrote. "But then the pictures were developed and the movies run through, and by the end of six weeks we had forgotten all our hardships and were raving in superlatives to all our friends about the unbelievable ski slopes, the sunsets, the flowers, and the big banquets of fresh heather-fed grouse." So their next attempt on Crillon began.

---

[2] *Appalachia* 50, no. 3 (1995).

Adventurers of all levels often call themselves crazy, but in truth, they mean that they imperil themselves at times. When they do, they gain much more than they risk. When women took such gambles, they looked kooky, sometimes, but not in *Appalachia*'s world. A considerable tribe of females has belonged to the AMC and written for the journal from its first days; they are well represented here. These women never approached their explorations with a self-conscious sense of being female, though they sometimes noted wryly that they'd encountered men who doubted their climbing abilities. Jan Conn opens her 1952 essay, "Manless Ascent of Devils Tower," with her moment of decision: "A brawny Minnesotan turned to Herb and asked, 'How does it work? Do you climb up to a ledge somewhere and then haul her up?' Herb's careful explanation was lost to me as I fumed inwardly at the stupidity of the human race and the quirk of fate which made me look like a pudgy schoolgirl instead of a tall, strapping Amazon." The deeper reason she climbed, of course, was the same one pushing every one of them: that she relished the challenge. She came alive in the mountains.

The best climbers never brag. They live with humility, and they respect the sport of adventures large and small. Climber Miriam O'Brien Underhill, who made a reputation for herself in the Alps and the western United States, started writing for the journal in the 1920s and edited it from 1956–1961 and in 1968. We include here her story about the "sporting" game she invented closer to home—climbing the Four Thousand Footers in the White Mountains in winter. A friend fell deep into a "spruce trap":

> *Then there was the time when Ken Turner, on falling into a hole, stretched his arms up above his head. All we could see was just the fingertips of two pairs of mittens waving for help. And a faint voice from faraway said, "Get me out of here, it's cold." Of course, you understand, pictures always come first in cases like these.*

Appalachia editors have long been climbers and explorers, and this allowed them to solicit stories that would make history. Underhill was a friend of high-altitude legend Fritz H. Wiessner, whose reputation had taken a hit after a failed K2 expedition in 1939, in which American Dudley M. Wolfe and three Sherpa guides perished. Underhill was able to persuade Wiessner to tell his side of the story in *Appalachia,* offering another chapter to the history of K2 climbs.

Adventurers know that the other side of growth is risk and loss. Michael Lanza describes a sudden rock fall on a Katahdin cliff that killed a friend and changed Lanza's attitude forever. Douglass Teschner and six others narrate a story of recovering a body from the slopes of Mount Washington in 1984. Dog-sled tour driver Blair Braverman risks her safety on an Alaskan glacier to protect human remains that her passenger had scattered in a place that would be plowed up. Japanese climber Masatoshi Kuriaki tells how he stayed alive on weeks-long solo climbs in the Alaska Range in winter. Christopher Johnson's push onto Frankenstein Cliff is no less dramatic because for him he must overcome his own fears that yawned as wide as any giant crevasse anywhere.

Through AMC, men and women of all educational levels, in most professions, and of all ages, come together in the mountains. These are not what I call "golly gee wow" adventure stories. All of these stories form around deeper revelations that erupt within the writer's mind usually after returning from the mountains. That's what this collection is all about: what adventure really does; what pushing yourself really means. And that you don't usually know what pushing yourself means until after you've tried.

A Note to the Reader

I have edited the articles for clarity, consistency, and length. I have added footnotes to clarify some points. In some cases, the author's original footnotes do that job. The accompanying photographs are as historically accurate as possible. In some cases, we were able to find images of the adventures described, but when we weren't, we explain that in the captions. We thank all of the writers whose adventures have come to life again here.

A CLIMB THROUGH TUCKERMAN RAVINE

M.F. Whitman

1877

Addressing herself to the hardy members of the one-year-old Appalachian Mountain Club, the young woman whose article below appeared in the third issue of Appalachia *showed the lighthearted toughness characteristic of the late-nineteenth-century mountain climbing boom. Women, part of the AMC from the beginning, hiked alongside men in their long skirts and did not think anything of it. On the mountain path, they made decisions together—at least, in this nerve-wracking near-disaster, they did.*

Of course, the word "hike" is a modern one that Whitman and her contemporaries never used. They would "tramp," "ramble," and sometimes "flounder." But even floundering they did almost with tongues in cheeks. The joke was always on them, unless it was on those greenhorn tourists they aimed to avoid. Whitman pointed out that she and her cohort felt very different from a typical tourist, relishing discomfort but remaining levelheaded when caught in a storm at treeline on Mount Washington. Up on the ridge, they knew the Tip-Top House, a hotel, sheltered guests from the cruel weather. The situation in which they found themselves reads like something out of the journal's Accidents report, if it had had such a report back then. What would an Accidents editor have thought of the fact that they carried only "two hard crackers and a very small pocket flask with not more than a spoonful of brandy," as they stood at treeline near dusk with the storm opening up, "wet to the skin and shaking with cold"?

THE RETIRING ADDRESS OF OUR LATE PRESIDENT, IN its appeal to members of the club for reports of their mountain work and experiences, even though unscientific, has emboldened me to offer you an imperfect account of a personal adventure among the White Mountains.

The attendant circumstances would have prevented accurate measurements of heights or distances in meters and kilometers, the taking of angles, or drawing of profiles, even had I been able so to do. Leaving that kind of work to those who have shown themselves not only able but willing to do it, I will confine myself to my narrative.

Our party had been camping among the mountains several weeks, our plan of operations being to select a good campground in an interesting locality, and with that as a base to make excursions to the various points of attraction in the neighborhood, and, in good time, to move on to another spot. In the middle of August we had reached the Glen House and were in camp on the clearing close to the Peabody River.

From this point one of our excursions, as a matter of course, was to Crystal Cascade and Glen Ellis. The tramp down the Notch Road was delightful; light fleecy clouds slightly obscured the sun, and the freshness of Nature, clean-washed by last night's shower, made every breath a delight. Emerald Pool, with muddy waters stirred up by the rain, showed no right to its name; but Thompson's Falls had gained a beauty from the same source, and the swollen waters leaped and danced with bewitching loveliness.

The grandeur of Glen Ellis, with its unbroken leap, held us entranced so long that it was past noon when we found ourselves back at Crystal Cascade.

While discussing our lunch on the precipice above, just out of reach of the guidebook tourist, one of the gentlemen in our little party, who had often been our leader in exploration, challenged us to follow up the stream to the snow arches in Tuckerman Ravine. I had long desired to explore this region, and, feeling great confidence in his powers as well as my own for the work, without hesitation announced my readiness to start upon the instant. The rest not feeling inclined to join, we left our heavy wraps with them to be taken back to camp, and divested ourselves of all but the most necessary luggage, which little we carried slung to our belts.

As snow melts in Tuckerman Ravine below Mount Washington, it forms the famous Snow Arch—shown partially collapsed in this old photo of seven hikers one July. Seeing the arch motivated the author's spontaneous late-afternoon dash with a friend.

At a little past 2 o'clock we started, promising to be back in camp at dark with true mountain appetites for a hot supper.

As has been stated at former meetings of the club, the old path is considerably overgrown, and in many places the blazes are obscure, but we rambled leisurely along, every step a revelation of beauty such as is only seen in the deep recesses of the unbroken forest. Rank beds of fern covered with a veil of loveliness the scars left by trees uprooted by the winter's storms, the beautiful *Linnaea* in many places bordered the path, orchids, both old friends and new, seemed to spring up in every direction luring us from our way in our eager search for floral treasures, beds of starry *Oxalis* tempted us to stop and revel in their beauty, while our indolence was awakened by the dainty upholstery of soft green mosses on huge old logs. But amid all these temptations we did not lose sight of our object. It was a constant climb, but so filled with delight, so brimming with invigoration and excitement, that we heeded not the work or the passing hour.

Neither did we heed what afterward proved a serious matter for us.

As we came out of the forest upon the cleared space just above Hermit Lake, we observed for the first time that the sky had become clouded and a dense blackness was fast settling down upon the ravine. The solitude of the place was awe-inspiring, the walls of the ravine rising so steep in front and on either side, the unbroken forest behind, and below us a lake whose black stillness seemed weird and dreadful. No wind seemed to ruffle its inky surface though the clouds were scudding rapidly over our heads. But we did not tarry long; neither was there a word said about turning back. We were accustomed to accomplishing whatever we attempted and the casual glimpses of the snow beyond, apparently so near, but which we found so far, encouraged us on.

We rapidly passed through the low growth of wood just beyond the lake, reached the alders, and were soon utterly lost. To those who have never traveled that road it is impossible to convey any definite idea of its horrors; added to the natural difficulties of the way, we had hardly struck into the alders when the clouds shut in around us, drenching us to the skin and weighing down the bushes so as to obliterate all traces of previous footsteps.

We floundered about wildly, first on one side then on the other, the wet alders lashing us with icy boughs as if resenting our efforts to force a passage.

We were finally compelled to take to the middle of the stream. At first we jumped from rock to rock, trying to keep our feet from the waters fresh from beds of ice. But we soon plunged boldly in, wading as we might, knee-deep and sometimes deeper. Those who are familiar with that stream—or those streams, for it constantly divides—remember that it is filled with boulders, some of them completely blocking the way. It is not pleasant to boost another up a slippery rock in the face of an ice-cold cascade, but this I frequently did and was pulled up afterwards, having but one boast to make for my part of the work, that in no case did I require assistance where I had not also to give it.

Out of the alders the snow arches seem close at hand, but benumbed with cold, weighed down with wet clothes, and with clouds freighted with rain dashing in your face, the scramble over the rocks is neither easy nor agreeable. I fear our course from Hermit Lake to the arches could hardly be called a pleasure walk, neither can we boast of our walking time, but at last we accomplished it and stood sheltered beneath a roof of ice and snow.

Under some circumstances it might have seemed a shelter in fairyland, and we should have lingered long, as we have since done, in examining its wonders. Above, the vaulted roof studded with a million projecting points, from each of which ran a tiny stream or hung a glistening drop; beneath, the streams dancing over the rocks, and the whole interior lighted by that strange greenish light which penetrates the roof; before the entrance, within a radius of 100 yards, a fine procession of flowers, from the curiously folded *Veratrum* just piercing the frozen ground at the edge of the ice, to the gold-enrod of late summer.

But now it seemed rather an abode of demons. The Thousand Streams had become foaming torrents and rushed down the precipice above us and through the ice caverns with a deafening roar. The winds howled, the clouds thickened and thickened as the storm every moment increased, and the black walls of the ravine seemed to be shutting us in closer and closer.

For the first time I fully realized our situation. Night was coming on, we could hardly reach the woods before darkness would be upon us, the only implement we had for building a shelter was the knife I wore in my belt, our stock of matches had become wet, and dry wood was not to be found. Our provisions consisted of two hard crackers and a very small pocket flask, with not more than a spoonful of brandy, and to increase the danger we were wet to the skin and shaking with cold. All this passed rapidly through my mind, but what was in the mind of my companion I knew not, for little had been said during the last hour and I would not by a question indicate to him that I had the slightest anxiety. At last he broke the silence. "To return is impossible; our only hope is to reach the top. Are you equal to it?" With no conception of the further difficulties before us, but reading the necessity from the tone and look of my companion, I answered, "I think I am," and without delay we started.

We knew nothing of the path from the ravine to the top and had no time to explore. All this time the clouds had been falling lower and lower, covering the tops of the cliffs and even obscuring their sides. But as we stood facing down the ravine we discovered on our left what seemed to be the bed of a spring torrent or the track of a slide. We selected this for our attempt. Up, up we went, clinging to twigs of spruce and willow, or when those failed us, to the very grass and ferns; often on our hands and knees, sometimes pushing and pulling each other in turn; carefully, for every step sent loosened stones bounding down, warning us by the sound how far a misstep might send us; often finding our way blocked by some steep cliff or huge rock whose vertical face offered us no hold for foot or hand, then a climb around to one side and then the other to find a way, but always up, till, at last, a climb which I cannot now look back upon without a shudder and which later examination convinces me we never could have accomplished had not our haste prevented our looking back and the darkness obscured the danger of the way, was ended.

But our perils were not yet over. As soon as we were above the protecting walls of the ravine the storm struck us with its full force, compelling us to cling to each other for support. Night was hard upon us and the clouds so dense we could hardly see a dozen rods ahead.

There was no time to be lost, and scarcely stopping to take breath we turned in what we supposed to be the direction of the carriage road. Almost immediately we were plunged into that dense sea of scrub which lies between the road and the ravine on the northeasterly side. We floundered helplessly, the wind driving us and the scrub with its Briarean[3] arms dragging us in. At last we escaped and hastily retraced our steps to the edge of the ravine. Again we started—this time following around the head of the ravine and striking off in a northwesterly direction, as nearly as we could guess, for the old Crawford Bridle Path, with which we were somewhat familiar, having passed over it but a few days before.

Let me say in passing that I speak of directions and localities from information afterwards gained; at the time I had no idea of the direction of the summit, the road, or the path, and knew not the intention of my companion, for little was said; he took the lead and I followed blindly.

Occasionally fierce gusts laden with sleet would strike us, compelling us to crouch and cling to the very rocks.

Bareheaded and with skirts close reefed, on we went, not daring to stop a moment in our chilled condition, knowing the necessity of speed, yet realizing the dangers of bewilderment and that a single misstep on those icy

---

[3] She referred to Briareus, the fabled giant who had 100 arms or 100 hands, depending on the source.—Editor

rocks might end in disaster, hardly daring to hope we were steering in the right direction, when suddenly, as our courage was at its utmost tension, and our helplessness in the face of the furious elements, and our loneliness on that mountain waste more and more drear in the gathering blackness, had become almost appalling, the clouds parted for a moment, revealing directly ahead of us the unmistakable outline of the summit of Mount Monroe.

With a cheery "We are all right," on we went with renewed courage, changing our course as much as we dared toward the summit but with slower and more careful steps in the increasing darkness until at last we came to the ridge of stones apparently thrown up by human hands, over which we stumbled and found ourselves on the Bridle Path. We were not a moment too soon, for our strength was nearly exhausted, and it was now so dark we could hardly distinguish each other's faces.

For the first time I knew where we were, and though remembering the difficulties yet before us felt that we were safe. A sigh of relief was the only outward expression of feeling from a heart too grateful for speech.

Many of you are familiar with the last mile up the cone and will appreciate the difficulties of traveling it by night in the blackness of a furious storm. How we did it I cannot tell. I only remember that we felt every step of the way—sometimes on foot, often on hands and knees—and that somehow we reached the old corral, the end of the Bridle Path. Here sheltered slightly from the force of the storm we rested for a moment and I was at last allowed the spoonful of brandy, which to this time had remained untouched in our flask—my companion dryly remarking that Lizzie Bourne perished even nearer the summit than we were. We soon left the corral and slowly dragged ourselves over those huge boulders which surround the immediate summit, with nothing to guide us save the sense of feeling and the knowledge that we must go up.

So thick was the night that we struck the platform which surrounds the house before we discerned a gleam of light. We hesitated a moment with a realizing sense of our ludicrous appearance, but finally opened the door and stood—hatless, with remnants only of shoes, stockings, and skirts, before the wondering crowd which surrounded the blazing fire.

Our kind host came at once to our relief, furnished us with dry clothes, hot food and drinks; and after a telegram had relieved our anxious friends and stopped a party of men from the Glen House who had started out with guides and lanterns to search for us, we were soon oblivious of our perils in that slumber which only comes to mountain climbers.

In the early morning a mountain wagon and six black horses—detained overnight on the summit by the storm—took us, the only passengers, and, driving at a gallop we drew up in style in front of our camp to breakfast with our overjoyed friends.

At another time our whole party visited the ravine by the same route, cut a path through the alders to the snow arches, and built a camp at Hermit Lake. At this time our explorations were favored by fine weather, and we enjoyed wonderful views of that natural coliseum by moonlight, which only the pen of a Byron can fitly describe.

A CLIMB ON MOUNT ADAMS IN WINTER

Samuel H. Scudder

1884

Samuel Hubbard Scudder (1837–1911), an entomologist who spent his life in New England, has been credited with starting Appalachia journal. *As a student at Williams College, he joined the first hiking club in America—the Alpine Club of Williamstown, Massachusetts. At age 39, he was a charter member of the Appalachian Mountain Club when it formed in Boston in 1876. He was 47 when he wrote this narrative of a winter climb in the White Mountains of New Hampshire. The 2-degree-Fahrenheit temperature and horizontal winds only added to the excitement, he noted. This expedition sought to answer a question that might amaze us today: Can reasonably strong people wearing "snowshoe creepers" (metal plates with prongs affixed to the bottom of their snowshoes) reach the top of Mount Adams in the winter?*

*A*MONG THE APPALACHIANS WHO VISITED THE northern side of the White Mountains last January were four gentlemen whose main object in seeking this region at this time was to climb Mount Adams. For this purpose the Ravine House, in Randolph, had been chosen as the headquarters of the party—a snug little inn where every preparation for our comfort had been made by the forewarned proprietor.

We reached the hotel on January 23 at a little after 7 o'clock, after a starlight ride from Gorham in a five-seated sledge of rough boards, made for the occasion. We found warm cheer awaiting us. Supper dispatched, we spent the evening discussing how and when we should make our ascent, and adjusting snowshoes. In this, as in everything relating to a mountain tramp, Lowe, who had dropped in for the evening, proved an adept. For ordinary use on level ground it is customary to fasten the toe of the foot to the shoe by a simple thong, but for steep ascents and descents more care is necessary; and before we parted for the night all the old boots at the place had been sacrificed to the needs of the occasion. A bootleg severed from the foot served for a single shoe-pocket; the cut end was securely fastened by thongs to the shoe, and the top split at both ends to adjust it to the bundled foot thrust into the loose opening. The straps of the bootleg then served as a *point d'appui* to fasten the foot into the pocket by thongs passed through them, behind the heel and beneath and above the instep.

Although the evening was full of promise, the next morning dashed all our immediate hopes. For two days it snowed. But the time was by no means lost. We practiced on our snowshoes—altogether an unnecessary procedure, unless to give us confidence against the coming day—and found a second guide to join Watson and ourselves, an accident to Lowe preventing his venturing with us. We visited a blacksmith and procured "creepers,"[4] to use in case of need on the upper mountain, where snow should give place to ice; and so when Saturday the 26th arrived, with its bright sky, we were not only up at an early hour, but all the little vexatious delays of an early party, hurriedly planned, were provided against.

It seemed as if there never had been such a morning. The mountain summits were clear, and the steady wind blew a delicate horizontal cloud of snow from the summit of Adams, adding the charm of defiance to our intentions. The thermometer stood only 2 degrees Fahrenheit; but we could laugh at that. Not one of us but had doubled his heavy winter underclothing, and had, besides, a cardigan or leathern jacket, and a cap that would cover the ears. Even against the brisk wind blowing over the open fields to be crossed before the woods were reached we had no need of our ulsters and other heavy wraps, and carried them slung, as superfluous baggage, across our shoulders.

---

[4] Creepers were pronged metal plates affixed to the bottom of the snowshoes for traction.—Editor

Three men carry their ice axes and snowshoes above treeline on Mount Adams.

We were off by 7:30, four gentlemen and two guides, Watson and Hunt, who each carried a basket on his back, into which went our lunches, hatchets, photographic apparatus, and other paraphernalia, with a rope for possible use on icy slopes. Each of us carried a compass and a spirit flask—necessary appendages of the cautious pioneer. Our course lay at first over the Moose[5] meadows to the woods, in a direction at a slight angle with the stage road, so as to hit a logging road which struck the AMC path[6] at the logging camp about a kilometer and a half [about a mile] from its base. The road, as it entered the woods, crossed a little brook, Cold Stream, then completely buried in snow.

Up to this point walking in the open fields had been over more or less compacted snow, leaving in many places scarcely a trace of our steps. We had only the wind and frosty air to contend with; and as these were only exhilarating we dashed along with perhaps more vigor than discretion. As

---

[5] We are assuming that Scudder meant meadows near the Moose River.—Editor

[6] We are not sure which trail Scudder is referring to here, though it was likely in the vicinity of the current Appalachia Trailhead.—Editor

we entered the forest all was changed, and the rare beauty of the scene, quiet and pure, disturbed by no breath of the wind, enticed rather to moderation or even to frequent pauses. The fleecy snow sank at least six and eight inches under our broad latticed shoes; and as we passed along in Indian file we left behind us a trench-like path more than two feet wide, with an almost uniform flat bottom of packed snow.

Our course was pretty direct, and of an almost uniform, easy grade. We saw neither bird nor quadruped, but the tracks of the latter were abundant. They showed that rabbits, squirrels, and mice abounded; sable and fisher, especially the former, were not uncommon, and now and then a fox could be traced in the various footprints that crossed our path or were freely distributed around a fallen log. One fox had chosen the logging road; and for a long distance our broad, straight track obliterated most of his vacillating steps. We imagined his surprise when he next passed that way! We heard a few birds, but their tracks were rare; they feed from the taller trees. Once, higher up, we came across a pair of plump crossbills, fearless of our approach. But everywhere, excepting in the two or three cleared spots we passed—as at the logging camp—the snow was covered with the marks of fallen sticks and other fragments, and most of all with those of the fallen clusters of snowflakes.

Nothing was more beautiful than the fleeciness of the snow. It had not been visited by rain, no sun nor thaw had reached it; but it lay as it fell, compacted only by its own dry weight. Every fallen trunk was crowned by a white wall of more than double its own diameter, as may be faintly seen in the lower picture on the plate. Every stump or other projection of the soil became a round-topped cone with gracefully sloping sides. And this was not here and there, but everywhere; the forest was made up of it. But so light and delicate and fluffy was this pure covering of the earth that when the breeze stirred the treetops where the snow had collected in quiet times upon the boughs, and scattered their almost weightless clusters of snow crystals, these flocculent masses sank deep into the snow mantle, dotting it so completely with little pits that nowhere could an unbroken square rod be found. The breeze did not reach the surface of the ground. Every flake that passed the treetops remained where it fell. The charms of the forest in winter are indeed exquisite.

Just before reaching the logging camp, so completely buried in snow, one of the party, wearing lighter snowshoes than the rest, caught one shoe in a half-buried snag and broke the hoop at the crossbar. This delayed us a few minutes only, the guides quickly repairing it by aid of a young sapling and a bit of wire, which one of us had carried for an emergency. These provident people are almost glad of an emergency.

We reached the logging camp at 9:20, and now the regular path and a little steeper climbing were before us. We all took turns at the lead, the foremost man having the most to do in breaking the way. When he began to fag, he simply stepped aside, waited for the whole party to pass, and took his place at the rear, where keeping up with the rest was but as child's play, walking on the more solid floor of snow. This, however, still yielded to the tread, but only enough to remind one of walking on springing moss. In this way, alternating at the lead, we were able, except in the steepest portions, to keep steadily on with only brief rests. The signboards also became a great moral help. We knew just how much we had done—just how far ahead the camp, the ledge, and the summit, lay. We who were accustomed to the path knew where the steep places were and gloried at each conquest. Yet the path differed from that we had passed over in summer. Then the little inequalities in the surface required ever an exact and even strain of just the same set of muscles. Then in the steepest places there were roots and stones to give at least the semblance of a foothold, and allow one to halt midway to seek securer footing or a better purchase; now the slight passage of the toe over the crossbar of the snowshoe did not serve in the slightest degree to check the backward slide over the powdery snow, and here and there a slender twig the hand might seize (and this often treacherous to the touch) was the only aid one could secure. The one way to scale these portions of our way erect was to plant the shoe flatfooted on the snow and trust to luck that it would not slip back when the other foot essayed a forward step. Many a fall did we have, and many an ignominious backward slide, to the amusement of those behind. Our turn to laugh would come when the hindmost would reach a battleground, where the scrambling of the leaders had scattered all the looser snow, which helped a footing, and where the only method of procedure was a hand-and-knee scramble till some rigid tree might lend its aid. This lively climbing occurred when we had reached about the third kilometer sign [nearly two miles], and its end brought us at 10:45 to the Appalachian camp. It had taken us more than three hours to accomplish what in summer would have taken us less than two.

We stopped at the camp, of course. The snow had penetrated every corner, and the rabbits had been sunning themselves under its shelter. With a snowshoe for shovel we dug three feet to reach the fireplace, which has cheered so many a climber, and melting some snow we soon had hot tea to accompany sandwiches and doughnuts. Photographs were taken, axes thrown aside, and provisions buried against our return. Here, exposed to the wind, with the thermometer just at zero, we were still comfortable, so warmly were we clad, and we feasted on the outlook toward Jefferson Hill[7] with a new delight. But after a rest of three-quarters of an hour, one after another grew impatient to be moving, and the actual cold began to test our toughness. One of us was soon discovered to have a frozen nose, and snow was at once applied. It was but the forerunner of similar experiences. Sooner or later each of us was somewhere touched—cheek, nose, ear, or wrist—the point of least resistance. And no wonder; we looked like a caravan of Santa Clauses. The moisture of the breath froze not only upon our mustaches and beards, but on our eyelashes, eyebrows, hair, and all our clothing above the chest. Hoary-headed fellows were we, and we bore the crown of glory with pride. Not only had each individual hair become frosted, but a fringe of icicles of frozen breath surrounded our mouths; one, at least half an inch in diameter and an inch and a half long, hung from the upper lip of one of the party. Another had one eye nearly closed by the freezing together of the lashes.

At noon we started again and repeated our wild scrambling as soon as we struck the steeper parts of the path; but here, where the trees diminish in size, their aid is more easily obtained, and had we been as fresh as at the start we should have passed more rapidly over the ground. The snow too was less light, and signs of moisture and of wind began to appear. On the lee side of rocks, of trees, and of twigs projecting from the snow, we would find little crannies filled with icicles—geodes bristling with the most delicate ice crystals. Rabbit tracks were everywhere seen.

Before we reached this point, however, our spirits received a sudden chill. The sun disappeared, and a gray mist suddenly enveloped us. We knew what it was. The clouds we had seen from the camp, about the mountains in the far west, had begun to roll upon our mountainside; and what the chances ahead would be could only be told when we had cleared the forest. We pushed ahead, the last steep climb past, every opening in the diminishing growth revealing sufficient cause for anxiety. Soon we saw the ledges ahead and made

---

[7] Mount Jefferson, which lies southwest of Mount Adams.—Editor

rapidly for the last dense clump of low timber, to escape the piercing, moisture-laden winds that now began to strike us. This we reached at a little before 1:30. Here we donned all our clothing: wraps and ulsters, hood and caps were well adjusted, light gloves exchanged for fur mittens, scarfs securely fastened, and out again we marched—now in the teeth of the wind. We clambered up the ledges, dodging around the rocks, avoiding the glary crust, and selecting each for himself the spots where the shoe might find a slight coating of snow, or the toe crunch a footing in some feebler crust. All was changed. There was hardly a flake of snow that could blow away, but the shallow gullies gave a tolerable foothold. We soon flanked the first ledge and gained the summit of the second, and now we could see the state of things. Off on the western horizon lay a dense mass of clouds. Rank upon rank, they filled the space between. One line had just passed us and we were in the sunshine; but we could see little on either side, excepting when an occasional rift revealed a scene of glory. So it would doubtless continue, and the chances of any views would diminish as the day wore on. Here, then, we divided our forces, half remaining and half proceeding, one of the guides with each party. Those who went no farther sought the leeward side of the ledge before descending and, picking out sheltered spots behind the rocks, sat for ten minutes, careless of the cold and wind, enjoying such passing glimpses to the north as could be gained. They then returned to the camp in a leisurely and comfortable way.

The others doffed their snowshoes and armed their feet with creepers. When ready again for the start, the clouds had fairly settled down upon the mountainsides, but the little cairns of white stones that mark the summer path could still be seen, even against the snow. This serves to show the small depth of the snow above the trees, save in the hollows, which the summer path naturally avoids. At times the passage was over the ice, or over a crust stiff enough to bear one's weight; while at other times considerable distances were passed over weak crust through which one sank halfway to the knee. With varying fortune, through mingled sunshine and cloud, the little party of three kept on until they reached the peak known as Adams 4,[8] which is about a kilometer [about a half mile] from the summit, and about one hundred and fifty meters [about five hundred feet] below it. Still they pushed on; but the

---

[8] The U.S. Board of Geographic Names renamed Adams 4 Mount Abigail Adams in 2010 following a petition submitted by New Hampshire native and writer Bethany Taylor.—Editor

difficulties increased. There was first a broad plateau to cross, with gentle, upward slope, over which a wind of 20 miles an hour, laden with frost, was blowing. Beyond that the sharp, steep cone of Adams, with its huge masses of jagged rocks. The clouds became more and more dense and obscured the landmarks. The moisture of the breath, freezing upon the wraps about the face, seriously interfered with breathing. So when, at 2:45, half the distance beyond 3.4 kilometers [2.11 miles] was reached, and a height of about 1,620 meters [about 5,315 feet] had been attained, a hurried consultation decided that prudence and the lateness of the hour demanded a return. "It seems a pity," said they, "to be so near and yet so far; but prudence is the wiser thing."

Uphill and downhill on the ice are two different things, and it was not long before the forest line was reached again. The wind, to be sure, was in their faces; but the descent to this point was mere child's play compared to the toilsome climb. It was not always safe to keep one's feet; so this was diversified by many a slide upon the back. If attempted erect, by balancing upon long legs, one was liable to mishaps such as befell one of the party, who cannot tell today just what happened, and nobody else knows. At the bottom of a stretch of ice some fifty or one hundred yards in length, while "going like a rocket," his foremost foot struck a projecting bit of ice, whereupon he shot forward in midair, and landed a rod or more below upon his face, rolling over and over until a snowdrift stopped further progress. This battle-scarred warrior was the recipient of unusual attentions that evening around the fire, his features lending veracity to his tale.

At the timberline the snowshoes were again brought into requisition, and proved as useful in descent as in ascent. In the steep places all one had to do was to stoop and shoot downward until a tree was struck or caught; so it became a series of zigzag dashes, in which one must be ever on the alert. On the less steep portions of the path one merely took long steady strides, which made the kilometer signs pass rapidly to the rear.

The Appalachian camp was reached at 4:15. Some of the first return party had already left, strolling leisurely down; but there was a fire at hand, and hot tea. It was curious to see how little effect the blazing fire had had upon the snow sides of the pit in which it had been built; and though the sandwiches had been placed beside the fire at the bottom of the pit for more than an hour, bread, butter, and meat were frozen solid, and the effect of crunching them was very peculiar. We spent three-quarters of an hour here, and then resumed the downward dash with less recklessness, for it was already growing dark in the woods, and when we left the forest it was hard to follow the more obscure trail across the meadows. But soon, the lights of the Ravine House coming in sight, no further care was taken, and by 6:15 the last of the party was safely housed, the ascent having taken seven hours and the return one-half that time.

It is the unanimous feeling of the members of the party that a complete ascent of Mount Adams in winter is perfectly feasible and not extremely difficult. The following day was perfect throughout, and had that day been chosen there can be no doubt that the summit would have been reached without much difficulty by the whole party. The start should be made by six, however, to give ample time. Heavy overcoats are not needed, even above the forest; but leathern vests and cardigans are recommended, and a not-too-heavy hooded coat, the hood projecting as far in front of the face as to readily serve to protect it from lateral winds. Most of the party wore extra footgear; but the writer simply wore arctics over his ordinary winter boots and did not suffer for an instant. With the experience we have had, another winter is hardly likely to pass until Adams is ascended from the valley of the Moose.

THE FIRST ASCENT OF A GLACIER IN COLORADO

F.H. Chapin
1887

Frederick H. Chapin (1852–1900) of Hartford, Connecticut, wrote often for Appalachia in its early days, especially about his explorations of Colorado. A few years after this essay appeared, Chapin climbed Longs Peak via the steep southeast side—which very few climbers had done. The Appalachian Mountain Club published his books, Mountaineering in Colorado: The Peaks About Estes Park *(1889), and* Land of the Cliff-Dwellers *(1892), which described the then-newly-discovered ancient settlements in the Mesa Verde area of Colorado. As Reuben Ellis has written in* Stories and Stone *(University of Arizona Press, 1997), Chapin visited Mesa Verde in the summers of 1889 and 1890 and was apparently so enthusiastic about the history of that area that, soon after, archaeologist Gustaf Nordenskiold named one of the flat-topped hills Chapin's Mesa.*

*W*E REACHED THE LIMITS OF THE GRASS PATCHES AT 9 o'clock and could ride no farther. Leaving the horses, we walked up the rather steep ascent, arriving at the foot of the snowfield in an hour. We had seen the upper snows for two hours but had no view of the whole mass until we were right upon it; for an immense rocky ridge heaped high around the base hides three-quarters of the snowfield until it is surmounted. All at once this scene burst upon us. A steep snowbank extended about a thousand feet above to the top of the mountain. The water which had collected at its base had been frozen again—not solidly, but with occasional open spaces in which large blocks of ice were floating around. As the force of the wind moved them, they were lifted up by rocks or firmer ice from beneath, creaking and groaning; then broken up into fragments, but only to form new floes. The long line of the lower edge of the ice and snow curled over in the beautiful combings as it hung over the open water.

The snow expanse is about half a mile in width and entirely fills a kind of amphitheater made by the main range of the Mummy [Mountain] and a spur which extends around the northeast. In some places it makes the sky-line, but for the most part pointed rocks and towers jut up from the snow. One shaft, which we judged twenty feet in height, could not have been more than twelve inches in diameter at the base and was of pure white quartz. The more easily decomposed granite had fallen away, leaving this firmer vein of rock standing alone.

The whole extent of the snow was covered with grooves, markings, and cracks; a large crevasse began near the south end and extended a long way into the center, and close examination revealed many more above and below it, running parallel with it. The longest of these was about a hundred feet above the water at the southern extremity.

A single glance at the series of crevasses was enough to convince me that we looked upon a glacier, and further examination of the ice confirmed the first impression. The great ridge upon which we stood was evidently a terminal moraine formed by the glacier in past ages. What debris comes down with the ice at the present time must fall into the lake. The surface of the glacier, however, is remarkably free from stones and boulders, caused, as we afterward determined, by the fact that the loosened masses about the ice fall to the west down that much steeper rockfall of the mountain; yet at one point the ledges are breaking away toward the glacier, and a few boulders are already embedded in the ice and are on their way down the slide.

Having taken two pictures of the glacier and lake from the moraine, accompanied by our leader, I carried the camera back from the ice and took more a distant view; meanwhile the Appalachian[9] had strolled along to the south end to look at the big crevasse. It seemed desirable to secure three negatives of this section of the ice; but as we had only one sensitized plate

9   Fellow club member George W. Thacher.—Editor

with us, I started back to the foot of the glacier, where we had left the lunch and other luggage, for another plate-holder containing two plates.

And now an episode occurred which for the time being quite eclipsed the pleasurable excitement of our discovery with one of a more thrilling, if less agreeable sort. I had gone about halfway when my companion called out, "A bear! A bear! Come here quick!" I turned, ran back, and saw an immense range grizzly standing on a rock about two hundred feet from us; he had just come out from behind a huge boulder. I took his picture as quickly as possible. This was probably the first time that "old Ephraim" had ever had his picture taken in his own haunts; and if he could only have known what was required of him, he might just as well have sat for it. I then saw the Appalachian standing very near to the bear, but back of him, looking at him through his field glass as coolly as could be. The bear was of tremendous size and must have weighted a thousand pounds. His color was, for the most part, brown, but his back and the top of his head appeared nearly white. He was of the species called by the hunters silver-tipped grizzly; and as the sun was shining very brightly directly upon his back, the reflection was such as to give it a silvery-white appearance. He was evidently trying to make up his mind whether to come down to us and take his lunch or betake himself off up the mountain—or, as the local phrase has it, "pull his freight." I had not thought of the bear's attacking us, though I had wondered at the Appalachian's coolness, but now the beast was growling and snapping. Suddenly my companion suggested, "Suppose he should decide to come and take us." Then I proposed that I go for the other plates and that he get his shotgun, our only weapon, at the same time, and load it with buckshot. "That would not be much use," he answered, "but we can do one thing. Here, take this knife!" and he drew a large butcher knife from his belt and handed it to me. "If he turns on us, I will wait till his nose touches the muzzle on the gun before I let him have it, and you must do the best you can for yourself with the knife; this will be our only salvation, but it will take lots of nerve to await the proper moment to shoot."

Our motions were so lively that when we got back to our position by the camera, the bear had decided to move off, and was soon out of sight behind a ridge, giving a sort of snort as he turned away. Our fear was now that he would run down the mountain to where the horses and mule were tethered and stampede them. If the animals should get a sight of the bear they would break their legs or necks in trying to escape. This catastrophe must be averted

This photo from the expedition captures climbers pausing as they cross Hallett Glacier in Colorado. Frederick H. Chapin said he knew he'd come to a glacier by the crevasses and uneven surface.

at all hazards, for without the pack mule we could never carry the camera and plates back to camp before nightfall, and a night at this elevation, without blankets, would be horrible. We started at a brisk run over the rocks, hoping to head him off. But he traveled so rapidly that before we saw him again he had covered a great distance in a circle around us and was about three hundred feet below our position, crossing a large snowfield, and luckily headed away from the horses. He stopped, turned, and looked at us. Standing out on the white snowfield, with steep ledges and jagged cliffs rising high in the background, his figure was certainly very picturesque. It was impossible to photograph him, as he was so far below us; so my companion asked—

"Shall I give him a shot?"

"Pepper him," I responded.

"He may turn on us."

"Pepper him," I said again.

Bang went the gun, and the beast jumped. Bang! Another charge of buck-shot followed, and the bear gave another leap forward, although the effect of the shot was probably no more upon him than the cut of a whip would have been if given at hand. However, the shot so accelerated his gait that he probably reached Wyoming in a very short time, for he went up the side of the mountain on a run and was over the top of the ridge and out of sight in ten minutes. I watched him for a moment on the ground glass of the camera, and his figure looked like that of a rat running up a wall. This quickness of motion in a beast of such bulk was marvelous; for later in the day it took us over an hour to gain an equal height, climbing over similar rocks. One can judge how utterly powerless we should have been if the conditions had been reversed and we had been chased by the bear.

The bear being disposed of, we returned to the glacier and roped ourselves together for an investigation of the surface of the ice, using a 40-foot lariat for the purpose, so that we had about twenty feet of rope between us. Then we crossed the snow to the big crevasse. This was fifteen feet wide in some places, and 20 to 30 feet deep, and large icicles hung down from the upper edges. After securing photographs of this, we went back to the rocks, where the Appalachian threw off the rope and separated himself from us to climb the final peak by the ledges. Our leader and I tied ourselves together again and began the ascent to the ridge by the glacier.

We were more than an hour upon the summit; the atmosphere was of rare transparency, and the view seemed limitless. We could see clearly the ranges far into Wyoming; Pike's Peak rose in the south, and peaks farther away to the southwest; but here, as from the ledges below, the chief joy was in looking toward the Sierras of the west. This was the only peak upon which we had not found a cairn, and I doubt if it had ever been climbed before.

It was 4 o'clock when we left the summit, and we ran down the face of the peak to where we had left our traps and extra plates. Collecting these, we walked to the north side of the glacier and climbed about halfway up. Part of the south side of the glacier is in shadow early in the afternoon, and on that account is very smooth and firm, while the north end is exposed to the sun's rays from early morning till much later in the afternoon; consequently, the heat has so melted the upper snows that the water runs down and causes deep grooves. While we had been examining the formation and shape of the curious ridges of snow, the sun had been obscured by high drifting clouds.

Suddenly it came out with dazzling brightness, and we beheld a remarkable shadow profile cast upon the pure white snow by the sculptured rocks. At first it was a startling apparition, and we stood there transfixed with awe as we gazed upon it, shading our eyes with our hands. The length of the profile traced on the snow by the varying shadow was fully 100 feet. The lines were clearly defined. Of course it can only be seen at a certain hour on sunny afternoons. The day is far distant when throngs of tourists will stream up the gorge to see the one true glacier of Colorado, and by that time perhaps the granite rocks will have crumbled away, worn by rain and cracked by frost, and the profile which we saw will have vanished. Meanwhile many will doubtless be glad that we succeeded in securing a photograph of the strange and beautiful scene.

It was now 5 o'clock. We reluctantly turned away from the glacier, and scrambling over the moraine to the large snowfield where the bear had crossed, we glissaded down for several hundred feet, then took to the rocks, and soon reached our horses and mule. On our way down, we shot seven ptarmigans. We reached camp at dark in a very tired condition, but a cup of strong coffee so revived us that in an hour we were contentedly lying before the blaze, the thick hedge of spruce timber at our backs keeping off the strong blasts of wind. Then we told stories of bear, and stories of elk, and stories of "bighorn," and smoked the pipe of peace.

Spruce firewood will always crack and snap, and this night the sparks rose high, carried far up by the wild wind, and then whisked down the deep gulch toward the plains. As I lay there looking at the black line of cliffs surrounding us, and then into the dancing flames, I thought of campfires long since burned out, of blazing pines in dark forests, of nights in deserted log cabins in the West or in the stone-roofed chalet in the far-away Alps. Then from the heights and distance came memories of moraine, crevasse, and bergschrund, of expanse of snow, of boulder waste, and the wary "bighorn," of spires of dock and domes of ice, and, losing my hold on consciousness in this strange chaos, I slipped beneath the canvas and was soon asleep.

THE CASUALTY ON MOUNT LEFROY

Charles E. Fay
1896

This essay is an early example of what one might call a climbing accident elegy, in which a climber who witnessed a fatal fall bemoans the tragedy, recounting the fallen climber's normal caution, considerable skills, and love of the sport. Long-time editor of Appalachia *Charles E. Fay wrote mournfully of the accident in which Philip Stanley Abbot[10] fell to his death while climbing Mount Lefroy in the Canadian Rockies. The group thought this would be "the largest enterprise in the way of mountaineering that has ever been accomplished on Canadian peaks." The accident jarred the mountaineering communities in the United States and Canada. Abbot's was the first death on an Appalachian Mountain Club trip and the first fatality in Canadian mountaineering. The pass called Death-Trap Col was renamed Abbot Pass.*

Fay, a modern languages professor at Tufts University, had become the journal's editor in 1879 and would keep that post for four decades. Like most Appalachia editors, he went into the mountains regularly. He was more a walker than a technical climber, particularly in the years of his editorship, but Fay arguably remains the most influential editor in the journal's history. He established a format that in many ways remains unchanged. He established a tone that grew out of his zeal for climbing. He took many trips to remote and unclimbed areas, and wrote conversational stories about his trips. He also philosophized about people's attitudes about nature. In the twenty-first century we take that sort of thinking

---

[10] Abbot, a 29-year-old Harvard graduate, had joined Fay and fellow AMC member Charles S. Thompson on the first ascent of Canada's Mount Hector in 1895. Fay noted that Abbot had been "familiar with the grandest mountains . . . of the globe."—Editor

for granted, but in Fay's time considering the wilderness as a place for personal improvement—that was new.

Fay's original essay began with a lengthy backstory of the Lefroy expedition planning. Three of the climbers had attempted Lefroy the year before. We pick up the narrative after the group—Abbot, Fay, S.E.S. Allen, and George T. Little—took a small boat across the misty Lake Louise, marched over rockfall and old winter snow toward the cliff of Lefroy, and climbed, roped, to an elevation of 9,850 feet.

*A*LMOST BEFORE OUR EYES HAD TAKEN IN THE WONDERFUL prospect that opened so magically—the sudden plunge of the western gorge, snowless in its upper half, its sloping sides and narrow bottom lined with scree from the heights above; the sea-green lakelets at its foot, 3,000 feet below us; the pinnacle of Mount Biddle leaping up like a petrified flame and pricking clouds that leveled with the tops of [Mounts] Green and Lefroy themselves; the remoter array of peaks unfamiliar in this new aspect—Abbot had scanned the western side of Lefroy, now for the first time clearly revealed to us, and joyfully exclaimed: "The peak is ours!" and surely his confidence seemed justified. From here an unobstructed way was seen leading up to the long summit arête, which still frowned nearly two thousand feet above the pass. The vast mountainside rose in a sloping wall, ice-clad for the greater part, yet with here and there long upward leads of rock[11] that probably could be scaled, as the dip was in the right direction. Assured of what it lay nearest to his heart to know, Abbot now turned his attention to the grand spectacle, and his enthusiasm found ample expression in that ever-happy smile, his beaming eyes, and his quiet remark—and what was ever so convincing as that confident, almost childlike mental repose?—that nowhere had he ever seen that view surpassed for striking alpine effects.

Immediately to the left of the pass the line of the watershed rose abruptly some two hundred feet over the promontory, whose farther side was a precipice but that towards us a steep slope utterly buried under large

---

[11] It is probable that these rocky spaces were under snow at the time of Abbot's visit.—Editor

The north face of Mount Lefroy loomed over a resting climber at around the time of the Fay expedition.

angular blocks of rock. As serious climbing would not begin until we had surmounted this height, we kept on, after brief delay at the col, to a point near its top, where we paused for our noon meal. This slight addition to our altitude (now 10,100 feet) had opened up new vistas: the alluring monolith of Mount Goodsir in the southwest; to the north Mount Hector, refusing to lay aside its summit-veiling cloud, as if to spite its vanquishers; the vastly extended outlook over the snowfields of the Waputik mountains, that we confidently believed our feet would press on the morrow; Mount Balfour, seeming to proclaim from afar the ease of the victory we might hope to win ere two more suns should set.

At 12:30 P.M., leaving behind us two of our rucksacks with the remainder of our food and whatever else seemed unnecessary for the hours that we were expecting to be absent, we again set forth to complete, as we fondly believed, the largest enterprise in the way of mountaineering that has ever been accomplished on Canadian peaks. Our record shows that in the first half-hour we made excellent progress, for at 1 o'clock our aneroid reading was 10,400, three hundred feet above our lunching place. The point at which it was made is one that will never fade from our memory—the top of a low cliff, beyond the brow of which and somewhat higher up lay a narrow plateau covered with scree.

Of the next four hours and a half the writer of this narrative has a very vague recollection. Did not our record exist as a corrective for deceitful memory, I should without question underestimate the period fully one-half, either because it actually passed so quickly, or because in reminiscence the monotonous affords few halting-points, and so falsifies time just as the plains and the open falsify distance. These hours were spent either in cutting steps in our zigzag course up ice slopes or in wary advance up the unreliable slopes of rock, the effect of a slip upon which would differ slightly in ultimate results from a slip on the ice itself. Usually one moved at a time, the others maintaining meanwhile as secure an anchorage as possible. Caution governed every movement, as indeed it always did when Abbot was at the fore. On this day we were all deeply impressed with its needfulness. Even our leader smiled at the enormous size of the steps that were left in the wake of the party after each one had contributed his vigorous chipping to their enlargement. Some-one, thinking of the possible lateness of the return and consequent necessity for speed, suggested that we might need all the advantage their size would offer when we came to descend. So indeed it proved!

At 5:30 we drew up under an immense bastion possibly seventy-five feet in height,[12] behind which lay the summit, of which as yet, owing to foreshortening, we had no satisfactory view. This frowning face rose sheer from a narrow margin of tolerably stable scree that lay tilted between its base and upper edge of the sloping ice that we had just left behind us. Looking past it on the right we saw, a few hundred feet beyond, the tawny southern arête, so shattered as to be utterly impassable. In one place a great aperture, perhaps forty feet high and five or six in width, revealed the blue sky beyond. Evidently our course did not lie in that direction. On the left the dusky northern arête rose with an easy gradient possibly an eighth of a mile away, but across an ice slope similar to that up which we had so long been toiling, and in truth

---

[12] The last reading of the group's aneroid taken at this point gave 11,300 feet. The preliminary calculation of the topographical survey gives to Lefroy an altitude of 11,260 feet.

a continuation of the same. To cross it was perfectly feasible, but it would take so long to cut the necessary steps that a descent of the peak before dark would have been out of the question.

But now, Abbot, who had moved forward along the rock wall to the limit of the rope, cheerfully announced an alternative. His view beyond an angle in the bastion revealed a vertical cleft up which it was possible to climb by such holds as offered themselves. Bidding Thompson and me to unrope and keep under cover from falling stones, he clambered some thirty feet up the rift, secured a good anchorage, and called upon Little to follow. This the latter proceeded to do, but while standing at the bottom of the cleft preparing to climb, he received a tingling blow from a small stone dislodged by the rope. A moment later a larger one falling upon the rope half severed it, so as to require a knot. As danger from this source seemed likely to continue, our leader had Little also free himself from the rope and come up to where he stood. From here a shelf led around to the left, along which Abbot now proceeded a few yards and discovered a gully leading upward, unseen from the point first attained, and this also he began to ascend. To Little's question, whether it might not be better to try and turn the bastion on the shelf itself, he replied: "I think not. I have a good lead here."

These were the last words he ever uttered. A moment later Little, whose attention was for the moment diverted to another portion of the crag, was conscious that something had fallen swiftly past him, and knew only too well what it must be. Thompson and I, standing at the base of the cliff, saw our dear friend falling backward and head-foremost, saw him strike the upper margin of the ice slope within fifteen feet of us, turn completely over, and instantly begin rolling down its steep incline.[13]

After him trailed our two lengths of English rope—all we had brought with us—which we had spliced together in our ascent over the last rock slope, in order to gain time by having less frequent anchorages than were

---

[13] How the terrible disaster occurred we shall never know. In all probability his foothold, or more likely his handhold, gave way; though it is not impossible that he was struck by a stone descending from above. The facts that no outcry preceded his fall and that the fatal wound was on the back of his head seem, however, to argue against this latter hypothesis. I know not how to account for my immediate impression, unless I actually saw something to create it during the momentary slackening of his swift rush past us, but it was an increase of horror lest a large stone, clasped in his arms, should crush him as he struck the slope. The visual memory itself is exceedingly indefinite as regards details.

The majestic Mount Lefroy in British Columbia, Canada, dwarfed two climbers, below left.

necessitated by the short intervals of one sixty-foot line. As the limp body rolled downward in a line curving slightly towards the left, the rope coiled upon it as on a spool—a happy circumstance amid so much of horror—for not only did this increase of friction sensibly affect the velocity of the descent of nine hundred feet to the narrow plateau of scree above mentioned, but doubtless the rope by catching in the scree itself prevented the unconscious form from crossing the narrow level and falling over the low cliff beyond. Had it passed this, nothing, apparently, could have stopped it short of the bottom of the gorge leading up to the pass from the western side of the Divide—a far more fearful fall than that already made.

You would not pardon me if I could find words to describe our feelings. A single instant of supreme emotion may equal hours of grief or joy less intense. A single instant only was ours to yield to it. Little was still in a critical position, particularly if his nerves were unstrung. To ascend such a cleft is far easier than to descend, and he had had the aid of the rope in going up. He must forgive me if I mention here the self-forgetfulness with which he called down to us: "Never mind me. Hurry to help Abbot." "Our help is for the living. To reach Abbot will require hours. Everything must be forgotten save care for the present moment. Come down as far as you can with safe holds, and, Heaven helping, we will do our part." Happily the footholds lasted until he was far enough down to reach with his hob-nailed shoe an ice ax held braced against a projection by one of us who had crowded himself for a purchase into the base of the cleft. Another ax under his thigh and such handhold as he could grasp aided the remainder of the perilous descent. It was 6:30 as we stood together with grateful hearts at the base of the fatal bastion.

A brief gaze to where Abbot lay so still, a mutual promise of self-command and unremitting caution, and we began our descent with ice axes only, each responsible for his own safety. Our ample footsteps were now a priceless safeguard. On the treacherous rock slopes we could indeed secure a tolerable substitute for seven feet of rope by attaching two ice axes together by their straps, a wholly inadequate resource for this dangerous passage. Thus for three hours and until the beautiful sunset glow had faded on the high arête of Lefroy, we worked our slow way downward and at length stood beside the motionless form that all this time had lain in full view. To our surprise life was not yet extinct. The fatal wound in the back of the head, evidently received in the short initial fall of perhaps twenty feet, was the only grievous outward mark, and the autopsy proved that not a limb was broken. A faint murmur, that my imagination[14] interpreted as a recognition of our presence and expression of gratitude that we at least had escaped from peril, alone broke the silence for a brief moment, and then we three bared our heads in the twilight, believing that his generous spirit was already passing. But a moment later the faint breathing was resumed.

If living, then of course we would bear him down with us, difficult as the labor would be. We now at least had the ropes, and with their aids such a task did not seem impossible. To tarry in this spot was at all events out of the question. With tender hands, having first disentangled the ropes, we raised him, and began the dreary descent; but we had scarcely reached the brink of the little cliff when he again ceased to breathe. Not satisfied with

---

[14] The autopsy revealed a fracture of the occipital and left parietal bones, with some depression of the former, which renders it practically certain that he was unconscious as he fell past us, and that he never regained consciousness.

this evidence, we tested pulse and heart. That all was over in the mortal life of our loved companion was subject to no manner of doubt.

The seriousness of the task we had assumed as a matter of course at once became evident. To lower even the lifeless body down this short precipice was a labor involving a large risk for three persons. Only with competent aid and by long daylight could it be brought from its lofty resting-place to the chalet we had left so hopefully that morning. Twilight was deepening into dusk as we decided to leave it here and descend as far as possible before darkness should prevent further advance. By the dim reflection from the sky and the snow we could faintly discern our upward footsteps in certain places; in others merely divine them. The general course avoiding dangerous precipices on our left we could make out without difficulty. We reached without mishap the tip of the rock-strewn promontory, but by a strange misfortune all three of us forgot that it was near this point, and not in the pass itself, that we had left our rucksacks with food and our only stimulant (excepting the flask that Abbot had carried, and which had been shattered into fragments in his first fall), together with an extra sweater—an oversight we had occasion bitterly to repent. Not until we reached the col and failed to find our belongings did the truth dawn upon us, and a return in the darkness failed to bring the seeker to the desired spot.

Assembled again at the pass—it was now 10:30 P.M.—we accepted the decree that we should here spend the reminder of the night.

The bare rock of the lowest point of the pass, upon which we now found ourselves, was at least preferable to the snow for a couch, so we lay down upon it face downward. Soon, however, the rising breeze drawing freshly over the col from the north made us long for some shelter from its chill. The cairn would offer a slight defense, and up to it we hastened. Seating ourselves in its lee one close before the other, each held the one in front of him in a close embrace to utilize, so far as possible, our bodily warmth. Often we would lightly pound ourselves, or one another, to increase the sluggish circulation. Now and then Little would rise to stop some chink in the cairn or even build an extension to our stony windbreak. I should not say that we suffered physically in any very serious sense of the term; we were simply de-cidedly uncomfortable. Our condition became somewhat the worse toward morning, when the sky became overcast and flakes of fine snow began to sift over us, the forerunners of a storm, the severity of which was fortunately delayed for some hours. The night wore on but slowly.

Occasionally one or another would doze for a quarter or half hour, then, waking, consult the watch and congratulate himself on his happy fortune. By 4:15 it was light enough, despite the cloudiness, for one to move about, and only too gladly I proceeded to overcome my numbness by recovering the rucksacks. Strengthened for the descent by the welcome food—we had eaten nothing since noon of the day before—we set out at 5 o'clock, and reached the chalet at 9:30 A.M. in the midst of a rainstorm.

The following morning, Thursday, a party of six bridge-builders, sent in by the management of the Canadian Pacific Railway, whose sympathy and offers of aid knew no stint, went to the point where we had left the body, accompanied by Messrs. Little and Astley, and bore it in a litter over the rough way to the head of Lake Louise and thence by boat to the little landing of the chalet. In the afternoon it was transported to Laggan and by the evening train to Banff, where on Friday it was embalmed and the autopsy and inquest held in accordance with the law. Then began the long journey across the continent. On Wednesday, August 12, the remains were laid to rest in Mount Auburn.

Thus closed the saddest episode in the history of our club, for this is the first fatal accident in its twenty years of existence. It occurs at the very dawn of a new era of genuine alpine climbing, for the extension of which among our young countrymen Abbot was so earnest an advocate.[15] Shall the incipient movement cease because he is no longer with us to work for it, or because he lost his life while engaged in furnishing a brilliant example

---

[15] Here Fay described Abbot's dedication to bringing together climbing organizations through *Appalachia* journal. "It was his ardent wish to unite by closer ties those of our club to whom alpine climbing most appeals and like-minded members of the Sierra Club," he wrote in his original footnote. "To work more effectively toward this end, he had himself joined that society—which mourns his loss with us—and in a visit to San Francisco last May had consulted with some of its leaders as to the possibility of a greater concert of action between the two organizations. It was in view of what he believed *Appalachia* might accomplish in this direction that he, after much solicitation, had expressed a willingness shortly to place his experience in editorial work at the disposition of the Appalachian Mountain Club."—Editor

of what he would foster? We who passed with him this most exultant of all his mountain days have no sympathy with such a conclusion. In our judgment, neither the region nor the boldness of the enterprise is responsible for his death. A similar fall with the same result might have occurred in the White Mountains, or even on the craggy hills of Mount Desert Island where in boyhood he went into training for the more ambitious climbs of his early manhood. It is not, of course, to be denied that such climbing as the Canadian Rockies offer involves a larger element of risk, nor that opportunities for a proper schooling are sadly deficient in our country. In certain respects, however, and notably as regards climatic conditions, the dangers here are distinctly less than among the Swiss Alps. We should deprecate, as much as any, a party's venturing upon such enterprises without, at the very least, a leader who has made a careful study of both crag and ice work under competent guides. But after duly weighing all that is urged against alpine climbing, and while appreciating, none more profoundly, the value of the rare life that went out on Mount Lefroy, we maintain that the gain therefrom for the general and the individual life in an age of growing carefulness for ease and luxury must be held to outweigh the deplorable losses, and that this casualty should not call a halt in American alpinism. That a man like Philip Abbot should love this form of recreation—and to him it was an education as well—argues for its nobility. Let his death, then, point no moral against it, but rather let it be regarded with the same unquestioning spirit, silent before the mysterious dispensations of the controlling Power, with which we stood a few weeks before when a life of extraordinary promise for the commonwealth and the nation found an early end.

A WINTER ASCENT THROUGH THE GREAT GULF (MOUNT WASHINGTON)

George N. Whipple
1905

George N. Whipple and two companions—legendary trail-builder Warren W. Hart and Harland Perkins—set out in this story to chop their way up the icy headwall of New Hampshire's highest peak in winter. To get a sense of the group dynamics, consider Whipple's service three years later—over five days in mid-September 1908—on Hart's crew that built the first trail through the giant boulders of the exposed Great Gulf below Mount Washington. Two of his crewmen— Whipple and Ralph C. Larrabee—took a detour up Mount Jefferson, presumably to check out the entire area the crew was trying to mark with cairns. Hart later wrote in Appalachia *that Whipple and Larrabee "reported that from the heights the Gulf appeared interminable, and that it seemed doubtful that we could complete our trail. They did not know, however, that in their absence we had advanced the path nearly one and a half miles." That remark shows the irrepressible, bull-in-a-china-shop Hart meeting the more analytical attitude of Whipple.*

WHILE NOT WISHING TO EXALT UNDULY THE ALPINE opportunities of our humble Appalachian system, it is believed that the usual route of ascents in the Swiss Alps includes few slopes, where step-cutting is required, of equal height and steepness with that of the Great Gulf on the northerly side of Mount Washington.

The Great Gulf in 1910, when climbers found it to be almost impenetrable.

The cone of the Wetterhorn, a snow slope of exceeding steepness, rises from six hundred to seven hundred feet above its base. The Weisshorn, much more strenuous, calls for continuous step-cutting of no greater amount. In his ascent of Les Ecrins in 1864, [Edward] Whymper encountered a steep slope seven hundred or eight hundred feet high which cost his party six hours' work, and his remarkable descent from the Col Dolent in 1865 occupied seven hours; of it he says: "For the first and only time in my life I looked down a slope more than a thousand feet long, set at an angle of about 50 degrees, which was a sheet of ice from top to bottom." When Leslie Stephen[16] crossed the Eiger Joch in 1859, his party climbed an ice slope about one thousand feet in altitude and with an inclination of from 51 degrees to 52 degrees, which required seven hours of step-cutting—a feat which Stephen deemed well worthy of record. The rim of the headwall of the Great Gulf cannot be far from fourteen hundred feet above its base and half a mile or more distant from it, and a party of three spent seven and a half hours in the invigorating exercise of step-cutting up its icy surface on the 27th of January 1905.

Comparisons aside, it is beyond dispute that this headwall in winter offers a capital climb to those who find enjoyment in that particular form

[16] Sir Leslie Stephen (1832–1904) was a writer, critic, mountaineer, and the father of novelist Virginia Woolf.

of "what some people call pleasure," and there surely must be something in a place that costs an hour's time more than is required for the ascent of the Matterhorn, even for a party as slow and inexperienced as we were.

I had had my eye on this particular expedition since February of 1903, when six of us had made a very sporting ascent of the headwall of Huntington Ravine; and therefore it was with peculiar satisfaction that I found myself starting upon it during our stay at the Mount Madison House in Gorham. This statement needs qualification. I know of nothing more discouraging to complacency, or more likely to sour, for the time being, a naturally sweet nature, than to turn out of a comfortable bed some hours before dawn on a cold winter morning, to indue an exaggerated amount of clothing, to begin a so-called breakfast about the time when the sleigh is announced, to hastily cram a few last necessities into an already over-filled rucksack (wondering at the time how many have been forgotten), to snatch an ice ax, and sally forth upon a quest sure to result in a plethora of toil, and sure of nothing else. Truly, as the psalmist says, we are fearfully and wonderfully made.

The hour was six, the air was cold; a dissipated, gibbous moon was plowing through a field of watery-looking clouds in the west, and the aspect of Nature did not stimulate hope. What Harland Perkins and Warren Hart were resolving I knew not, for we were morose and uncommunicative; but that third member of the trio marveled, as he had before on like occasions, at his unaccountable infatuation, and felt capable of sympathizing with a candidate for a first-class asylum for feeble-minded youth. This lasted perhaps an hour, when a magical touch transmuted all. A turn of the road brought us in sight of Madison, then of Adams, and then of Washington, and we all sat up and wondered. The "rose of dawn" flushed their pure snows with radiance ineffable. They soared like mountains of dream in the blue heaven, wondrous in color and in form, and of texture delicate and evanescent. They seemed like clouds that the wind would blow away, as fleeting as thistledown that a breath might scatter. Our spirits, revived, our self-respect returned, and we fell to discussing our most sane and delightful trip.

Our plan was to enter the Gulf by way of the West Branch of the Peabody; and at 7:45 we slid down the steep bank at the junction of that branch with the main stream, which flows from Huntington Ravine, and were fairly embarked. This junction is about half a mile north of the Glen cottage.

We found fulfilled the promise of those tickets on which we had traveled to Gorham—"Good going Jan. 21st to the 27th." The going was good. We were able to keep in the bed of the stream, or rather on its counterpane, practically all the way, avoiding all brush and scrub. Hart, possessing a superior knowledge of the route and an ambitious nature, led the procession, and the only incidents that diversified this part of the trip were his occasional partial disappearances. Without the slightest warning he would suddenly subside, sometimes as far as his waist, sometimes as far as his shoulders, carrying down with him a large segment of the roof of the stream. The first time this happened Perkins and I rushed to his assistance in considerable alarm, as it is no joke to get one's feet wet under such circumstances, but were met with such imperturbability and *sangfroid* that the subsequent proceedings interested us no more. His feet entirely fast in the mass of debris rapidly being converted into slush, he would survey the landscape in a meditative manner, hazard the prediction that the water must be at least four inches deep, extricate his snowshoes by the aid of a remarkable mountaineering

In this slide from the 1920s, two adventurers ascend the steep slopes of the Great Gulf in the White Mountains of New Hampshire.

implement in the shape of a long-handled boat hook which he affected, and clamber out to repeat the process farther on.

Our course upstream led us a little north of west for three or four miles, and then, north of the spur of Washington which starts from above the Half-way House, bent round to the southwest for another three or four miles to Spaulding Lake. The first part of the way we were opening up views of the Carter and Carter–Moriah range behind us, while later, first ahead and then behind, Madison and Adams played the drama of "Box and Cox." The grade was very easy for most of the way until we struck the waterfalls a mile or so below Spaulding Lake, and there were no difficulties whatever on the entire route. We halted for a second breakfast about eleven, and reached Spaulding Lake at 12:45. The weather had not improved. Light snow began to fall soon after our second breakfast, and we cowered under a ledge on the shore of the lake to partake of luncheon, a fierce squall swooped down, blotting out all but our immediate surroundings. It seemed very cold, though the glass showed only 14 degrees. We would have parted with the chances of our success for a small sum at that time; but the squall passed, the scenery, such as it was, came back, and we decided to have a try at the thing anyway.

At 1:30 we got under way, and in a few moments found it wise to exchange snowshoes for creepers. Only a few feet of the thick growth above the lake, which is such an obstacle to progress in summer, projected above the snow, but the cliffs of Clay and of the headwall were thinly coated and looked very forbidding. From the lake the dim disk of the sun had been seen for a few moments over the neck of Clay, and when we reached the cluster of boulders, which form in summer such a generous cave, we had a most inspiring burst of sunshine, but it was the last effort on the part of that luminary, who was forced out of business by his more active rival the snow squall. A sort of shelf had been formed in the snow by the action of the wind just at the base of these boulders, and we took this last opportunity to sit down and gather strength for the fray. The view from this point, raking as it does the Northern Peaks, extending into the wooded depths of the Gulf, and bounded by the blue mountains of the horizon, is superb and well repays the effort required to gain it.

A detailed narrative of the succeeding hours would be monotonous and unprofitable. Chop, chop, chop. Chop, chop, chop. The bits of ice and crust went hissing down the slope; the snow squalls descended and enveloped us;

the dark rim of the wall above us certainly seemed no nearer than an hour ago. How slowly we moved! How slowly the time went by!

It may be said that not so much of it would have gone by had our creeper equipment been equal for all, but unfortunately one of us was poorly provided in that particular, and the speed of the party became the speed of the slowest member, for it was necessary to keep together. On this account practically every step had to be cut. There were stretches where with good creepers and good nerve one might have walked without step-cutting, but the one who, wearying of that exercise, essayed to do it, essayed it but once. For a while he made great progress, an object of wonder and admiration to his fellows, and then like Lucifer he fell. And yet not like Lucifer, for after a slide of what seemed to him like a hundred feet and was actually much less, he was able to bring himself up with the aid of his ax, and held the mountain in a most tight and loving embrace for fifteen minutes before evincing any desire to proceed.

Step-cutting was resumed for all, and we took turns at it. The labor was severe, for the crust had nothing beneath it but crust and was very hard. From eight to twenty strokes were required to fashion a step, the smaller number on the lower and larger on the upper part of the wall. The inclination was probably 40 degrees a considerable part of the way. Toward the top, where real ice was encountered, the Architect said 60 degrees. It became too dark to see the steps. We had to feel for them with our axes and drag ourselves up into the utmost care. The top of the wall had long ago disappeared. We began to doubt its existence. The higher we got the steeper it grew, and the particles of ice seemed to hiss more loudly as they tobogganed down. Our situation resembled that of Leslie Stephen's party on the climb to Eiger Joch. He says: "The ice was very hard, and it was necessary, as Lauener observed, to cut steps in it as big as soup tureens, for the result of a slip would in all probability have been that the rest of our lives would have been spent in sliding down a snow slope, and that employment would not have lasted long enough to become at all monotonous."

As this is not a novel by the ingenious philosopher, Henry James, there will be no description of our thoughts on this occasion. Had we been so unfortunate as to be characters of his, we might have reflected on the Evil Spirit that drags men from fairly comfortable homes to climb mountains in winter; we might have tried to reproduce the phraseology of our maternal parents could they have seen us; we might have asked ourselves just what particular business we had in that particular spot; we might have made mental photographs of just what we would not do when we got out of it. Being ourselves and thoroughly delighted with what we were doing, no such thoughts escaped our lips. On the infrequent occasions when we did use our valuable breath for words, the latter were jocular and congratulatory. Our humorous instincts came out strongly. At this distance I fail to recall any of the jokes; but I know that they were received with appreciation and think that they were probably better than many that are printed.

At last we pulled ourselves over the rim of the wall and struck a match. It was 9 P.M. What might have been called in Boston a blizzard—but on Mount Washington was merely a zephyr—was in progress, and the air was thick with snow. We decided to make for the summit and spend the night as best we might in the adobe of luxury, the stage-office. And here a curious thing happened. Hart omitted mention of it in his *Globe* article[17] because he thought it would not be believed. We had located the railroad without difficulty and started along the line of telegraph posts on its eastern side. We could just make out the post ahead of us as we moved from one to the other; but we were actually for some time in doubt as to whether we were going uphill or down. We stopped and experimented and talked it over and finally decided that we must be going uphill, whether it seemed so or not. The outcome proved that we were, for in fifteen or twenty minutes we reached the top and the shelter of the stage-office. Soon we had a fire going, which quickly raised the temperature from 10 degrees to 30 degrees. We melted some snow and had a delicious drink of hot chocolate and ate a portion of the small amount of food remaining. We then brought in the old slat bedstead with its delightfully cool straw mattress, from the adjoining room, placed it with its foot to the stove, and addressed ourselves to undressing for the night. This function was brief and stopped with the removal of our creepers. Under most circumstances we prefer a bed to ourselves, but for this night only, no one objected to having two bedfellows. We wrapped the drapery of our couch about us (consisting of a charming piece of second-hand carpet which someone had thoughtfully stored in the building), and lay down to pleasant dreams. At

---

[17] See *Boston Globe,* "Appalachian Club's Winter Excursion to White Mountains," February 19, 1905.

least it sounds well to say so. We not only slept but overslept, for we had planned to start down at three, and we did not wake until four. The fire had been replenished during the night by one of the party whose modesty forbids my naming him (it was not myself) and was still alive, and the thermometer still stood at 30 degrees.

Breakfast was even more sketchy than the preceding meal had been, for the commissary department had gone to pieces. We always begin with fruit; and in spite of our limited menu we were able to maintain this habit. An apple frozen in its passage up the mountain as hard as a stone had been placed on the shelf behind the stove the night before and was found in a delicious state of pulpiness. A few mouthfuls apiece were quite sufficient. For a second course I think we had half a sandwich, not quite as juicy as the fruit, but very good. At 4:45 we emerged into the cold world, finding the weather much as we had left it. It was dark and it was thick, and for the first half-mile of the Carriage Road we had to move slowly and with extreme caution to avoid losing our way. Once, however, round the bend at the point where the road comes nearest to the Great Gulf, we found ourselves as Parker would say, "on Easy Street," and trotted merrily down to the Glen, which we reached at 8:15, and refreshed ourselves with hot milk and crackers. It was a good ending of a great trip.

This narrative has but one moral. If you wish to climb Mount Washington in winter from the Great Gulf, be sure of the commissary department, and do not shrink from an early start.

SNOWBOUND IN SEPTEMBER

Robert Whitehill
1917

This essay, about a predicament that many have faced in the White Mountains, is the only article Dr. Robert Whitehill ever wrote for Appalachia. *The other writing he did was about healthy teeth. He was a dentist in the early 1900s; his office was at 175 Newbury Street in Boston. He served as president of the Harvard Odontological Society for a period, and he wrote in an article for a dental journal that healthy teeth matter not so much for appearance's sake, but because people must be able to chew and benefit from healthy food that requires chewing. He rallied his colleagues to realize that "millions are, through a crippled condition of the organs of mastication, failing to get from the food they consume the heat, the energy, and the power which make life worth living." One can imagine what kind of a mountain explorer Dr. Whitehill must have been. We speculate that Dr. Whitehill refers to himself in this story as the character Mr. Bob.*

*I*T IS THE COMMON LAMENT OF MOST OF US MORTALS, WHO never wander very far from our own firesides, that "nothing ever happens to us." To minds which have to depend upon the adventures of Jack London's creations or the perils of the motion picture heroine for the thrills which are needed to quicken the circulation, it does indeed seem that existence is all too tame. Little do we realize that at any time we are likely to encounter some situation which will give us more real thrills than fall to the lot of the heroine in the jungle scene, protected as she is by an invisible wire screen and a half-dozen sharpshooters. Yet the exciting evening's entertainment or the thrilling adventures in the printed page have one decided advantage over the other kind: one can end the story when he has had enough, and go to sleep in his own bed before the clock strikes twelve.

The great storm of September 1915 furnished the unexpected "stage properties" for the scenario about to be unfolded, and furnished the amateur actors with more than they had bargained for in registering the various emotions while the crank was being turned.

This storm, lasting several days, made its fury felt from Canada to the Gulf of Mexico. It was especially severe in the White Mountain region, where the terrible gale devastated forests as no storm has done for many years. In the Franconia and Crawford notches roads were rendered impassable by the fallen trees, while in some places heavy growths of timber for a mile or more were cut off, as if by the stroke of a giant scythe. The good old Peak House on Mount Chocorua, which has sheltered many happy trampers during more than a quarter of a century, strained at its moorings for the last time, and the place of its anchorage knew it no more. On Mount Washington the old stage-barns, which have stood more windy buffeting than almost any buildings on this continent, had finally to submit to broken roof chains, blown-away doors, and one, to the bursting of its entire side. The Halfway House, four miles below on the carriage road, suffered only the blowing in of a door and a window. The stage-office on the summit withstood the storm without the loss of a single one of the architectural beauties, save the breaking of one of its roof chains. It did, however, have one of the roughest voyages in its history as it rose and fell to the music of the spheres. That its passengers were not lost, in their desire to gain terra firma, was due only to the presence of mind of the skipper, who guarded the exit with an ax. Down below, in the erstwhile peaceful vales, on the worst night of the storm, some of the more prudent of the good people kept their clothes on all night, ready to board up broken windows or to make a try for the cyclone cellar if all else failed. Such was the setting that was being arranged for the amateur actors "on that pleasant morn in the early fall" when this story really begins.

It was, indeed, a beautiful autumn morning, such as only those who know the crisp tang of mountain air can appreciate. Knapsacks had been packed, a fine breakfast dispatched, and the big seven-passenger car stood chugging at

In the days before technical gear, getting caught in a snowstorm at the Appalachian Mountain Club's Lakes of the Clouds Hut meant pulling out blankets and huddling together. In this image, taken during the same fall snowstorm which Whitehill describes in his article, rime ice covered the side of Lakes of the Clouds Hut.

the door in front of the Wilson Cottages in the lovely town of Jackson. Five eager passengers climbed aboard and stowed away their dunnage, ready for the start. First came "the Veteran," so called because climbing Mount Washington was no new thing to him. In fact, half a century and more had passed since, as a boy, he first saw its glories in company with his father. During the later years he had been content with the lesser climbs, as a variation from his literary labors. It is whispered that the Veteran is writing a book. Next came Ottilie, a lady prominent in the society and club life of famous Milwaukee. To her the Canadian Rockies and most American mountains are as old friends, while she knows the White Mountains as thoroughly as a California school teacher knows Boston after a week's visit. Next in line is Parker, alias "the Timber Cruiser," so called because he has learned the lumber business, from the logging camp to the finished product, his more recent years having been spent in British Columbia near the lofty peak of Mount Robson. Next comes his sister, "Mrs. Bob," a vivacious young matron, who believes in having something doing every minute. Last of all is Bob, who has no distinction other than being the husband of Mrs. Bob.

Just as the car is about to start someone sees the wistful look on the face of David, the eight-year-old son of the Bobs, and asks why he cannot come too; so he gleefully climbs in, to have the ride to the foot of the trail and come home with the driver. To be sure, he hasn't had his breakfast, but there are sandwiches in the knapsack, and what is breakfast compared with a ride in the big car on such a morning? Away they go, with the farewell cheers of the chaffing guests giving the party a proper send-off.

Down the steep hill, through the village, across the Ellis River and along the smooth and winding Glen Road the big car swiftly travels. The ten miles to the foot of the mountain is made in but a fraction of the time it used to take with the plodding horses. Arrived at the foot of the Tuckerman Ravine Trail the party alights, with instructions to the driver to come to the Glen House for them Monday night at 5 o'clock, the plan being to spend Saturday night at the Lakes of the Clouds and Sunday night at the Madison Spring Hut.

David's parents kiss him a fond goodbye, knapsacks are shouldered, and the procession starts. As they leave the road the ravine shows up before them with startling clearness, a peculiar gray appearance of the rocks through the clear air causing the party's pessimist to make mental observations that this beautiful weather is good for one day only. He doesn't dare to say so aloud, however. In the woods the trail leads, until in a few minutes a little bridge is crossed, from which is viewed the beautiful Crystal Cascade. The perfect waterfall is worth going miles to see, and a stop of a few minutes is made, as it is unusually good on this particular morning. The call sounds to "hoist packs," and the march begins at a moderate pace, as everyone wishes to have the Veteran take it easy and enjoy this trip, which is his first ascent of the mountain by the Tuckerman route. As all who know this trail will remember, the first part is through real forest, at a fairly steep grade, with most delightful streams crossing the path. Each one of these streams is an invitation to stop and have one little drink of delicious water, noting with interest that the water is a little cooler at each stopping place, until one feels sure there must be ice somewhere in the vicinity.

Reaching Hermit Lake Camp, the group rests while Ottilie photographs the group. The camp, which is nothing but a bark-covered log shelter, is clean and cozy withal, and it is noted that there are the materials for a fire and enough odds and ends of food stuffs to keep a stormbound traveler from starvation for a day or two. The great boulder before the open side of the camp, against which the fires are made, could tell great stories of the campfire tales it has heard these many years. It is a wild and picturesque location, surrounded by scrubby forest, which somewhat screens but does not hide the frowning ramparts on three sides of the hut. The walls tower perhaps fifteen hundred feet above the spectator in rugged perpendicular fashion, which makes the novice wonder if there is any possible safe ascent.

On leaving the camp the party divides, as Ottilie and Parker are planning to make the still more strenuous ascent of Huntington Ravine, the trail to which is a short distance below the camp. During their ascent they have several thrills, and on meeting the rest of the party at the summit, tell of fighting their way against a terrific wind between the headwall and the top of the mountain. Meanwhile the Veteran and the Bobs make progress at the moderate rate up Tuckerman's. Mrs. Bob's youthful enthusiasm finally gets the better of her, and she goes on ahead to the top of the headwall near the Fall of the Thousands Streams, where she impatiently waits for the plodders.

On the way along the narrow ledge near the top of the ravine, Bob is interested to observe the spot where he nearly went over the edge some years previous, when making the climb alone. At that time he was trying the stunt which proved fatal to Lot's wife, that is, looking backward. He saw out of the tail of his eye some perfectly good-looking grass on the narrow path. As it happened, the grass had no soil under it but was growing out over the edge, so, of course, as he stepped on it, over the edge he went; and he might have kept on going, had not his bare right elbow caught in time to allow him to hang there and think over his sinful life, as he tried to climb back safely.

At the top of the headwall, Mrs. Bob starts out at a lively pace on the climb up the rocky cone to the summit. The plodders still plod and reach the top a good half hour later than she. In her joy at finally seeing them she knocks out a pane of glass from the stage-office window, and the keeper of the house, placated with half a dollar, immediately begins to put in another pane. It is well that he does too, for the poor old stage-office will need whole windows for the next few days, if ever.

The party here is reunited and makes a rush for the new Summit House, which is just being closed for the season. Through the kindness of some of the guests still inside, in spite of the inhospitality of the management, the doors are unlocked and hungry travelers are enabled to have their belated lunch and much hot coffee. After a comfortable rest in front of the big fireplace, they sally forth to go down via the Crawford Bridle Path to the Appalachian Club's new stone hut at the Lakes of the Clouds, where they are planning to spend the night. Little do they imagine for how many nights they are destined to be grateful to the shelter of its walls from the raging of the elements!

To shorten the distance to the hut a cutoff is taken, which leads straight down over the great masses of broken rocks on the cone, and here the ever-increasing wind strikes them with such fury that jumping from rock to rock is something of a feat. The three speedsters leave the Veteran in the rear with Bob, and the latter wonders at times whether his senior partner is going to make the ticklish steps without being blown over. This is no joke, for a mis-step may mean broken bones.

As they are halfway down the cone they see a fleet-footed antelope sort of a chap coming up the treacherous rocks on the run. This proves to be the caretaker of the Lakes of the Clouds Hut with a knapsack on his back, on his way to the top for provisions—provisions which never came and which might have served to make the long sojourn more endurable had they been available. Before the plodders have reached the trail at the foot of the cone, the redoubtable George, for such is his name, passes them on his way down, and still on the run.

As the hut comes more plainly into view, a figure capped with an oil-skin "sou'wester" can be seen pacing about in front of the stone house near the little lakes. This gentleman, later known as "the Scientist," is to play an important part in our drama and to make the others glad that the fates sent him along to share their joys and sorrows. The Scientist has just come up via the trail from Crawford Notch laden with a knapsack, two cameras, and various other impedimenta, some of which proves very useful to the party during the next few days.

By about 5 o'clock the six travelers are inside the house enjoying the warmth of the cookstove and the prospects of a good supper by and by. The house, the particular pride of the Appalachian Club, is the last word in shelters of its kind. It was opened on August 7, 1915, at which time printed announcements of the opening were distributed, stating that it was built by voluntary subscriptions and dedicated to the use of "those who enjoy the higher altitudes." It is a fine structure of stone, capable accommodating 36 persons with sleeping quarters. It is divided into two rooms; one with twenty-four folding bunks for men, and one with twelve for women. One feature of the house which is very attractive in fine weather is the view to be obtained from the unusually large windows. Some of these are from five to seven feet high, and nine or ten feet long. From one, a magnificent view of the hotels and golf links at Bretton Woods may be had, also the Base Station on the cog railroad, the trestle known as Jacob's Ladder, and beautiful distant views of the town of Jefferson.

On this Saturday night the sunset was a gorgeous sight, and everybody enjoyed the beautiful views and explored the surroundings, though the high wind was too chilly to make long stops out of doors comfortable. Aside from the exposed situation the location of the hut is admirable, for the little lakes are but a few rods distant. From them the narrow stream which supplies the camp with drinking water pours down the beautiful Ammonoosuc Ravine, to emerge later as the well-known Ammonoosuc River. Near at hand the peak of Mount Monroe rises several hundred feet above the camp and adds greatly to the picturesqueness of the scene. The daylight does not linger long, and the chief entertainment for a while is in watching George, the caretaker, get supper ready. It is a real supper too, and one that is recalled in the lean days that are to follow, for there is real bread and real butter and real potatoes, things that later are as scarce as icicles in a boiler room.

That first night in the new camp was a jolly one. In spite of the high wind prevailing, everyone was reassured by the brilliant red sunset and had the feeling that the morrow might be fine. The proposed trip over the northern peaks—Clay, Jefferson, and Adams—to the Madison Huts was eagerly antici-pated; so at a fairly early hour George let down the folding bunks, arranged the blankets, and everyone prepared to turn in. Owing to the fact that the ladies' dormitory was shut off from the heat of the fire and seemed rather cold and cheerless, the two ladies of the party elected to take a section of the larger room.

For a party of seven the night was a very quiet and restful one, aside from the roar of the wind rushing up the ravine outside the house. Such few snores as could be heard were of a very refined and considerate sort, and all awakened with a feeling of gratitude to their fellow voyagers for not "mak-ing night hideous." Breakfast was had in good season, and plans were dis-cussed. Sunday had not dawned as pleasantly as could be wished—far from it. A stiff wind was blowing, about all that one could stand against, and the clouds were scudding low and thick. The more optimistic and venturesome members of the party were in favor of starting anyway, but one old croaker protested and asseverated that a big storm was brewing, one which might last four to five days. He urged everyone to sit tight and enjoy the beauties of the rainy day in camp, with the hope of getting out by Friday. The croaker was promptly voted a nuisance, especially by the ladies, who dubbed him a "calamity howler." The calm and imperturbable Scientist came to his rescue, however, and read a few extracts from the *Appalachian Guide Book*[18] as to the dangers of the Gulfside Trail in bad weather. This seemed to have the desired effect, and everybody calmed down and made the best of the situation. Rain was soon beating against the exposed windows and the wind steadily increased in velocity, keeping at it with violence until late in the afternoon, when the clouds suddenly parted and spirits rose. The sun attempted to come through and things looked decidedly better.

In spite of the fierce wind, somebody dared somebody else to take a run up Mount Monroe, which is only a fifteen or twenty minutes climb from the camp. All hands voted in favor of it and started up the east side of the peak, which was the lee side as the wind was blowing. Ottilie, who was the featherweight of the party, was firmly grasped by George, the guide, or she might have been blown away. As she neared the top, the wind seized her tightly tied veil and tore it from her head, carrying it straight up for several hundred feet, and then chased it at the rate of a mile a minute over Boott Spur in the direction of Jackson. A minute later, when she gained the summit, the gale might have made her follow suit, had not George rescued her. The Bobs, who were following, for once thanked their *embonpoint*, which was sufficient to keep them from going skyward. On the summit no one could safely stand, and all beat a hasty retreat toward the hut. They were not a minute too soon; for, by the time they were safely housed, the real storm began, a storm which raged without cessation until Thursday morning.

It was on this night that the Chocorua Peak House disappeared and that the greatest damage was done throughout the entire mountain region. The caretaker at the stage-office on the summit of Washington estimated the wind velocity on that night at 175 miles an hour, and this does not seem incredible,[19] as the United States Weather Bureau recorded 186 miles an hour at the time

---

[18] Likely the first edition of *AMC White Mountain Guide*, published in 1907.—Editor

[19] The U.S. Weather Bureau, asked to ascertain the probable wind velocity on Mount Washington during the storm of September 1915, stated that from comparative records of velocity and of barometric pressure at adjacent stations during the years when a weather station was maintained on Mount Washington, it may be assumed that the velocity of the air did not get below 100 miles per hour for several days of this storm. The department also stated that it may have reached the high record of 1878—that is, 186.5 miles per hour.

it maintained a station there, and this storm of 1915 was said to be the worst for thirty-five years.

Suffice it to say that one who has not experienced such a storm can have no conception of what it means to be where the wind is traveling from two to three miles in a single minute. Had not the Lakes of the Clouds Hut been most strongly built, the uneasiness of its occupants would have been much greater. As it was, apprehension prevailed, for the huge windows offered a splendid target for the fury of the gale. The steel window sash with its quarter-inch panes was firmly embedded in masonry, but a tendency to bend and buckle could be noted with half an eye, as the savage gusts crashed against the glass barrier with the force of surf breaking on the rocks by the seashore. These ominous crashes served to make everyone reflect upon the consequences, should the windows give way. With windows gone there would be more real shelter in the lee of the masonry on the outside of the hut than there could possibly be within. Fortunately these foreboding were not realized, and in spite of doubts and fears all turned in at a seasonable hour. For the most, it was afterwards confessed, there was little sleep. Aside from the regular crashes of the gale there was a vibration of the entire stone structure, which required no seismograph to record, as it could be plainly felt by the would-be sleeper lying in his narrow bunk.

Monday morning came at last, with the hurricane still doing its worst. To add to the general discomfort, the temperature had dropped greatly during the night, and investigation showed that the thermometer on the sheltered side of the house registered 18 degrees Fahrenheit. Within it was not much warmer, before the fire was built; while, later in the day, an indoor temperature of 38 degrees was the standard at a short distance from the stove. One of the most comforting features of the situation was the ample supply of charcoal fuel. The food supply, however, caused serious thought of the future, should the storm continue, as now seemed probable. A consultation on this important subject, and an inventory of the scantily stocked larder, made it appear that a decree prohibiting more than two meals a day must be issued. It was done forthwith. Breakfast, thereafter, was changed to "brunch."

It began to appear that the most comfortable place to spend the day, as well as the night, was in bed; so most of the boarders of the hostelry kept under cover of the heavy blankets and whiled away the hours by reading the few magazines which some thoughtful people had left in the camp. To hold a paper for more than a few minutes one wanted his gloves on, while the frosted breath of the occupants and the heavily frosted windows lent an Arctic air to the scene. The Veteran, who rather spurned the comfort of his couch in the daytime, felt the need of exercise to warm his feet on the chill concrete floor. Many miles he paced up and down the avenues between the bunks—a picturesque figure, with his blue stocking cap pulled down over his ears, a blanket pinned tightly about his shoulders, and on his hands a pair of large and fuzzy gloves.

As the day wore on, gloom settled upon some of the party, as they realized what anxiety might be felt for them by their families. This was the day that they were due to be at the Glen House at 5 P.M. and failure to be there to meet the automobile would at once cause all sorts of fears as to their safety. They knew, of course, that the home folks could not tell whether they had been overcome by the storm on the trail over the Northern Peaks, or whether they were still safe in the shelter of the hut. Nothing could be done about it, as the only means of communication with the outside world, a wireless telegraph outfit (which had been in use for a short time at the opening of the hut) had been dismantled. To attempt to escape through the raging gale seemed but to invite certain death.

At times the gloom gave place to gaiety, when some lively little incident or some humorous story enlivened the whole party. The hawk-eyed George, for instance, captured a mouse which he tossed to Mrs. Bob, thinking to frighten her. To his surprise, she proceeded to make a pet of it, and George was obliged to make some holes in a baking-powder tin to serve as a cage where Mr. Mouse could live in comfort with a supply of cheese to feast upon.

Monday passed with no change in the weather. Such bits of out of doors as could be seen within a few rods of the house were thick with snow and the beautiful frost-feathers. It was quite possible to run, for exercise, for a couple of minutes outside on the sheltered side of the house; but let one venture beyond the corners and the gale would knock him flat. Somehow George and the hardy Parker at times managed to crawl to the stream for water. On one occasion Parker started with a full pail but the wind sucked out the contents, except for enough to cover the bottom, giving him a drenching that required hugging the stove for some time.

The generous providers of the furnishings of the hut had been wise enough to equip the place with 85 blankets, and it was well that they did, for by Monday night they were all called into requisition. Some, of course, were placed as mattresses and some for pillows, while each person was covered with a mountain of them; but, in spite of the fact that all slept with their clothes on, no one was too warm. The searching wind made such unhindered progress through the hut as to make it necessary for most of the guests to sleep with a cap on or to cover their heads with a blanket.

On Tuesday morning Bob wakened with the recollection of a dream freshly in mind. In his vision he had seen a front page of the *Boston American* with the words "Peary Volunteers" in huge headlines. On reading further, it developed that the enterprising sheet had started a relief expedition led by the intrepid explorer; while, not to be outdone, two other national heroes, General Funston and ex-President Roosevelt, had wired that they were on the way. This dream served to create some amusement; so, that whenever an unusual noise was heard outside, someone was sure to shout, "There's Peary!"

Tuesday was much like Monday, only the food supply was getting lower. At this juncture, the Scientist recalled a box of food which was pressed upon him as he came up the Crawford Trail on Saturday by Dr. Blake of Boston and his party, who were on their way down. As luck would have it, it contained some sliced chicken, which the ladies fried. They also made a peculiar but edible kind of bread from some package flour. This was eaten with some spoonfuls of melted bacon fat left over from the cooking, and the second and last meal of the day was voted a success. The Veteran was unkind enough to smuggle some samples of this bread into his knapsack, which he later took home and exhibited as geological curiosities.

Throughout all this time, let it not be forgotten, the storm was raging in earnest; though the fact that the windows had held thus far gave assurance of safety that enabled the prisoners to feel more calm. The continued roar of the wind, however, had a wearing effect on the nerves, and the worry over the anxiety of those left at home was ever present. Lack of exercise, in itself, is enough to upset the equanimity of most individuals, while a poor and scanty diet goes far toward keeping the circulation sub-normal. At times the cold seemed to get into one's bones in a paralyzing fashion, so the party formed in a ring and marched around, each slapping the shoulders of his neighbor in front until all were again thoroughly warm.

The bedtime hour was an interesting time for George, who certainly earned his salary in arranging the many blankets and tucking everybody in. In this he was quite expert, as he folded them in such fashion to make a sleeping bag effect and keep out the chill breezes to the best possible advantage. It was voted many times by the party that the camp was fortunate in having such a versatile and well-qualified caretaker. In the first place, George was a native of the mountain country and familiar with it from boyhood. He had also had great experience in the woods, both as a lumberjack and as a licensed guide. These were only a few of his accomplishments, as he was a licensed chauffeur, a motorman, a carpenter, and a blazer of trails, having done trail work for the Appalachian Club for several years. In addition he was a good cook—when he had the necessary raw materials to cook.

Monday and Tuesday were long days, but Wednesday stretched its length even further, as the shelves containing the supplies were now nearly empty, and uneasiness was rampant. Plans were discussed as to what might be done in case the wind abated; but it was finally agreed that no move would be made until the weather was such that all could go and the party be preserved as a unit. The ladies busied themselves in cutting the remnants of an old blanket into strips wherewith to make puttees, for they knew the snow would be deep on the trail and no one was equipped for Arctic travel.

During the day when the wind lulled a bit, the ladies, who were anxious to see whether travel in the storm might be possible, sallied out a few rods from the house toward the Crawford Trail. In an instant they were lost in the thick scudding clouds. One of the others inside had an inspiration and seized a cowbell which was kept for the purpose of signaling. This he rang violently in the doorway, and in a few minutes the adventurous girls returned. They afterwards confessed that they were hopelessly lost, although only a stone's throw from the camp. Wednesday night at 11 o'clock the last night-owl had retired. The storm was still raging with no sign of abatement.

At 5:15 on Thursday morning the first slumberer to awaken gave a shout of joy, which caused every sleepy head to emerge from its cocoon. A miracle had happened. The wind had ceased. The sky was clear. Instantly everyone was out of bed in a rush to the door. The imperturbable Scientist for a moment forgot his calm demeanor and dashed out into the snow in his stocking feet. The chorus of "Ohs" and "Ahs," which arose as the magnificent scene began to be comprehended, might have been heard a mile away in the clear air.

In the eyes of some tears of joy could well be imagined. Perhaps they were even there. The heavens overhead were a fleckless dome, the valleys below showed a glorious green, save for here and there a dainty cloud of purple chiffon. Rising lofty and impressive above the Lakes of the Clouds the great cone of Washington appeared in spotless white, resembling a huge frosted cake made for the king of all the giants. On the weather side of the stone hut marvelous frost-feathers covered the walls in wonderful patterns to a depth of a foot or more, while every rock to which these could attach had its Indian head-dress of eagle plumes in perfect white. In many cases their wonderful formations stood to a length of several feet. As the rising sun began to approach the horizon, a roseate glow crowned the summits of Lafayette and the more distant Adirondacks, while far to the north the mountains of Canada were easily discernible. With all this display of magnificence it was difficult for the overjoyed party to eat the necessary breakfast and make the preparations for the flight from their erstwhile prison.

At 7 o'clock all were ready for the march. It was decided to go up the cone to Washington summit, thence down the carriage road to Glen House. George volunteered to pilot the party. It was well that he did, too; for, while one might go almost anywhere over the snow, it was almost impossible for one but slightly familiar with the trail to follow it closely, with all the landmarks in a similar disguise of feathers.

A notice was left on the door, giving the roster of the party and information as to where they had gone. This was read a couple of hours later by the rescue party sent to find the Scientist, and they gave up their search—otherwise a party of twenty volunteers, which had been organized, would have been called upon to take affairs in hand. The climb to the summit was wonderful, affording as it did every instant some new and undiscovered glory. As the ocean, gleaming in gold at Portland, came into view, cheers were given to show the grateful feelings of the party, not only at being discharged from their dungeon, but in being liberated on a morning in ten thousand. Words fail to describe the happiness of that climb and the descent on the other side of the summit. Though feet were cold in wading the drifts in canvas sneakers, as some of the party did, hearts were warm enough to make up for it.

Arrived at the summit, mirrors were flashed, to signal news of safety to anxious friends in Jackson. The response was amazing; not only from Jackson but from beyond and from either side answering flashes were noticed. It seemed as if all New Hampshire must be watching the fairy scene on that perfect morning.

The story of the thawing of chilly bare feet in a shovel of snow at the stage-office, the description of the view from the summit, the bidding good-bye to George, the meeting of the rescue party near the Halfway House—all these things might be forgiven if one were writing a book; but this is just a little tale of what happened to people of humdrum lives, "even as you and I."

OVER ICE AND SNOW ON THE EQUATOR:
AN ASCENT OF KILIMANJARO

Paul Simpson McElroy
1932

This climbing feat seems unlikely enough as to have been dreamed up. But as far as we can ascertain, Paul Simpson McElroy (1902–1989) did achieve this amazing climb of Africa's highest peak with little experience, no planning, and not much gear. Appalachia *editor Robert L. M. Underhill noted at the time, "This climb, made September 3–8, 1928, with the summit attained on September 7, seems clearly to be a first American ascent. The author is heartily to be congratulated on the enterprise with which, lacking suitable equipment, he undertook this climb and the persistence with which he carried it through."*

This is the only article McElroy wrote for the journal. We believe that this is the same man who became a Lutheran pastor and edited an edition of Thomas à Kempis's The Imitation of Christ.

I

"*L*ET'S CLIMB THE HIGHEST MOUNTAIN IN AFRICA!" I remarked somewhat flippantly to my three traveling companions as they peered through the train windows in search of the lofty summit, which can be seen on cloudless days en route from Nairobi to Mombasa.

"Impossible," explained Curtis. "Why, do you know that no American has ever been to the top of Kilimanjaro?"

"What do you mean?" burst in Alden. "Climb up a snow-capped peak when dressed as ruffians for the tropics? Not on your life!"

Just then Harold, who had been consulting a guidebook, interrupted by reading to us that "Kilimanjaro has the longest continuous ascent of any mountain in the world, rising as volcanic cone from a plain 4,500 feet high to a peak of 19,710 feet."

"Isn't it strange, too," added Harold, "that a mountain three and a half miles high should have been totally forgotten from the time of the Greeks until as recently as 1848; and that when it was rediscovered the scientists of that day had so conclusively proved that snow could not exist on the equator that the report was discredited?"

In spite of the protests, I reiterated, "Let's climb the highest mountain in Africa!" By the time we had reached the coast I had ascertained the cost and looked up possible train and boat connections; the challenge was too great for me, and just twenty minutes before the train was to leave Mombasa I reached my decision—my friends thought it a wild one—to make the 500-mile detour into Tanganyika Territory and undertake this ten-day excursion alone. In the short interval before our separation I confiscated and hastily transferred to my kit our canned goods and edibles and cabled for boat fare to the American University at Cairo, where I was teaching, trusting that it would be awaiting me on my return.

Almost before I realized it I had bidden farewell to my three traveling companions and was alone. As the train bore me away from my friends toward the cold and hazardous peak, I confess that my heart grew faint. But so enraptured was I with the wild tropical luxuriance around me, and so enthralled by the prospect of doing something never before accomplished by any of my countrymen, that I was lured on.

Returning to Voi, the junction, I managed to get permission to ride to Moshi, at the foot of the mountain, on a special water train that was leaving due to the season of drought. (Trains run only once a week, Sunday, on this line.) It took me ten hours to ride the one hundred miles. As I sat in a comfortable coach and listened to the puffing of the wood-burning engine, it was hard to realize that, only a few years before, wild lions had killed scores of natives engaged in the construction of the road.

Unable to get much information when I arrived at Moshi, other than that I should need provisions—which I bought, estimating them the best I could—I resolved to go on to Marangu, twenty miles away, to consult a German missionary to whom I was referred there. He was said to have made the trip before. So I hired a dilapidated Ford and carted supplies and equipment over. At Marangu my porters, eager to rid themselves of my heavy packs, went in advance and to my embarrassment deposited my luggage at the home of this German missionary. It was with diffidence that I tapped on his door a half-hour later. But before I could apologize for the unannounced appearance of my baggage or explain my presence, a pleasant soft-voiced gentleman greeted me by saying, "Come right in. It is a treat for me and for my wife to see you. I presume that it is Kilimanjaro that has attracted you to these remote regions?"

"Yes," I admitted, "it is."

"What a coincidence!" said Reusch. "Tomorrow I am starting up the mountain myself in the hope of establishing a record.[20] Would you like to join me?"

Excitedly I replied that I certainly should, and then the horrible thought occurred to me that I had to be back at Moshi in five days to catch the weekly train for the coast. Could it be done?

My hopes sank when Reusch told me that the trip would probably take six days, although it might be done in five. Should I take a chance on making the trip in five days?

I did.

II

While we were making preparations for our expedition Reusch told me much about the mountain.

"Naturally," he said, "on a mountain whose base is larger than England itself it is exceedingly difficult for me to give a clear picture of the surrounding topography. You will see two peaks or craters on the mountain. Kibo is the higher, dome-shaped and covered with snow. Mavenzi, which is about

---

[20] That is, a record number of trips for one man. Richard Reusch had already been up the mountain three times at the time of the original writing. Also, Reusch's first name was originally omitted from this article. During his lifetime, he summited the peak 65 times.—Editor

Somehow Paul Simpson McElroy made it across the Uhuru Glacier—then known as just a glacier beneath Kaiser Wilhelm Point—wearing English army shoes he'd bought in Cairo.

seven miles east of Kibo, is irregular, rugged, and studded with spires—the highest of which is named after me, since I had happened to be the first to climb it. Mavenzi rises to a height of 17,400 feet and Kibo to one of 19,710. Connecting these two distinct volcanoes is a plateau five miles broad, known as the Saddle."

As Reusch was talking I glanced out of the door and noticed that a couple of natives were watching us. A few minutes later I looked out again and to my surprise saw that there were several standing in the doorway. These natives, who had mysteriously gathered around and were peeking in at us timidly while we packed, interested me greatly. Many of them carried a blanket slung over one shoulder like a toga or draped over the head in the fashion of a cape. Their feet were bare and had apparently become so toughened that they were immune to prickers, sharp stones, and cold. Strangely enough, their kinky black hair was always bared to the penetrating rays of the torrid sun, yet it was dangerous for one of us to step into the open for a short time even on a cloudy day, lest we succumb to sunstroke. An occasional sly smile often revealed a set of filed teeth, with perhaps a lower front tooth extracted in order that life might be sustained in case of such illness as lockjaw, which is common. Of such were our porters.

These porters, nineteen of them, took enough supplies to last us at least six days: 72 pounds of rice, 105 pounds of flour, 60 pounds of raw meat, 10 pounds of sugar, 38 blankets, and 3 lanterns, in addition to our personal equipment. No porters are eager to toil up a mountain with a burden of about forty pounds on their heads, but when accompanying white men who climb up and back for nothing, they are more than reluctant to go. To climb simply for the sake of climbing is a sport unknown to the native. The fact that he can make the trip barefoot and with a heavy load on his head makes the white man seem a weakling in comparison. Admittedly, the native is able to undergo extremes of hunger, fatigue, heat, and cold much better than the white man; but for prolonged endurance the European will outdo him.

III

Because of the difficulty in procuring the nineteen porters our departure was delayed until evening, and darkness added considerably to the weirdness of the climb. With only a flickering lantern to light the elephant path, we stumbled along as best we could. The hillside forest up through which we wound our way was thickly carpeted with tall elephant grass and densely packed with bushes, twisted vines, and saplings, while huge moss-draped trees with far-spreading branches formed a continuous interwoven canopy so solid that even the stars were not visible. Only an animal as powerful as an elephant could have forged a path through such a jungle. Numerous depressions, deep elephant footprints, were filled with water from the afternoon's rain. Our lantern did not really illumine the route, it only served to guide those who followed; and as we felt our way along the sinuous path in the darkness it was not uncommon for us to fall into these watery depressions. Not only were the elephant footprints there, but not infrequently we heard the elephants themselves signaling to one another on opposite sides of our path. And no sooner did we feel ourselves out of the area guarded by these powerful sentinels than we heard the screeches of baboons.

All along the way one of the porters, Ndesangusio, of the Wadschagga tribe, had been jabbering incessantly—for the purpose, I had supposed, of warding off any prowling animals that might be lurking about our trail. But it was not long before Reusch turned to me and said, "Listen to what

Ndesangusio has been telling me. 'The old Wadschagga legend about the mountain,' he says, 'is that once in ancient times, when both peaks were smoking their pipes, that of Mavenzi became extinguished. He went to his bigger but younger brother, Kibo, to borrow fire. A short time later while he was taking a nap the fire in his pipe went out, and again he went to borrow from Kibo. But this time the latter became very angry and thrashed him so terribly with his club that even now one can see his bruised, battered, and torn surface, and sense the attitude of austerity he adopted after his unjust treatment. The Wadschagga believe that Mavenzi is ashamed of his appearance and, therefore, covers his face with clouds at every opportunity.'" And, indeed, it is seldom that one sees Mavenzi without clouds.

The night's excitement had been so great that, weary as I was, I could not sleep when we reached Bismarck Hut (8,400 feet), a camp beside one of the countless rivulets of melted ice which flow down the mountainside. Even though we were over a mile and a half high, the foliage was still so thick and lofty that we could not get a clear view of the surroundings.

IV

As we journeyed the next day from Bismarck Hut on up to Peters Hut (11,500 feet), we noticed that the vegetation gradually diminished in size and abundance. On the way we passed through acres upon acres of shrub land—bushes bedecked with red and white straw flowers, rhododendron, and the rare Johnstonia. Along the path we saw astonishing numbers of fresh spoor, which we identified without the slightest doubt as those of leopards. Mountain lions, too, obviously inhabited this country. All that day, so far as we knew, the fog never lifted enough to give us even so much as a glimpse of the peak; in fact, we were so busy scanning the landscape for ambushed leopards and lions that we missed any momentary view of it we might have had. After tramping for about ten miles we discovered that we were only a little over one-half mile higher in altitude than the day before.

Inside Peters Hut we found hay to lie on, and a woodstove; but even then the room was none too cozy, with the temperature outside 5 degrees below freezing. In order to prevent the latchless door of the shelter from banging all night and disturbing our slumbers we fastened it with a piece of string, leaving it partway open so as to secure sufficient ventilation to keep the odor of the 60 pounds of raw meat hanging inside from becoming obnoxious. We could not sleep soundly in that altitude, in spite of our being very tired, and the various and mysterious noises that reached our ears seemed painfully distinct in the clear, crisp air. About midnight a loud scratching sound on the door annoyed me so much that I arose to see what was causing it. It stopped before I got to the door. But I reached this just in time to see a leopard bounding away in the bright moonlight. When I got back in bed Reusch remarked, "Did you realize that we only have one revolver among us for protection?"

At dawn we found ourselves on the very shore of an unbounded sea of fluffy clouds. Although I had been in the vicinity of Kilimanjaro for six days, I had not had so much as a glimpse of Kibo, for either clouds or fog had constantly kept the frosted peak from view. But now that we were above the clouds the peak stood out in all his majesty. Kibo, in his morning grandeur, invited one to climb. It seemed incredible that the silvery dome, so near at hand, should still be, for us, two days' journey away. We could also see clearly the brother, Mavenzi, seven miles away from Kibo.

V

Our next day's journey was to take us above the vegetation belt, which meant that we should have to carry fuel and water enough to last until we could get back. At best we could only hope to take enough of the former for cooking. And not only were we to be deprived of the warmth of a fire in this colder climate but we were to have no hut in which to sleep.

We had not been climbing long when we noticed eagles apparently oblivious to the cold from which we were suffering, soaring majestically around the jagged spires of Mavenzi. Before the day was over I realized my childhood wish: I saw not only snow, but a snowstorm, on the equator itself.

Up in this intemperate land one would not expect to find game; but giant eland, the largest of all antelopes, frequently pass the night on the open saddle, where ambushing leopards and lions cannot attack them. So unsuspecting are the eland that we were able to come within a stone's throw of a herd of fifteen while we were crossing the saddle, and so long as we did not molest them they merely stood by and watched.

Our destination for that night was "the Caves" (about 15,000 feet), a barren spot nearly as high as the highest peaks of the Alps. These crude, cruelly cold caves are at the western end of the saddle, just at the foot of Kibo's truncated cone. The name "caves" is scarcely justified, as it connotes more protection than this exposed shelter affords. Had I said that we slept in the open, sheltered only by a roof of stone made ages ago by colossal rocks tumbling together, it would better describe our lodgings.

VI

After we had been shivering for hours in our "shelter" it was a relief to crawl, at 3:20 A.M., out from under the chilly blankets and make ready to start, even though it was for colder regions. From 4 A.M., when we started, until sunrise it was so bitterly cold that we walked with blankets wrapped round us. At sunrise we took off the blankets and sent back the two porters who had thus far accompanied us, with them, to Peters Hut for a rest. Much as we needed the wraps we had to part with them, for they were altogether too cumbersome in that altitude. Although we were in better spirits and more jubilant than ever before, we could not break out into laughter and song as we had been doing, because we needed to save our breath. The economics professor who told me that air was a free commodity because there was so much of it had certainly never been up Kilimanjaro.

Our ascent was made up an inclined trough formed by a glacier. On either side of this glacier-formed passageway huge boulders had been heaved upon one another, and the last half of the broad pass lay between masses of thick ice. The comparative absence of snow was due to a current of warm air. The final part of the route was up a slope that is just as steep as it is possible for loose gravel to be piled, making the ascent of Kibo strenuous, but not as sharp as that of the rocky Mavenzi.

We climbed along silently, by lantern light, until sunrise and in those two hours our feet became numb. The stones were chilled below freezing temperatures and, step where we would, we couldn't move off that cold, cold floor. Under normal conditions we could have kept warm by stamping our feet and swinging our arms vigorously, but up there we had no breath to spare on fatiguing exercises. Then, my discomfort was intensified owing to the fact that I was equipped for the tropics and not the Arctic regions.

At first we took 100 steps and then stopped for breath, but the cold was so intense that the pauses had to be short and consequently we were forced to journey on without sufficient rest. The exertion necessary for advancing became increasingly difficult as the atmosphere became more rare. After every 100 steps we were veritably gasping for air, yet this air was so thin that even after our halts it was impossible to breathe normally. Walking in gravel on the level is hard enough; it is trebly hard going up a slope in an atmosphere so rarefied. We estimated that for every yard-step that was taken on this gravel mountainside we slid back to such an extent that the actual progress made was only from six to ten inches. We soon had to reduce our allotment to 80 steps; then to 60, 40, 25, 20; and before we reached the top it was impossible to take more than ten steps without stopping. At the rate we breathed, puffed, and gasped for air we knew that our lungs and hearts—the latter pounding and thumping at the rate of 132 beats a minute—must be in good condition to stand the strain. Luckily, we did not succumb to the nauseating mountain sickness so prevalent in high altitudes.

VII

After exactly twelve hours of arduous climbing, Reusch suddenly exclaimed to me, "Is that scene worth the effort? You can consider yourself among the very few ever to have viewed it." When he spoke I knew that we must be standing on Gilman's Point, on the rim of the crater, for I saw stretched before me a miniature arctic zone, a veritable sunken garden of ice. Nature has carved parts of this white expanse into colossal temples, bulwarks, and palaces. One section had cracked away and exposed a glossy vertical surface of ice over three hundred feet thick and 0.25 mile long. The rays of the sinking sun decorated these fantastic, crystalline shapes with myriads of sparkling diadems and lighted up the tips of gigantic icicles, turning them into beacons in a sea of ice. Perhaps the natives were not far wrong, I thought, when they imagined this beautiful region to be the home of the gods and, as such, a place not to be disturbed.

Not infrequently a wrathful boom would disturb the serenity as a gigantic crack occurred in the ice. That, and a terrific wind howling across the very top of the crater's edge, awed one with the cruel and merciless spirit of the place.

Although we were on top of the world, a point on the western edge of the crater, diagonally across this white basin, seemed just a bit higher than the Gilman's Point where we were standing, and this was our destination. Part of the course around to that western peak—Kaiser Wilhelm Point,[21]

---

[21] Now known as Uhuru Peak.—Editor

as it is called from the days when Tanganyika Territory was German East Africa—is on the inner and sheltered side of the crater, but the greater part is over glaciers on the outside wall. Safety devices such as a rope and nailed shoes, essential as they really were, we did not have (I was wearing ordinary English army shoes, purchased in Cairo), and furthermore they would have been very cumbersome at that fatiguing height. Our only climbing aid was the alpenstock, and upon that staff all depended.

As we started out, a terrific gale nearly swept us both off the crest, whence, once started, we would have slid down the icy crown of Kibo for a quarter-mile or more. Frantically trying to hold on to our tropical helmets with one hand, for fear of sunstroke in that equatorial frigid climate, and holding fast to our alpenstocks with the other, we forged ahead, zigzagging across the windswept dome.

Much of the surface was wind-furrowed, resembling the leaves of an open book. These thin, flaky sheets broke off at each step and we sank down before we could get a firm footing. There were smaller cracks, which we jumped over, but because of the exquisite beauty of the surroundings and of my eagerness to reach Kaiser Wilhelm Point, I had become oblivious to any real danger, when we found ourselves standing before a huge crevasse. By following the tapering divide far enough we came to a narrow vantage point, where we would cross, but time was too precious to waste on many such detours.

One might well have been cold up there even in heavy woolen garments, but to me, clad only in thin cotton ones, the low temperature was unbearable. Had this been something other than an *ex tempore* expedition, undertaken in a mood of adventure, I should not have had to resort to a pair of socks for mittens. Unfortunately, it was not possible to hang on to the alpenstock long enough with one hand at a time to let the other hand get "thawed out" in my pocket. But I expected discomforts when so inadequately equipped.

As we poked along we saw numerous dark, icy caverns. The slanting leaves of flaky ice so hid these holes from view that we nearly stumbled into one such enormous, bottomless pit. When we came upon this particular opening, Reusch, who, though a fearless man, has enough of that saving sense of caution which makes a man a hero instead of a fool, said, "I think we had better go back. It is getting dark." I saw no reason to be afraid of darkness with what seemed, save for a few holes, to be at least three hundred feet of solid ice beneath us; so I pleaded with him to go on in order that we might attain the longed-for goal. He consented. After that it would have been impolitic to admit that I inwardly doubted if my limbs could carry me further, so I trudged on. Rapid breathing for a short time is enervating; when kept up for several hours it becomes utterly exhausting; yet in spite of extreme fatigue we pressed on. Careful as we were in placing our footsteps, we suddenly discovered, while looking down into another fathomless dungeon, that we were standing not on its side but on the edge of its overhanging, thin shelf. Lying prone in order to distribute our weight as evenly as possible, we crawled off this edge like boys creeping off from thin ice.

With darkness rapidly approaching the chances of safety were running against us. But after having traversed near to Kaiser Wilhelm Point my alpenstock began to break through the ice at every step. Out of curiosity I halted to investigate. Leaning over one of the series of holes it had made, I found to my horror that we were standing, not on three hundred feet of solid ice, but rather on a thin shelf with enormous cavities beneath. From far below the sound of running water faintly reached my ears. Where next to step was the question.

The sensation of being thus almost suspended in midair was rare. Perhaps, since fear could scarcely have increased our heartbeats, our feelings of this sort may have been diminished; but I doubt if the sensation of actually plunging down into the cavern could have been more realistic than our imaginings. While we were thus marooned on this frail roof, Reusch turned to me and said, ironically, "I think it is best that we try to go back." This time I did not dispute the wisdom of his words and we retraced our steps as best we could.

It was fortunate that we did turn back, though disappointed to do so, for soon after we had set foot on solid ground again (about 8:30 P.M.) Reusch had a severe outbreak of malaria. Shelter was still five hours away. In this emergency we took the chance of racing down the long incline in the darkness. What it had taken us twelve hours to go up, we descended in two. We had no lantern and the moon was not out, but somehow we pushed along. The Southern Cross was the only marker familiar to us. Two of the porters were waiting on the saddle to guide us back to Peters. They used that uncanny sense, which all natives possess, of finding their way in a strange district. They took us aimlessly around stones, over stones, and beside stones, on what they called the path; farther down the mountain they took us past clumps of grass, over clumps of grass, and around clumps of grass, on what they still claimed was the path; yet, though they wandered about as they did, I would not swear it was not the way, for to my surprise we eventually reached Peters Hut.

We had been going steadily from 4 A.M. until 2:30 A.M. the next day, 22½ hours; and during that time, due to loss of appetite at the high altitude, we had eaten and drunk nothing.

VIII

On Saturday morning I bade farewell to my companion and left Peters Hut with two porters, via a different route, direct for the railroad station at Moshi. The descent as far as Johannes Hut (about the same altitude as Bismarck Hut on the other route) was uneventful save for unique weather conditions: dense clouds were both above and below us, yet the intervening space was clear. From Johannes Hut we again followed elephant trails; more truly, judging by the freshness of the tracks, we were following elephants. When I thought we were nearly "out of the woods," all three of us instinctively stopped short, and ever so distinctly we heard the panting of some big beast. As we were unarmed, it was to our great relief that the animal soon turned and retreated into the brush entanglement.

We emerged from the woods at a place five miles from my destination, which delayed my arrival at the home of a hospitable missionary on the outskirts of Moshi until 10 P.M. My host informed me that I should have to leave at 4:30 in the morning in order catch the 7 o'clock weekly train from Moshi to the coast. When all ready to start, all my persuasion and threatening would not induce my porters to travel in the dark without a lantern. To confiscate my host's lantern would have been highly discourteous, and to have missed my train disastrous; the only solution was to hire the porters to return the lantern and trust they would do so. On the way to the station, about a half-hour after starting, a leopard crossed the road and sneezed or coughed at us from the embankment. It is said that an animal will never attack a moving light, and I was indeed glad that the porters had insisted on carrying a lantern.

The low morning clouds, which shut off a view of the mountain, gave me the feeling, as I rode away, of leaving a dear friend without bidding farewell.

THE ATTACK ON CRILLON

Bradford Washburn

1934

Brad Washburn (1910–2007) was in his early 20s with most of his illustrious career—as mountaineer, mapmaker, and founder/head of the Museum of Science, Boston, from 1939–1980—ahead of him when he made this attempt on Mount Crillon, in the Saint Elias Mountains of Alaska's Fairweather Range. As this story shows, the Harvard alumnus already could write very well.

Washburn's devotion to high peaks began even earlier. He told Appalachia[22] that he climbed Mount Washington with a cousin at age eleven, but that the French Alps gripped him starting in 1926. He once said that he would have lasted only about thirty minutes if he had tried to climb solo. But as a leader, he had nerves and muscles of steel. He pioneered many first ascents and new routes in Alaska, and he made new maps of the Grand Canyon, Mount Everest, and the Presidential Range in New Hampshire's White Mountains.

Washburn, who remained involved with the AMC most of his life, wrote a healthy handful of feature articles for Appalachia over the years, including the story of the route he pioneered on Mount McKinley (Denali) in 1945. Washburn climbed and made maps with his wife, Barbara, at his side. Most of his life, Washburn lectured, wrote, and explored (for, among other places, National Geographic*) as a way of making extra money. Late in life he noted that his salary at the Museum of Science, Boston, in the 1940s was in the neighborhood of $3,000. It is unlikely that he earned anything writing the essay below, however, since the journal was then entirely volunteer-run. (Today, it is mostly volunteer-run.)*

---

[22] Doug Mayer and Rebecca Oreskes, "Mountain Voices," 53, no. 4 (2001).

Just a month after this article was published, Washburn and Carter made a fourth attack on Crillon and successfully reached the main summit.

T HE IMMEDIATE REACTION TO OUR DESPERATE STRUGGLES [in 1932] with Mount Crillon and its August storms was that none of us ever wanted to see Alaska again as long as he lived. But then the pictures were developed and the movies run through, and by the end of six weeks we had forgotten all our hardships and were raving in superlatives to all our friends about the unbelievable ski slopes, the sunsets, the flowers, and the big banquets of fresh heather-fed grouse.

By January plans were already under way for another attempt on Crillon. This time we knew the mountain and its problems infinitely better than before, and we had several months ahead of us to plan to meet every possible contingency.

The stupendous northwest wall of Crillon, in the southern group of the Fairweather Range, lifts itself 7,000 feet in one unbroken 50-degree precipice of ice and rock from the head of the North Crillon Glacier. The eastern approaches to the summit ridge are a continuation of this same unscalable cliff, which at not a single point, over a distance of nearly fifteen miles, reaches an altitude of less than 3,000 vertical feet. The few buttresses and ribs which jut out from this precipice are either too steep to be practical for transportation routes or are blocked at their upper ends by immense cornices and walls of avalanching ice. The southern approaches to the great Crillon plateau appear fully as dubious as those to the north and east, an endless series of hanging glaciers and icefalls dropping from the summits of Mount La Perouse to the smooth surface of the Brady Glacier 7,000 feet below.

From the Pacific Ocean, however, it seems as if one could force a way to the plateau by following the edges of the great icefall of the La Perouse Glacier, which cascades 6,000 feet to the sea from a deep gap between Mounts Dagelet and La Perouse. Here, for a distance for a little over a mile, the barrier cliff of the plateau is broken and, in the winter and spring, smooth snowfields lead unobstructed to the upper reaches of the great peaks.

Although so much lower than Fairweather, Crillon and its massive cliffs present to the climber one of the most knotty problems of the whole range. A group of lesser peaks, ranging from 5,000 to 7,000 feet in height, lies slightly to the west of the barrier cliff, completely hiding all routes of approach to its base. Without the use of an airplane, the reconnaissance of Crillon had proven to be an immense undertaking the first time we tried it in 1932.

The equipment was intensely complicated, for we planned to do a great deal of surveying and photographic work in addition to the climbing. In general, everything we had taken in 1932 went on the second expedition with only a few slight alterations. Probably the most interesting of the minor changes was made in the preparation of our "willow wands" for trail-marking in the snow. As used originally by the Mount Logan Expedition, in 1925, these had been true willow twigs, which were jabbed into the snow at regular intervals to mark the trail in case of the obliteration of foot tracks by high winds or blizzards. In 1930, on Fairweather, we had found these too fatiguing to push into the snow, for the twig always twisted under pressure. In 1932 we had used quarter-inch maple dowels 36 inches long, dipped in black paint to make them visible in the snow. But these had proved a failure for, although one could insert them by merely pushing on the upper end, without leaning over at all, their color attracted so much heat from the sun's rays that they invariably melted themselves into little pits and disappeared from view in only a day or two! In 1933 a simple remedy for this was found by dipping only eight inches of one end of these dowels in the paint. This sole difference in preparation made the trail-markers such that they stood up for periods as long as ten days without the slightest bit of attention.

The food and other supplies were packed at the close of April and shipped west via the Panama Canal. On June 23 the advance guard, consisting of William S. Child of Philadelphia, Charles S. Houston of New York, H. Adams Carter[23] of Boston, and Russell Dow and Howard Platts of Woodsville, New Hampshire, left Juneau by boat and took all the supplies to Cenotaph Island at Lituya Bay. On the 29th of June the remainder of the

[23] Editor of the *American Alpine Journal* from 1960 to 1995.—Editor

party, composed of Walter Everett, Robert Bates, Richard Goldthwaite, and myself, reached Juneau, and on July 1 flew in to Cenotaph Island, covering the same course as a twenty-hour boat trip we'd taken two years before, in exactly an hour and ten minutes. Five airplane relays were made from Lituya Bay to Crillon Lake, and, shortly before noon, everything was in the base camp, the tent was up, and our pilot was again on his way home. What a wonderful boon the airplane is to the Alaskan traveler! In a few short hectic hours we had accomplished what it would have taken us close to a month to do by boat and on foot.

On the morning of the 2nd of July the backpacking grind commenced, and on the night of the 8th, after one day of rest, we had moved 30 days of supplies to Camp II in the site we'd set in 1932—now buried deep under the winter snow. The route from Camp II to the Knoll, at 5,600 feet, was the more arduous pack on the whole mountain. Leading first over very steep slopes of hard-packed winter snow and then along a wide arête of rocks and heather, it finally concluded by ascending a narrow rock ridge which always demanded the utmost of caution and in one place necessitated the use of a fixed rope, so delicate was the climbing. The rock was treacherous and rotten; in fact, conditions were as nasty as one could hope to find anywhere for the transportation of 75-pound loads of food and equipment. But on the 11th of July Camp II was broken and the last load of supplies went to the Knoll, where Camp III was established on a sheltered ledge. Goldthwaite, who was to spend the summer at Crillon Lake working on a geological survey and studying the glaciers, now left us, with his assistants Dow and Platts.

The second attempt on Crillon now began in earnest. At daybreak on the morning of July 12, Charlie Houston, Bob Bates, and I started for the South Col on skis. The winter of 1933 had been rather mild—at least so far as snowfall was concerned—and we were surprised to find that the route into the lower end of the Great Valley through the snow of Klooch Corner was already almost as badly broken up by cracks as it had been a month later in 1932. But we had no great difficulty in entering the valley, where perfect crust conditions prevailed. The crevasses below the South Col were entirely filled by winter snow and at 10:30 in the morning we skied in triumph over the crest of the col and had lunch. At noon, in beautiful weather, we commenced the ascent of the rock cliff over the exact route planned by Paumgarten, Everett, and me on the 1932 reconnaissance.

Two in Brad Washburn's party navigated Mount Crillon in 1932 on the unsuccessful attempt that left them eager to try again the next year.

But the cliff did not turn out to be so easy as it had appeared from a distance! What had seemed to be sturdy metamorphic rock turned out in reality to be a very rotten and weatherworn granite with a flow texture that had fooled us into thinking it was slate. The slabs were large and rounded by the constant weathering that a southwest slope is always bound to undergo. Crossing the schrund was a major problem at the start and we were nearly an hour in getting from the glacier onto the lower part of the cliff—an operation that was effected by an extremely delicate *courte-échelle* and 30 feet of climbing with scarcely any handholds. Forty minutes of this hour were spent in desperate efforts to pull Bob Bates (who was last) up over this overhang, with Houston and me towing from above, perched on microscopic platforms.

The first ledges of rock led to a very steep snow slope (47 degrees), which in turn ended at the foot of a gigantic overhang. Three hours of climbing brought us to the top of the snow some five hundred feet above the glacier. By now the sun was full on the cliff and the occasional *whir-r-r* of a pebble coursing by from above warned us that the danger of avalanches was not by any means absent. As we started to skirt the final overhang, which now tottered above us like an immense leaning wall of rock, the barrage of pebbles continually increased. A halt was called and fifteen minutes later we decided that to continue was not only dangerous but a waste of time. Stubbornness alone would have led us to go on to the plateau, for this route, with all of its obvious climbing difficulties, was far too delicate to use for reaching the upper part of the mountain. A vast amount of climbing remained once the plateau had been gained, and our route up the cliff must not only be easy enough to permit us to start this climb in moderately fresh condition, but it must not be so difficult as to be dangerous for an exhausted party to descend on the return from the summit.

Accordingly we beat a hasty and dangerous retreat to our lunching place on the glacier and sat down to survey the possibilities of another route farther to the right. The ice slopes that intervened between the end of the rocks and Mount Dagelet were effectively barred by immense cornices which lined the edge of the plateau—some of these as long as 60 feet or more. In one place only, along this two-mile barrier, the cornice narrowed down to a width of about four or five feet. A route leading to this spot up the ice slopes was our only remaining chance. The problem then remained whether the cornice could be cut from underneath, for the slope was considerably steeper than the one which we had just been on, and, although I had considerable experience on snow and ice, I did not relish too greatly the prospect of excavating a tunnel through a cornice, balanced in a small foothold at the top of a 1,500-foot, 60-degree ice slope, with occasional outcropping rocks below. When we skied back to camp that afternoon it was, however, with the conviction that this route should be attempted.

The skis were marvelous. We had not had them in the Great Valley the year before, and whereas then it had taken us nearly three hours to descend to Klooch Corner on foot, we covered the same ground now in only twenty minutes of easy skiing.

The following day was spent in resting and in moving more loads up the crest of the Knoll, a few hundred feet above the camp. Then, in the evening, all six of us started out by moonlight. We each carried 30- to 40-pound loads of provisions and rope and intended to climb the cliff and discover, if possible, the nature of the problems the upper part of the mountain above the plateau had in store for us. In fact, we planned to push ahead until we became too tired to go any farther.

The weather, which had looked a bit dubious at sunset, remained overcast with high cirrus clouds throughout the night. We reached the base of the cliff just at dawn, put on our crampons, and started out at 5 o'clock. The first rope was composed of Carter third, Everett second, and myself as leader. The route first led us up some two hundred feet of avalanche cone until we reached the schrund. This was totally impassable except in one place—exactly where the avalanches, by running across it, had carved out a narrow declivity in its upper lip. Even there it was necessary for the leader to climb on the shoulders of the second man and be pushed on up over the lip of the schrund on the end of the third climber's ice ax.

Once on the slope above, we left a picket with 60 feet of fixed rope hanging over the crack and climbed on without any great difficulties for several hundred feet. The ascent with hard frozen snow would have been terribly arduous, but after a fairly warm night we were able to make most of the footholds by kicking. At 7 o'clock we had reached the halfway point and a little more care had to be taken on account of the steepening of the grade and several little patches of ice-covered rocks across which we had to climb. The slope became continually steeper as we approached the underside of the cornice and, when we finally reached it, we were standing on a grade that measured between 60 and 65 degrees.

The boring operation was extremely delicate. I dug a deep platform on which to crouch directly under the four-foot cornice and one smaller hole well off to one side from which Everett could belay me. The cornice itself had to be chipped away in tiny pieces, for fear that the concussion from the harder blows might make it all come off at once. A half-hour of gentle pecking and the last hunk of snow finally dropped away. I poked my head up through the hole and there was the plateau stretched out before me. Once on the plateau we placed 300 feet more of fixed rope for future use and then started out beneath somber skies toward the base of Crillon, now completely enveloped in mist.

An hour later we had lunch and, owing to the extremely poor weather, gave up plans for proceeding any farther toward the mountain. Returning to the edge of the plateau, we descended the ice cliff the way we had come up. It was not till three in the afternoon that we reached the flat glacier below the cliff, after spending much time permanently fixing two 300-foot ropes to speed us on our next ascent.

The continual glare of the sun, which was breaking through the mists, had fogged my glasses and I had been forced to take them off repeatedly to supervise operations below, while the ropes were being attached. That night, when we reached the camp, I suddenly lost my sight entirely and for four days was unable to see anything at all but the difference between light and darkness. During the time I was sick some further packing was completed. I went into harness again on July 23 and we immediately moved camp, first to Klooch Corner, and then through the crevasses into the Great Valley. On the 25th of July we sledged the whole camp (900 pounds) up the valley to the South Col, there establishing our sixth camp at an altitude of 6,800 feet.

The following day we made an attempt at the cliff, but this time the night had been too warm and it had not frozen sufficiently to make carrying loads up it safe. We left our packs at its foot and skied back to camp, where we were storm-bound in a light snow all the next day. On the evening of the 27th the clouds cleared and at 3 o'clock the next morning we started out again. We had great trouble in relocating our fixed ropes and the whole upper half of the cliff, including the excavation of a newly formed cornice bigger than the first, had to be done again without their aid. We reached the edge of the plateau at eight in the morning, with the skies clouding over fast and a gentle southeasterly breeze picking up. Snow flurries commenced, and we busied ourselves with making a wall of blocks of frozen snow to shelter our tiny refuge tent. By 10 o'clock our 8,000-foot bivouac was firmly set up and we were all dozing inside waiting for a shift in the weather. Big fluffy cumulus clouds drifted lazily across the plateau, hiding Crillon entirely from view. Everywhere to the south and west an endless sea of silvery fog stretched across the ocean. La Perouse, Dagelet, and the Twins occasionally broke through the mists that seemed to hang closely only about the mountain peaks.

By noon the clouds began to disperse and, counting upon one of the evening clear-offs so typical of the Alaskan coast, we packed our sacks and set out for Crillon at 2 o'clock in the afternoon. Our plan was to traverse the plateau during the afternoon and climb to the eastern end of the final ridge toward the west peak, which is some 340 feet higher than the central summit, reaching its top just after daybreak.

All went well crossing the plateau. The footing was excellent—an inch of slush over a firmly frozen base—and the visibility fair, although occasional clouds obliterated everything and made us advance by dead reckoning for short distances. Instead of becoming clearer as sunset approached, however, the fog seemed to be settling down closer on the mountain, and by the time we had crossed the three miles of plateau and commenced to climb the steep rolling snowfields that led to the ridge we were moving entirely by guesswork—the basis for the guesses being a very thorough knowledge of the airplane photographs taken of this part of the mountain the year before. Much of the time, however, the mist was so thick that I could scarcely pick out the figures on the second rope just behind us.

We wormed and twisted about among a myriad of large, snow-covered cracks, the first bearing gently to the right, then straight ahead. Once in a while we were forced to retrace our steps and try a different route after being blocked by some yawning chasm in the glacier. As we climbed higher the fresh snow grew deeper and deeper. At first we had taken turns at leading, the first man holding his position for a half-hour. Then the time shortened to fifteen minutes and, by 7 P.M. when we had attained an altitude of about 11,000 feet, we were plowing over our knees in windblown powder and changing the lead every 30 steps!

At 7:15 the wind, which had been increasing in force continually as we mounted, rose to a near gale. The gray mist about us was suddenly changed to a gorgeous pink and melted away into the twilight. The spectacle which we witnessed for the next fifteen minutes was a sight which I shall never forget. The plateau, now 3,000 feet below us, appeared momentarily between streamers of flying fog. An endless sea of clouds stretched out across the Pacific as far as the eye could reach. The superb peaks of Dagelet and La Perouse lay below us, now bathed like everything else in a marvelous glowing pink. Above us and to our left rose the summit of Crillon, cold and gray in the shadows, a tornado of mist and blowing snow swirling about its ice cone.

We were almost at the ridge. Every now and then it loomed up just ahead of us through the eddies of flying snow and frost. Two more schrund-like cracks separated us from it, and we redoubled our speed in an attempt to reach it and map out our route before the light should be gone.

But the mountain was playing a wicked joke upon us. The proud old hill had no intention at all of giving us a friendly welcome. Scarcely had the clouds dispersed than the blustering wind increased to a veritable hurricane from the north. Another bank of fog, filled with driving snow that cut like buckshot, swept down upon us from above, and we were lost in the midst of a howling blizzard.

We floundered on for twenty minutes around the cracks and at 8 o'clock the grade lessened. Huge cornices appeared just to our right, and we knew that we had reached the ridge. We were at an altitude of 11,500 feet, just 1,200 feet below the summit, but to continue, moonlight or not, through this inferno was utterly out of the question. The snow, even on the crest of the ridge, was soft as flour and threatened to avalanche at every step. Lingering only long enough to be sure of where we were, we turned and started to flounder downward once more. Five minutes below the crest to the ridge our trail was gone—obliterated completely by the swirling snow. But those godsent willow wands stood out like telegraph poles ahead, guiding us unerringly through the gathering darkness. Twenty minutes of pell-mell descent and we were out of the wind and storm and below the clouds once more. We sped onward to the plateau and, speechless with disappointment, reached the bivouac at 11 o'clock.

Not a breath of wind stirred about us. The moon had risen, and by its light one could trace the outline of a long, silvery cloud that lay draped peacefully on the ridge of Crillon. Hardly could one believe that beneath that quiet frosty mantle a wild storm still raged on.

We crawled into the tiny tent and, huddled close together, snatched a few hours of fitful sleep. At 2 o'clock I wriggled to the door to have a look at the weather. A gentle northerly breeze coursed across the surface of the plateau. The stars were shining brilliantly, and not a cloud was in sight. Two of the others came out, and we held a council of war. Our difficulties on the cliff and the trouble with my eyes had put our schedule far behind. The August storms were fast approaching, and we must make another attempt at the first possible moment. Two of the others felt that they should not try again at once, but, with the weather clear, we agreed that some of us should start immediately in another attempt to reach the top. We decided therefore that Child, Carter, and Houston should stay at camp as a support party and try to climb Dagelet in the morning. Bates, Everett, and I were to strike out once more for Crillon.

The others helped us pack our sacks and then at 2:45 in the gray of dawn we started out again across the plateau. Walking as fast as we felt safe, we reached the base of the mountain in just over fifty minutes. After a moment's rest we continued toward the ridge, along the windswept trail of the night before. Day was breaking and streamers of windstorm snow swirled high in the air above the summit of Crillon. The cold became more and more intense, and, as we approached the ridge, gusts of frigid ice-laden wind came rushing toward us down the slope.

The others had started for Dagelet. The sun was just touching its peak, and we could discern three tiny specks progressing at a snail's pace in the deep shadow below its mighty schrund. For half an hour we crouched in the sheltering hollow of a deep crevasse, waiting for the sun to reach us and warm our freezing faces. Then we set out again and at 7:15 reached our limit of the night before.

The view to the east was stupendous. An appalling precipice of ice and jagged rock dropped to the sources of the Johns Hopkins Glacier 5,000 feet below us. The vast snowfields of the Brady Glacier, the waters of Glacier Bay, and even the rugged mountains behind Juneau stood out clearly through the transparent atmosphere of early morning.

Our route here swung sharply to the left, following the crest of the ridge as closely as possible. The powder snow was even deeper than the night before, and we wallowed along in it, often nearly up to our waists. Changing the lead every 30 to 40 steps we progressed slowly but steadily and at 8 o'clock had reached the beginning of a short but very steep arête of blue ice. Here we spent nearly an hour chopping steps. The gusty wind was a nuisance, its blasts more than once causing me nearly to lose my balance while cutting a short traverse in the ice to avoid the crest of the ridge.

At 9 o'clock we were on level going once more, and at 9:45, after another session of snow-plowing, we reached the summit of the central peak at an altitude of 12,390 feet. At first we thought that we had reached the actual peak of Crillon. Just after leaving the ice arête we had plunged into a dense frost cloud through which we were unable to see more than a hundred feet at most. We had traversed an immense length of ridge and had climbed a cone in many ways resembling the actual summit. Also, our unreliable aneroid registered well over 13,000 feet. But a few minutes after 10 o'clock our happiness was suddenly cut short when a heavy blast of wind swept the cloud away for a moment, disclosing the real summit about a half-mile farther on ahead! As we were enveloped by only a local wind-cloud, which hung along the very crest of the ridge, we decided to continue toward the top in hopes that the heat of the sun might soon cause the weather to moderate.

We descended a couple of hundred feet into a notch between the west and central peaks of the ridge and then began to traverse a fast-narrowing arête toward the summit of a small intermediate peak, which appeared slightly lower than the one that we had just been on. The farther we advanced, the sharper and more treacherous the ridge became. It seemed everywhere to be underlain by a thick mass of immense frost feathers, such as one finds on Mount Washington in winter, only ever so much larger. Over this crumbling base lay deep masses of drifted, corniced powder snow. In several places the ridge was honeycombed by transverse cracks completely hidden under the snow and feathers. I fell into one of them up to my neck and was duly hauled out on the rope. These holes were quite unavoidable, as not the slightest undulation marked them on the surface, and it was necessary for the last two men to keep prepared for a sudden jerk at any minute.

At 10:45 a halt was called at a point where the ridge rose into a sharp gendarme. To our right a 60-foot cornice of crumbling frost feathers overhung the abyss that dropped to the Hopkins Glacier. On the left lay a 50-degree slope of feathers and powder snow that dropped several hundred feet into a maze of snow-filled crevasses. Up to this spot we had been able to traverse to our left whenever the top of the ridge was corniced. Here this was quite impossible. We had our choice of traveling a knife-like arête of waist-deep powder along the tip of the cornice, or slabbing a 50-degree slope of avalanching frost feathers.

It would be folly to continue under such conditions. Moreover, if we were lucky enough to cross this gendarme and another which followed it, we were bound to find similar conditions that would stop us on the steep slopes below the summit. We munched some corned beef and crackers, sitting up to our necks in the fine flour-like snow. The summit appeared now and then through the driving mists, its icy slopes wreathed in whirls of eddying snow. It seemed as if it were laughing us to scorn swathed in its treacherous frosty mantle and playing hide-and-seek before us in the clouds.

We sat for half an hour, dazed it seemed, hoping that something might happen, but nothing *could* happen. It would take three days of furious gales before climbing would be safe on such a ridge. By that time the August storms would be upon us and we dared not risk the chance of spending the winter on the plateau.

We turned and fought our way back against the wind to the summit of the central peak. There we lingered to take a few pictures and then started the long tramp back to the bivouac. Not a breath of wind stirred on the plateau. Trudging onward under a blistering sun we reached the tent at 2 o'clock. A note in the camp told us that the others had made the first ascent of Dagelet. They had gone down to Camp VI and would return the next day with more food if we deemed it wise to continue our stay above the cliff. We who had weathered the August storms the year before had no desire whatsoever to see them over again at close range. Fresh snow on our cliff might maroon us on the plateau for several days. We decided one and all that we had shot our bolt. The weather might hold another day, but neither we nor the mountain would be ready again for three or four.

The cliff was a sea of slush in the hot afternoon sun, and not until 9 o'clock that night did we dare start the descent to the South Col, tossing the tent and extra clothing 1,500 feet to the plateau. A glorious harvest moon was sinking into a sea of clouds to the west as we let go the last fixed rope and glissaded the avalanche cone to our skis. It was midnight when we crossed the South Col. What a wonderful feeling it was to have a fresh, cool breeze soothing our scorched faces as we gathered momentum on that glorious 800-foot ski run down to camp. Weary legs and total darkness do not combine to make for perfect skiing, but in a jiffy we were home and once more reclining on our mattresses, gorging bowl after bowl of hot cereal and klim.

Before turning in Bob and I stood for a moment together before the tents. The cliffs of Crillon towered above us, black and impressive. The snowfields of the summit outlined cold and gray against a myriad of stars that twinkled overhead. An avalanche rumbled ominously in the distance. Rocks clattered ceaselessly down the cliffs. Among the Alps one feels as if he were craftily outwitting sleeping giants. Here in Alaska the mountains seem to be alive.

THE BIETSCHHORN IN A THUNDERSTORM

Elizabeth Knowlton
1937

The writer and climber Elizabeth Knowlton (1895–1988) first explored the White Mountains of New Hampshire in the summer of 1903. She was 42 years old when this account appeared in Appalachia, *for which she wrote articles and poems. These biographical remarks are based on information at the University of New Hampshire's Milne Special Collections, where her papers reside in 27 boxes, and on an article by the climber Willy Merkl in the* Himalayan Journal.[24]

Knowlton was born in Springfield, Massachusetts, and first climbed in the White Mountains at seven. She earned bachelor's and master's degrees from Vassar College and worked as a journalist. At 36, she joined eight climbers in the German-American Himalayan Expedition, which tried to climb Nanga Parbat in Pakistan in 1932. She told the press that on the trip she lived for more than a month in a tent higher than 20,000 feet, which made her one of the few women then to reach that elevation (the first was Fanny Bullock Workman). Knowlton was grief-stricken when expedition member and fellow American Rand Herron died in an accident on a pyramid in Cairo later in 1932. She wrote the story of the German-American Himalayan Expedition in her book The Naked Mountain *(Junior Literary Guild, 1934). She remained single her entire life and continued to hike even in her old age. She died in Scituate, Massachusetts, at age 93. She also published a volume of poems,* Grief Is a Lonely Journey *(Comet Press Books, 1952).*

---

[24] *Himalayan* Journal 5 (1993).

*O*N ONE OF THE FEW FINE DAYS IN THE ALPS LAST SUMMER, I was lucky enough to be tramping up the long length of the Loetschental, the valley of the Bietschhorn.

Beside its connection with that great peak, the Loetschental has other claims to fame. Tucked away in the heights by the Gemmi Pass bordering the Oberland, it has managed to preserve almost unspoiled its old costumes and customs, and its religious festivals and processions are well known to the lover of the old Swiss tradition. It has been safe from the ubiquitous tourist, partly because there is a road only for the first hour of the five hours' length of the valley.

On this bright August afternoon the Loetschental was a delight to the eye, the archetype of the picturesque valleys of Switzerland. Steeply V-shaped, with a rushing glacial torrent in its depths, its sides at the level of the path were green with patches of cultivated ground and of hay which the peasants were not cutting, and here and there one came to a little village with brown-roofed chalets and high-spired church. Above, the mountains rose in shaggy wooded slopes to peaks of gray rock and white snow, sharp against the upper blue.

I spent my first night in the Loetschental at the very head of the valley, at Fafleralp by the foot of the snow pass that leads to the Great Aletsch Glacier, where the ice comes down to the edges of the summer pastures. Fafleralp is an idyllic spot, with gnarled old fir trees, and alpenroses, and the distant sound of cowbells.

For the ascent, I engaged Alois Bellwald, one of the best local guides. The Bietschhorn is to the Loetschental what the Matterhorn is to the Zermatt region, and I am sorry I cannot boost Alois's reputation by telling the exact number of times he had climbed it. But as he is a guide of fair age and of experience, it was somewhere well up in the scores. The shortest approach to the Bietschhorn is from Ried, halfway down the valley, so I turned back and spent the night at the little hotel there.

Now I found myself in the shadow of great tradition. The Bietschhorn has been a favorite of mountaineers since the earliest days of climbing history, and the inn at Ried has sheltered in its day many of the most illustrious names in mountaineering annals. The host proudly brought out the old guest books of the 1860s and 1870s, and I spent a delightful afternoon in his little garden, first reading the accounts of the earliest ascents, and then raising my eyes from the reading to look up greedily at the peak of which they told. I ought to have taken notes on the early history of this famous mountain. All that now sticks definitely in my memory is that the first woman to climb it was an American girl, and that she was taken up by Coolidge in the very first years of Bietschhorn's story. I admired her courage, to defy convention as boldly as women must who climbed in those days, and I envied her opportunity to know the Alps when they were still fresh and virginal.

The writers spoke frequently about how well kept was this little inn at Ried. I wish I could say the same now, but food seemed to be the problem. I feel that the table nowadays might well have inspired those famous lines—"They will dine on mule and marmot, and on mutton made of goats."

The sun was still shining bright from a cloudless sky—all too bright, alas—as next afternoon we wound up the steep opposite slopes, through forest and pasture land, to the Bietschhorn hut. It is a new and comfortable stone building, and we had the luxury of having it to ourselves. Alois arranged the supper just according to my taste. Already I was discovering that he was indeed, as the girl from Lausanne at the Ried hotel has said, *très gentil*. But the completest test and proof of this was to come the following day.

When we rose and looked out of the window about three the next morning, heat lightning was gently playing in the far night sky over the peaks along the Rhone valley.

"What do you think?" I asked Alois.

"We can start," he said, "and see what it is at sunrise."

An hour, following the lantern up the steep rotten rocks behind the hut; a half hour or so, traversing a high glacier around under the ridges of our peak; then steep rotten rock again, leading up toward the Nord Grat, a snow ridge; and a gray dawn and a gray sunrise had come and gone unnoticed. We stopped to eat, and gazed out at thick gray clouds hanging over the distant peaks.

"What do you think now?" I asked Alois.

"It will not be a good day," he said. "What do you wish?"

"It is a fine mountain, and I should enjoy climbing it," I replied. "Of course we ought not to do anything really dangerous. But otherwise, I should like to go on."

The snow ridge was a very pleasant and spectacular knife edge, with bits where cornices suggested a certain caution. As I watched Alois negotiating these places, I felt a complete confidence in him; he moved and handled himself like an old wise guide, who has never perhaps attained the brilliance of technique that makes one famous through all Switzerland, but who thoroughly knows his own mountains, their snow and their rocks, and who takes no chances.

Moving along this ridge that leads gradually to the summit, we were in a position to see the magnificent formation of our mountain. Roughly starfish shape it stood, with numerous sharp rock ridges converging steeply to its peak—(ours was the only snow ridge)—ridges rising from the valleys in abrupt lower buttresses and a network of subsidiary ridges. Their crests were now darkly impressive against the sky, and the bare rocky gullies between were masses of black shadow, in the gray storm light.

We reached the summit in about six hours from the hut. The mountains among the clouds showed now a more interesting aspect than when ranged in the neat blue and white panorama of the perfect day. Rock and snow summits, near and far, emerged gigantic, only to vanish again in the gray drifting masses of mist—mighty shapes, now brightening, now darkening, in the rapidly changing light. Sometimes a window in the clouds would open and give glimpses of a far range of serrated peaks, sharp-cut against a lighter sky, or of the profound blue shadows of some valley floor eight or ten thousand feet below. Toward the east, the sky was brighter and more open, and the Aletschhorn showed up magnificently. Here and there, where the clouds gathered thickest and darkest, toward the west, played occasional lightning.

We did not let the weather possibilities unduly hasten our lunch. If a storm were going to break, it would happen long before we could get down those lengthy ridges. Fortified by cold meat, bread, tea, and chocolate, we turned to the rocks of the West Grat. The top bit offers the most interesting rock climbing of this route, but even that, technically considered, would not seem striking to those acclimated to Storm King or the White Mountains. The main interest is given by the depth of the gulfs waiting beneath one's boot soles.

We crawled cautiously downward, and had reached a part of the ridge where we could occasionally move together, when the storm broke. Driving icy pellets of snow beat against our faces, a wild wind tried to tear us from the ridge. My eyes were so lashed that I could not see, until I donned dark goggles to protect them. With heads bent against the wind, half feeling our way, we fought on down. Still we held to the crest of the ridge, for in spite of the wind, that way offered the easiest route: the sides of the ridge were precipitous and their rock rotten.

Many *Appalachia* writers and readers explored the Alps in the 1920s and 1930s. Above, a climber, Anna E. Holman, and guide, on one of the peaks.

The thunder and lightning began. First a muttering and crashing in the distance. Then the intervals between flash and roar grew shorter and shorter. Then our ice axes began to sing. This was the moment when by common consent we moved off the crest on to the unattractive steep rotten sides, as far down as we could get—which was only some fifteen or twenty feet. And here the "*gentil*-ness" of Alois first began to show itself conspicuously. He is the only guide with whom I have ever been who did not act excited and irritable, taking out his nerve strain on his tourist, when caught high up in a thunderstorm. Alois's soft and pleasant manner remained unchanged: you would never suspect from it that anything untoward had happened.

We had a little heart-to-heart talk about all this in the hut later. He explained that of course he knew that interminable ridge was no place to be climbing down in a thunderstorm (high rock ridges attract the lightning), and that naturally we ought to have stopped and parked our ice axes at a distance (the metal attracts lightning), and taken shelter in a safe spot, till the worst was over. But since there were no safe spots to stop, he thought we might as well keep on, without making any fuss. I explained that I had seen the matter just as he did.

So as the lightning flashed and the thunder roared around us, we exchanged not a comment but kept on skirting our ridge downward. It was great fun in many ways. I had all the pleasure of leading a first descent, for, as we had left the regular route along the crest, Alois knew no more than I did where to find the easiest way. I thoroughly enjoyed vanishing around some projecting rock, clinging with toes and mittened fingertips, to see the holds that I had hoped might be there all working themselves out happily ahead, and to shout proudly back, "It will go, here."

But the situation was not without its drawbacks. The ridge went on without end; the rocks were getting slippery, and the loose stuff was becoming treacherous under the wet clinging snow; and I could not help jumping occasionally when the bombardment of the heavens would seem to land directly on my head. Once as we walked down easy rock, some twenty feet below the jagged crest, suddenly what looked like a big ball of fire hit, and shattered with a tremendous crash, on its nearest pinnacle.

"Did your scalp prickle or anything?" asked Alois, as we talked in the hut later. "I felt for a moment as if my head had been plunged into a hot oven." I, apparently less sensitive, had felt nothing physical, but I had found it a thrilling sight. However, at the time, neither of us said a word about it. We seemed agreed that the only way to treat such a rude event was tactfully to pretend not to notice.

On and down we went. The ice axes continued their humming duet, but in a milder key, for the thunder was withdrawing. Soon it was only a menacing mutter in the distance. We resumed the crest of the ridge. And still it went on, interminably downward. The snow changed to rain as the hours passed, and we were thoroughly soaked even before we crossed the glacier to descend the rock wall behind the hut. Still in dripping discomfort the *gentil* Alois was gay and cheerful and remained so even through the final contretemps of the day. When the way became absolutely simple, he suggested he should go ahead at the double-quick, to get a fire started in the hut before my arrival. And—(advertisement for the bowline)—the rope, which he had tied in the ordinary square knot beloved of guides, now in its soaked state would not untie. He struggled with my waist knot for about ten minutes, while we both laughed at his efforts. Then I suggested that I would bring along the rope, if he could only get out of his own end. Another lengthy struggle, till I had begun to think we were permanently attached together. Still Alois joked and smiled.

At the hut there was a final wrestle with the rope, much and prolonged eating, and a pleasant exchange of lightning reminiscences. Then a long walk, partly in darkness, before we were at last able to shed our sodden garments in the haven of the hotel. It all remained on the same cheerful key.

Next day as we shook hands and parted, while Alois regretted that I had missed the view, we agreed that it had made the climb of the Bietschhorn much more unusual and interesting to do it in a thunderstorm.

THE K2 EXPEDITION OF 1939

Fritz H. Wiessner
1956

This account of the second American expedition to K2, in 1939—in which American climber Dudley M. Wolfe and three heroic Sherpas died—first appeared in Appalachia *over fifteen years later, in 1956.* Appalachia *editor Miriam Underhill explained in its introduction that the expedition members had preferred to be reticent about their troubles and difficulties. Aside from two 1940 articles—a confusingly brief article in the* American Alpine Journal *and a story in the* Saturday Evening Post *by climber George Sheldon, who had waited out much of the climb at base camp after freezing his foot—nothing firsthand about the summit attempt appeared in English until Underhill obtained permission to publish this translation of expedition leader Fritz H. Wiessner's side of the tragedy, which had damaged his reputation. Wiessner (1900–1988) was born in Dresden, Germany, and immigrated to the United States in 1929. He was living in Vermont when, in 1955, he finally published a book in Germany about the K2 disaster. Underhill believed that the silence about the climb "had the unfortunate consequence of permitting much adverse criticism of the expedition," and she arranged for a translation of the story.*

    The climbers were: Wiessner, then age 39; Chappell Cranmer, 21; Oliver Eaton Cromwell, 42; Jack Durrance, 28; George Sheldon, 21; and Dudley M. Wolfe, 44. Two other climbers had been unable to join at the last minute. The Sherpas, led by Pasang Kikuli, numbered nine. Lt. G.S.C. Trench was the transport officer. An Indian teacher called Chandra served as a middleman between the team and the hired Sherpas.

    They established base camp on the Godwin-Austen Glacier on May 31. By June 21, Camps I, II, III, and IV were set where the first attempt in 1938 had stayed. A furious storm raged for seven days. The climbers established Camp V just before another three-day storm, then pushed on to camps VI and VII. Wiessner and two Sherpas waited at Camp VI during a third brief storm. The story, as published in the journal, begins at this point.

The bracketed phrases in Wiessner's account were added by Underhill when she originally edited this essay. (She also detailed much of the chronology now repeated in this introduction.)

Many years later, in 1989, mountaineers Andrew Kauffman and William Lowell Putnam published a new account of this tragedy, relying on Durrance's newly released diary. Appalachia *makes no claim as to which tale is correct and believes that the future could bring new interpretations of the 1939 K2 tragedy.*

*O*N THE SECOND DAY THE WEATHER CLEARED IN THE afternoon. As we were short of provisions and no one had brought us support from below, we descended quickly to Camp V. Here Wolfe had been alone for the last four days; the support from below had failed to arrive. Every day Wolfe had gone as far as the House Chimney, whence one can look down upon Camp IV, but no one had arrived there. This was a great disappointment to us, for we had set up the camps according to plan up to an altitude of 7,400 meters [24,300 feet] and needed only loads of about 400–450 pounds more from Camp II in order to be able to establish the last high camps and start in on the attempt for the summit. In order to get the support operations running again I went down alone to Camp II on July 9. The men there had been very anxious about us and were delighted to see me again. The report of our progress above on the mountain brought new life and energy into the group, who had been depressed by the storms.

On July 11 we—Cromwell, Durrance, Trench, and I—with two Sherpas climbed to Camp IV, picking up at Camp III the last loads needed above. The next day Trench and Cromwell returned with a couple of Sherpas to Camp II, while the rest of us—three sahibs [including Wolfe, who had been at Camp V] and seven Sherpas—climbed with heavy loads to Camp VI and on July 13 to Camp VII. Above Camp VI Durrance no longer felt well and turned back.

In this image from the 1930s, Fritz Wiessner climbed Crow's Nest Cliffs, just north of West Point on the Hudson River.

We had made the following plan: we would send four Sherpas back to Camp VI that same day; on July 14 we ourselves with three Sherpas would go to Camp VIII and later to Camp IX. On July 14 Durrance was to attempt to climb to Camp VII with four Sherpas and if possible join us again higher up; in case he should not feel well he had only to send the Sherpas on up. As it turned out he was ill and on July 14 went, not up, but down to Camp II; unfortunately he took Pasang Kikuli and Dawa with him. Pasang Kikuli had hoped to be able to go to the summit with Wolfe and me. Since, however, he had frozen his toes on our first ascent to Camp VII, his wish now was only to oversee the final support operations between Camps VI and VII. He was unhappy not to be given this job as planned.

On July 14, as intended, Wolfe and I with three Sherpas climbed on the steep slopes from Camp VII. Each of us had a load of from 40 to 44 pounds. (From Base Camp on, all the sahibs had carried loads along with the Sherpas. For one thing, in order to establish the camps quickly, and for another, because we thought that hard work would help us get into good form. This turned out to be the case.) We struggled along up in the direction of the southeast shoulder, for the most part sinking up to our knees in breakable crust, until we reached a flat bay. Here we set up Camp VIII in the midst of the snow at an altitude of 7,710 meters [25,290 feet]. We had hoped to be able to get higher, but the bad snow conditions and the heavy loads made this impossible. We sent two Sherpas back to Camp VII. They were to make connections there with the group expected to come up from Camp VI and to join these the next day in bringing up the final supplies intended for Camps VIII and IX.

During the night it began to snow again. We were well sheltered in our camp, dug into the gentle slope of the bay, so that the two-day storm bothered us little. On the third day, July 17, the weather was sunny again. Wolfe, Pasang Lama, and I continued the ascent. About 80 meters [260 feet] beyond the camp we had to cross the bergschrund. Above it a short, steep snow slope led to the broad southeast shoulder. As we approached the schrund the snow became deeper and deeper, and finally bottomless. After two hours of the hardest conceivable work I succeeded, almost by swimming, in getting up across a snow bridge and then treading out a belaying stance on the steep slope above the bridge. Even at a lower elevation, say on a four-thousander in the Alps, such unfavorable conditions would have required the output of all our energy. Pasang Lama followed in my trench but almost disappeared in the snow before he reached me; he too needed an hour. Now came Wolfe, by far the heaviest of us three. He was not able to master this place and suggested that he return to Camp VIII, only 100 steps away, and follow us with one or more of the supporting party the next day, when the tracks would have become firmer.

By the short slope, which at the top became more gentle, we reached the crest of the shoulder. Done up from wallowing in the deep snow, with our 35-pound loads, we rested here a long while. We were now at the height of about 7,840 meters [25,710 feet]. Ahead of us rose the great ice cliff, where the summit névé breaks off in a vertical wall of 60–80 meters [200–260 feet]. . . .

[This rocky platform] looked as if it were near at hand, but we had soon to realize that after our long spell of wallowing in the deep snow and with our heavy loads we could no longer make it. Somewhat below . . . we prepared a sheltered camping place beside a large rock. Here we spent the night. Next morning we broke camp and carried our loads up the platform. The way there seemed very long to us. As expected, the platform offered an excellent campsite. It was the only one (except for Camps II, VII and VIII, which were entirely on snow) where we could erect the tent without first building a platform of stones. As further protection we built up a stone wall around the tent.

The view from this spot was inconceivably magnificent. . . .

Because of the good weather and the slight chance of finding a campsite nearer the summit I decided to strike for the summit the next day from here, with Pasang Lama. Our situation on the mountain was favorable. We had established a series of fully equipped camps; tents with sleeping bags and food for many weeks stood ready in Camps II, IV, VI and VII. In addition there was Wolfe in Camp VIII with further supplies (unless he was already on the way up to us), and here in Camp IX there was food for six days and a supply of gasoline for a still longer time. So, in case bad weather should again set in, or we should arrive dead tired and without packs in one of these camps, we could count on finding complete protection there, and that, even in case connection with the supporting camps or the Base Camp had meanwhile been severed. This formed the backbone of our plans; the experience of past expeditions had taught how hopeless the situation can become if a safe line of descent does not exist.

After a quiet night and a warm hearty breakfast we left camp on July 19 no earlier than 9 o'clock. Pasang carried our crampons and the reserve rope, 75 meters [245 feet] long and 9 millimeters [⅜ inch] in diameter; I had the rucksack with food, pitons, carabiners, and warm extra clothing. Climbing on the 35-meter [115 feet] rope, 12 millimeters [½ inch] in diameter, we mounted the lower and relatively easy rocks of the southeast ridge. After the good long night and the brief work of the preceding day we were in the best of condition. In two hours we were already at the foot of the buttress, the last part of the way having lain over a small ridge of ice. Thus we had gained 240 meters [785 feet] of elevation. Since even here we had no good view of the ice cliff, now to our right, I decided for the route to the left, which was safe from the ice avalanches. Rounding a small rock that had broken off from the wall of the buttress, we climbed to the west into a black couloir. . . .

The black verglaced[25] couloir soon became very steep and terminated in an overhang. With piton-protection I was able to overcome this obstacle by traversing to the left under the overhand; the rock was very difficult and covered with verglas in places, but the weather was so warm that I could climb without gloves. Now came a short ridge of rock and snow, then for two rope-lengths the climb was made straight up, under piton-protection, over friable, verglaced, and very difficult rock. At that point I succeeded in traversing right to a steep snow slope. This slope terminated in a steep, smooth angle of rock just beneath the crest of the ridge. We tried to climb the slabby right side of the angle in order, in about 10 meters [33 feet], to regain the southeast ridge, now at a point high above the ice cliff of the summit snowfield. But the slab was too steep and lacking in holds; we could not climb it. To be sure, our shoe-nails were badly worn down; with modern cleated-rubber soles this bit of friction climbing may be possible.

Thereupon I traversed, 5 meters [16 feet] lower down, to the broken-up left wall of the rock angle. This wall is climbable, but it is somewhat longer than the right wall, since it reaches the crest of the ridge higher up. It begins very steeply, but after 12 meters [39 feet] slopes back toward the ridge. From the point of attack I climbed up with great difficulty for about 8 meters [26 feet], putting in two pitons for security. Pasang belayed me from a position still on the snow.

There would have been a section of about 8 meters [26 feet] more of this going, so difficult at this height (we were at an altitude of about 8,390 meters [27,510 feet]), but these 8 meters would certainly have been climbable. Pasang however was unwilling to go farther and urged that we turn back. He held the rope tight when I wanted to climb to the next stance and said

---

[25] Meaning ice-covered.—Editor

with a smile, "No, Sahib, tomorrow." At the same time he made a sign in the direction of the other possible route of ascent. For farther down, at the top of the black couloir, we had been able to examine this other route and the ice cliff which threatened it and had regretted that we had not tried our luck over there. The last ice avalanche which had come down from the wall of the cliff had left a perfectly smooth cleavage, so that this easier line of ascent was at that time exposed to no objective danger.

I now tried to make clear to Pasang that the difficulties would be over in a few meters, and that we could then have a long rest upon the ridge; further, that in the clear night and over easier terrain we could go on to the summit and descend in sunshine the next morning. But I could not change Pasang's mind; he did not understand that this would be easier than to descend to the camp in the evening—and probably even in the night—and the next day attack the summit by the other route. Then too Pasang, who was a lama in his native village, was no doubt afraid of evil spirits, which according to Buddhist belief reside on the summit during the night. He had been a splendid comrade, very capable, faithful, and always ready to do his full part; the weather was good and would doubtless be reliable for days; the other and no doubt easier route would require less time—so I gave in.

Fritz Wiessner perched during a climb on the East Ridge of Mount Edith Cavell, in Alberta, Canada, the year before the fateful 1939 K2 expedition.

The descent turned out to be unexpectedly difficult, and night came on even while we were roping down over the overhang into the black couloir. While Pasang was hanging in the air during this rope-down the rope became tangled in our crampons, which he was carrying on his back. He succeeded with difficulty in freeing it, but in the process the crampons fell off down the mountain. That was a severe blow for us, as later events were to prove. Although it was clear, windless, and not very cold (I estimated -3 to -5 degrees Celsius [-29 to -30 degrees Fahrenheit]) at our great altitude, still the descent continued to be difficult; it was 2:30 A.M. when we reached Camp IX. No one had arrived there from below. In spite of the long day and the lack of rests—we had never been able to rest sitting down—we were in good shape. Cooking was soon in progress and at 6 o'clock we were lying in our sleeping bags in sunshine. Later on it became so warm that I could take a sunbath completely naked—at an altitude of 8,000 meters [26,200 feet]! At 3 o'clock we felt fresh again, so that we decided to go to the summit next day by the easterly route. I had no doubt of our success.

On July 21 we left camp as early as 6 o'clock. In two hours we reached the point beneath the buttress where the routes separated. A somewhat rising traverse brought us to the foot of the ice cliff. First came verglaced slabs, sprinkled with scree, then steeper, firmer rock where, however, all the hand- and footholds were covered with snow or ice, since we were in the shade. That meant difficult climbing; I had constantly to put in pitons for bringing up Pasang and for my own security. At the end of this traverse a short, completely verglaced chimney brought me directly under the vertical wall of the ice cliff and so at the beginning of the snow gully which led up between the ice cliff and the buttress of the southeast ridge. This gully runs eventually into the summit snowfield just to the right (east) of the southeast ridge.

Because of the difficult conditions which I have described, we had required two hours to this point from the fork of the routes. The snow in the gully was hard as rock, the lower portion was steep, and we had no crampons. I worked up a short distance by cutting steps but realized that it would be impossible to accomplish the entire ascent in this manner. With crampons one could have walked quickly up, but as things were we should have had to cut 300–400 steps and for that, at this altitude, we should have needed over a day. So we had to return to the fork. We reached this point at 11:30, too late to ascend again by our first route on that day. We had therefore to go down.

On this day as well no one had arrived in Camp IX from below. Our supplies had shrunk. I therefore decided to descend to Camp VIII the next morning, unless in the meantime someone came up to us from below. With Wolfe's help, I wanted to bring up fresh supplies from Camp VIII, so as to be able to hold out a new storm here if necessary. Furthermore, we could there obtain crampons from the people in the expected support party. Pasang Lama seemed much pleased by this plan. He asked me whether he could be relieved in Camp VIII by another Sherpa for the next attempt on the summit; this I naturally promised him. Since the day before he had no longer been his old self; he had been living in great fear of the evil spirits, constantly murmuring prayers, and had lost his appetite.

On July 22, toward 10 o'clock, we began the descent. Since I intended to return we left everything in Camp IX, except that Pasang took along his sleeping bag. As we were traversing the hard névé of the southeast shoulder Pasang slipped off. It was only with difficulty that I could hold him on the rope, since my Tricouni nails were almost worn down. Arrived on the east side of the shoulder we soon saw the tent of Camp VIII close beneath us. Wolfe was standing there and called to us. He was greatly pleased to see us again but considerably put out that no one had come up from below. Two days before his matches had given out, so that for drinking he had had only water from melted snow which he had caught in a fold of the tent.

We cooked a warm lunch and celebrated our reunion. Since the supplies in Camp VIII would have sufficed three men for only four days, and since in Camp IX too there was food for only one day more, we started quickly down for Camp VII, in order to bring up more food. The main part of our supplies was there, enough for weeks and for a fresh provisioning of Camp IX.

During the descent, shortly before reaching Camp VII, we slipped off as we were traversing a slope of hard snow. I had scratched a step with the ice ax and was just in the act of taking a step forward when suddenly a sharp jerk by the rope from behind pulled me out of balance. I slipped off, and Wolfe could not hold me when the rope tightened. As came to light later, he had inadvertently stepped on the rope, which had then become wound about his foot. Under these circumstances my fall brought about his, and Pasang, who had not been sufficiently on guard, was likewise pulled off. We all three plunged down the steep slope, where the snow became harder and harder. By means of my ax, and my boots scratching against the slope, I succeeded in obtaining a hold. I held the rope with the strength of desperation and thus was able to check the fall of my companions. Luckily for me, at this point the snow was somewhat more soft; a few meters below, where Wolfe and Pasang were hanging on the rope, it was again so hard that both of them required help from the rope in order to climb up to me. Only about 60 meters [196 feet] below us were the great ice cliffs of the summit snowfield and beneath these the east wall plunged down over 2,000 meters [6,500 feet] to the Godwin Austen Glacier. During the fall we had all three of us given up hope of being saved.

Due to the fall we had lost much time, so that twilight had already begun to come on when we reached Camp VII. Here there awaited us the disappointment of our lives. Not a human being was in the camp. The two tents, which nine days before we ourselves had set up with the help of seven Sherpas and had furnished with many supplies (food, petroleum, extra sleeping bags, air mattresses), were in the worst condition. The flaps had been left open, one tent had great holes and was half broken down, the other was full of snow; most of the food had been dragged out and was frozen into the snow. The disappointment was well nigh unbearable. The wildest ideas tormented our minds. We could find no rational explanation for this unexpected state of affairs. A great part of our reserve food and all the sleeping bags, which we ourselves had lugged up by hard work and which formed the backbone of our expedition, had vanished.

It was too late to descend to Camp VI. We cleaned one tent and set it up again. The remainder of the scattered food, which we collected, would still have sufficed for about fourteen days. Fortunately for us the evil spirits had neglected to carry off the big can of oil, so that at least we could prepare ourselves a warm supper. Then began the night, and we shall never forget it: three men in a cold tent at an altitude of over 7,500 meters [24,600 feet], without air mattresses, and with only Pasang Lama's sleeping bag to cover our knees. The night was a very bad and cold one. Morning dawned raw and windy, for the first time since July 16. Toward 10 o'clock the weather cleared and the wind went down. With only one sleeping bag we could not stay here in Camp VII, so we decided to go to Camp VI and fetch sleeping bags from there. One of us, to be sure, could remain up here with Pasang's sleeping bag, get a rest, and so spare himself the trip down and up. Wolfe suggested that he stay, to recover from the unpleasant night and be in better shape to take a load to Camp VIII the day after tomorrow. As leader of the expedition I, myself, had to go down to Camp VI to get the support operations going again and find the explanation of the unheard-of occurrences. Pasang was to be relieved.

I therefore agreed with Wolfe that next day most of the Sherpas in Camp VI—there must be six of them there!—with Durrance if possible, should bring loads to Camp VII; for the day following Wolfe planned to provision Camp VIII fully again with a part of the Sherpas, while I intended to take a day of rest in Camp VI and then on July 25 climb directly to Camp VIII without a load. In that way by as early as the 27th or 28th we should again have had a firm basis for the summit climb. As a matter of fact the good, warm weather held till July 30; on July 31 came the first storm. Two partly cloudy days followed, while on August 3, 4, and 5 fine weather reigned again.

At 11 o'clock, I left Camp VII with Pasang. On our arrival in Camp VI we found this also broken up. Only a cache of two folded-up tents, gasoline, and food was still there, while in this camp too the reserve sleeping bags and air mattresses were missing.

Our situation now became very serious. We could not go back to Camp VII, since there was only one sleeping bag for Wolfe there, and this would not have been sufficient to keep the three of us from freezing. Camp V, according to the expedition's plans, had not been prepared as a support camp. So only one course was possible, the descent to the big Camp IV. But, a thing inconceivable to us, there too the reserve sleeping bags and air mattresses had vanished! Well-nigh desperate, and at the end of our power of resistance, we threw ourselves upon the empty tent platforms. But we had to go on, the fight for our lives had begun.

According to the plans of the expedition, the next camp with complete reserves and sleeping bags was Camp II. The sahibs, also, must be there. . . . So, onward!

Almost exhausted, mentally and physically, we reached Camp II at nightfall. Here two large tents were standing, but they were unoccupied; one was completely empty, the other half filled with food. The sleeping bags and air mattresses were missing! With our last bit of strength we took down the empty tent and used it as a covering for the night. The cold tent cloth, however, gave no warmth, and we shivered miserably; our toes and fingers, frostbitten in the preceding night, became much worse.

Next morning we went down past Camp I, which according to plan was not supposed to have reserves, to Base Camp. For the last kilometers on the nearly level glacier we could only just drag ourselves along, and often we fell to the ground. Shortly before we reached the camp, Cromwell with several Sherpas caught up with us. They had been searching the glacier higher up, under the precipices of the Abruzzi Rib, for our bodies! It now came to light that we had long been given up for lost by a fall.

The following had occurred. On July 14, the day on which I went from Camp VII to Camp VIII with Wolfe and the three Sherpas, Durrance, who was feeling ill, descended from Camp VI to Camp II. He took with him, as already mentioned, the Sherpa headman, Pasang Kikuli, and the Sherpa Dawa. To the other Sherpas in Camp VI, namely Pinsoo and Kitar [Tsering?], Durrance gave exact instructions as to what loads they were to take to Camps VII and VIII. There, along with Tendrup (who had been appointed leader of the four Sherpas by Pasang Lama) and Kitar, they were to maintain the connection with the group in the front. On July 15 and 16, however, there was a slight storm, and so they stayed in Camp VI. On July 17 Tendrup and Kitar, who had waited in Camp VII for better weather, came down to them, instead of carrying more loads to Camp VIII as I had arranged. As reason for this change in plan Tendrup alleged that Wolfe, Pasang Lama, and I had undoubtedly perished at Camp VIII in an avalanche. He therefore proposed that they should all four now descend. Pinsoo and Tsering, however, were not convinced by this invented story of an avalanche and stayed on in Camp VI when Tendrup and Kitar descended next day to Camp IV. In Camp IV these last two found the Sherpa headman, Pasang Kikuli, and Dawa, who had been sent up there that day from Camp II by Durrance, to fetch the reserve sleeping bags. Durrance was assuming that, the weather being so fine, everything would go well up above and we would have no difficulty in bringing the valuable sleeping bags down with us from the higher camps. Pasang Kikuli was indignant that Tendrup had come down and ordered him to go back with Kitar to the high camps. Thereupon they climbed back to Camp VI, where Pinsoo and Tsering were still staying, and on July 19 to Camp VII. There they called up to Camp VIII, which however was beyond calling range. Since they got no answer this gave a greater probability to Tendrup's story of the avalanche; we were definitely given up. The two of them now broke up Camp VII, threw most of the stored supplies into the snow, and left the tents open. Only the sleeping bags and air mattresses were all taken along down to Camp VI. There Tendrup convinced the other two Sherpas that his avalanche story was true and ordered a descent. Later on, in Base Camp, the Sherpas called Tendrup a devil, who had deceived them with the avalanche story and wanted to wreck the expedition. I myself suspect that the strong but often lazy Tendrup was tired of packing between the high camps and therefore had invented the avalanche story.... At the same time he probably thought the sahibs in Base Camp would praise him for bringing along the valuable sleeping bags from Camps VII and VI.

On the morning of July 22 the four Sherpas arrived in Base Camp with all the sleeping bags from Camps VII and VI. There Durrance, Kikuli, and Dawa had already come in on July 19 with thirteen sleeping bags, or all those from Camps II and IV. Thus it happened that on July 22, from Camp VII (where Wolfe, with Lama's sleeping bag, was waiting for support), on downwards not a single sleeping bag was any longer on the mountain.

Due to the great confusion in Base Camp, to my mental and bodily collapse, and to the catastrophe that shortly ensued—the catastrophe which caused the loss of three faithful Sherpas and my good comrade Wolfe—the reason for the events I have described was beyond my understanding. It was only three months later that many things became more clear to me. After my recovery in a New York hospital I came upon a slip of paper which enlightened me. This had been left by Durrance for Wolfe and me in Camp II on July 19. I had at that time put it among my expedition papers, but in my then condition not paid any attention to it. In this note Durrance began by congratulating us on having attained the summit. He then went on to write that on the day before (July 18) he had had all the sleeping bags carried down from Camp IV by Kikuli and Dawa, and that they all would now descend with these bags and with all those from Camp II, thirteen in all, to Base Camp. Thus, he said, there were no longer any sleeping bags on the mountain from Camp IV on down; he was expecting us to bring bags with us from higher up. Naturally, when he wrote this note, Durrance had no means of knowing that Tendrup and his party would take away the sleeping bags from Camps VII and VI, as well, on July 20 and 21.

The Indian member of our expedition, the teacher Chandra, had already become anxious on July 19 when Durrance arrived in Base Camp with the sleeping bags from the lower camps. He was dismayed when, on July 22, Tendrup's party brought down all the bags from Camps VII and VI. Since he had his doubts about Tendrup's avalanche story he, along with Pasang Kikuli, proposed that sleeping bags should immediately be sent up above again. They both knew that according to the expedition plans the summit group could count on finding bags in Camps VII, VI, IV, and II. But Tendrup's report of what he gave out as our certain death produced such a feeling of shock in the members of the expedition at Base Camp—Cromwell, Durrance, and Trench—that they had no doubt of our death and gave no consideration to the proposal of Chandra and Kikuli.

An immediate return of the bags to Camp II, better still to Camp IV, would have saved Pasang Lama and me from collapse during the night of July 23. Furthermore, in view of our good condition and excellent acclimatization, it would again have been possible for Wolfe and me to resume our final attack on the summit, of which I felt so confident. A cruel fate determined otherwise, and therewith ended the hardest fight, the greatest hope, and at the same time the greatest disappointment of my climbing career.

At Base Camp, in the firm conviction that Wolfe, Pasang, and I had perished, it had been decided to begin the march out on July 25. This plan had to be altered somewhat when Pasang Lama and I dragged ourselves into camp. Pasang was quite broken down and I, too, had reached the end of my strength. During the last two days I had suffered from frostbite and in addition had developed a severe inflammation of the throat, so that I could hardly speak. It was only with the greatest effort that I could make myself understood by whispering. Toward evening, however, I was again able to make decisions; indeed, I had hopes of being able to organize another attack. The weather was still very good, and I hoped to be able to climb up again myself after a rest of two or three days. In the camps up to VI there was still sufficient food, enough to supply the higher camps as well. Only sleeping bags, air mattresses, some tents, and some food to round out the reserves were needed up above.

We decided that Cromwell and Trench should start off down to Askole next morning with the porters who had come up to carry out the loads. Durrance, Chandra, and I, with all the Sherpas except Tendrup, who had invented the avalanche story and who the other Sherpas called a devil, should remain for a further attempt. Durrance, who felt himself in good shape, intended to go next day with three Sherpas to Camp VII as fast as possible; they needed to take only sleeping bags from below and could pick up food in Camps IV and VI. From Camp VII Durrance, Wolfe, and the Sherpas were to provision Camp VIII. I myself would try to follow on the third day with the other Sherpas and join up with Durrance's and Wolfe's party.

Durrance and his three Sherpas arrived in Camp IV on July 26. Here again Durrance could not stand the altitude, and Dawa also seemed to be sick. Next morning therefore Durrance decided to return to Base Camp with Dawa; he instructed the other two Sherpas to go to Wolfe in Camp VII and explain the situation to him. I myself had been unable to recover and after the three days in Base Camp was still in bad condition. Pasang Lama had not left the Sherpa tent at all and required constant care.

When Durrance arrived I knew that now any hope of attaining the summit must be given up. If Wolfe was not already in process of descending, he must at once be informed. I resolved to climb up next morning with Pasang Kikuli, in spite of my bad condition and in the hope of improving, but Pasang declared I was still too sick to do so. He offered to climb to Camp VI the next day with a second Sherpa, without packs, and on the following day to go to Camp VII if Wolfe was not already descending. Pasang Kikuli, accompanied by the Sherpa Tsering, actually accomplished this great feat of ascending to Camp VI in one day; in Camp IV they picked up the sleeping bags left there the day before by Durrance and Dawa and reached Camp VI in the late afternoon. There they found the two Sherpas who had gone with Durrance to Camp IV. In spite of his precise instructions they had not climbed up to Wolfe in Camp VII.

On the following day, July 29, Kikuli and two other Sherpas went up to Camp VII without food or sleeping bags. Wolfe had already given up, no doubt from disappointment, anxiety, and perhaps fear that the supporting party would again fail to arrive. He no longer seemed to have courage even for the descent to Camp VI. He lay apathetically in his sleeping bag. Three days before he had used up his last matches and since then had been unable to cook anything. On these days he had no longer gone out of the tent. . . . The Sherpas got him up, prepared tea, and wanted to bring him down. Wolfe, however, refused and said he would not go down until the next day. Without sleeping bags and food the Sherpas could not stay with him. They descended to Camp VI and planned to return the next day and bring Wolfe down. During the night, however, there came a storm, which continued the whole of the following day (July 30) and made the ascent impossible. On July 31 the weather cleared up again. Pasang Kikuli, Pinsoo, and Kitar climbed up to Camp VII,

Tsering stayed in Camp VI and had instructions to keep tea ready until noon. They expected to be back early enough to be able to descend farther.

On this day toward 10 o'clock, through the telescope in Base Camp, Durrance observed three persons ascending just below the ice traverse at Camp VII. Next day, through the glass, he saw a single person at Camp VI. On August 2 Tsering came back alone to Base Camp from Camp VI. He reported what had happened on the mountain during the last days, so far as it was known to him—in particular, the ascent of Kikuli, Pinsoo, and Kitar to Camp VII on July 31. The weather this day was windy and partly cloudy. When the three did not return in the evening he thought that evil spirits had killed them. Since they had taken with them no sleeping bags and no food they could not pass the night in Camp VII. Pasang Kikuli had said before their ascent that they would return at noon in any case, even if Wolfe should again refuse; in this event they would ask the sahib for a written confirmation of his refusal. Tsering continued to wait in Camp VI through August 1. During the night of August 1 the weather was cold and stormy, and Tsering thought the evil spirits were raging around his tent. On the morning of August 2 he fled down the mountain, driven by fear.

After Tsering's report we had to give up hope of seeing our comrades again. Nevertheless on the following day, August 3, the weather being warmer again, I started out once more from Base Camp. I succeeded in dragging myself, with two Sherpas, as far as Camp I, and on the next day in reaching Camp II. Since my strength seemed to be slowly returning I had hope of perhaps reaching Camp VII after all, but on the night of August 4 the weather broke. The storm howled about the tents, and by morning we already had 30 centimeters [12 inches] of fresh snow. The storm continued and more and more snow fell.

On August 7 I gave way to the insistence of the Sherpas and had to realize that even the last glimmer of hope had vanished. Through snow up to our hips we worked our way down to the glacier and returned to Base Camp.

The most loyal of my comrades and three of the best Sherpas, among them their tried and true headman, Pasang Kikuli, had remained behind on the mountain.[26]

---

[26] Wolfe's body was found in 2002. As of this writing, the others have not been found.—Editor

ON ARIZONA'S SAN FRANCISCO PEAKS

Dorothy May Gardner
1944

Dorothy May Gardner (1917–2011) was in her mid-20s and at the start of a long career working in and wandering the West when Appalachia *first printed this story. She is best known to the world as Gale Burak because she used her nickname, Gale, and her second husband's last name for most of her life. She grew up mostly in the Boston area, married briefly at age 20, moved West, divorced, and then began roaming in the deserts and mountains of the Southwest. She supported herself as a hotel clerk, cook for a mining company, and studio assistant for the Curry Company in Yosemite National Park. In 1942,* Appalachia *published her short article, "Crossing the Grand Canyon on Foot." In 1945, on a backpacking trip near Half Dome, she met the man who would become her second husband, service station owner Ted Burak. They had three children and lived in California at first, but in 1955 they moved to Lincoln, New Hampshire, in the White Mountains. She returned to the Grand Canyon regularly to explore and volunteer for the National Park Service, and later worked as a ranger and on the staff of Phantom Ranch. She was a friend of and caretaker for the Grand Canyon photographer Emery Kolb before his 1976 death. She died in North Woodstock, New Hampshire. Her papers, including an oral history, are housed at Northern Arizona University.*

*M*Y RESTLESS FEET IMPELLED ME IN THE SUMMER OF 1943 to Arizona's highest range, San Francisco Peaks, some 12,600 feet above the hot, shimmering desert. Until on gaining the summit I found the stained register in an old coffee can buried among the rocks of the cairn monument, I did not realize that I should be the first since the previous November to ascend the queen of our western volcanic majesties.

Jogging along the hard tar road out of Flagstaff in mid-July with a full packboard pushing backbone into hip sockets, I was thinking of the grandeur which soon would be spread before me when I reached Arizona's highest point. I did wish, however, that I had had enough sense to start over this hot, straight stretch before the heat of the day had set in. Even a dude would know better than to start in midmorning. No cars were coming out from town, either, though plenty were going in. Just my luck, for a lift now would take me to the foot of the mountain within six miles of my home-to-be for the next few days: a ski cabin perched at 10,000 feet among the spruce, just below timberline. And there was that old mountain, looming and beckoning way up ahead of me several foothills distant, hinting at all the enticing mysteries I was about to explore. No wonder that I was impatient to be rid of this monotonously level road and all the people gaping back at me from their car windows.

It wasn't until after I'd stopped at the Museum of Northern Arizona three miles out, for a drink and chat with the Hopi attendant there, that a pickup truck finally showed up and stopped. A round, jolly Chinese face popped out and smiled at me. "OK, hop in back."

The ride rested me a bit and did wonders for my morale, for when he let me off at a ranch by the side of the valley, there was the mountain directly ahead and above me. There, too, was the new mountain road leading to the Flagstaff Ski Lodge which I was to follow up partway to an old tote road heading straight up a chain of steep meadows below Spruce Cabin, my objective. Well, I did tramp along it for a mile or so while it headed uphill, but when it started looping in loose tedious switchbacks meant for autos traveling under winter's icy conditions, I welcomed an old overgrown wagon trail veering up the slopes.

I felt like a frontiersman following a worn old Indian trail through the forest, so that even week-old tracks of a shod horse didn't prepare me for a gray, weathered sign saying "Deerwater Ranch" and indicating a low roof or two up to the right among a grove of aspen.

The very name "Deerwater" suggested a local supply of some kind, so I set about looking for it. Sure enough, against a low cliff beyond the build-

Dorothy May Gardner, whose nickname was Gale, in 1943. She later remarried and was known for most of her life as Gale Burak. Northern Arizona University collected her papers and photos.

ings lay a small built-up pond of fairly fresh-looking water. And under the cliff itself was a tiny, stone spring house with a deep concrete basin inside its cool walls to trap the water as it bubbled out of a cleft in the rock. Any kind of water is so rare around those parts that finding the oasis was better than anything else I could have asked for. The dust and sweat of all my miles dissolved in its reviving refreshment and were forgotten.

Finally I turned back toward the old road again, realizing that the afternoon couldn't promise too many more hours and that I wasn't even sure where my cabin would be. Then suddenly I thought I heard a tinkle. I couldn't have; but yes, there was another, a lower one, and still another. My curiosity was too much for me; time be hanged. Having hitched my pack on again with grunts and contortions, I sneaked through the underbrush and trees toward the sound, and, topping a little knoll, found myself face to face with seven fat burros, one carrying water kegs and another carrying their Mexican driver. I don't know who was more surprised, I'm sure, but he at least recovered first.

He pointed diagonally up the mountain toward the good road. That was where I should be heading, I knew; he evidently realized it, too, for with a look at the size of my pack and me carrying it, he said with raised eyebrows, "You jus' wait, *sí*? I feel thees an' thees," gesturing toward burros and water kegs alike. He prattled on while untying his burros, filling his kegs, and fashioning me a rude halter from a bit of handy rope.

Soon our procession up the shoulder toward the road was under way. My new friend and I, with our feet dragging in the grasses, were each leading a burro, mine carrying my pack and his having water kegs bobbing about on its back. The rest wandered along behind us at their own pace, tinkling with each step and nibble of grass.

Juan's chatter filled the woods around as we jogged along. It's a good life for a man there on the mountain, he said; lonely, to be true, but sheep are easy animals to get along with. He and his partner herded over a thousand sheep there on the lower mountain flanks, moving every few days to new grazing grounds. Had I known the trail on up to the cabin, I might have accepted their repeated urge to stay for supper in their neat, cozy camp and enjoy an evening of songs from Old Mexico. But it was already 5 o'clock, and I knew that the next few miles would be tiring and difficult to find after dark. Promising to stop in on my way back to town, I set off.

———

When the white-trunked aspens gave way finally to hemlock groves and spruce on either side of the meadows, I knew I hadn't far to go. Sure enough, there was an end of the last meadow merging with the pine border. And here through the trees was a shiny spot of tin roofing. Standing in the center of a small, lupine-filled clearing was the cabin, a little bleak and lonely, perhaps, but with a welcoming door sagging wide to greet me.

It looked as forlornly weather beaten and battered as any of the ski cabins and old Appalachian Mountain Club shelters that I know and love in the White Mountains back East.

There wasn't too much time before dark now, so I went afield with my hatchet to cut a deep springy mattress of hemlock boughs that converted the rough, boarded bunk shelf into a bed fit for a queen. After that it was the work of but a few minutes to open out my bedroll, empty the pack, and get ready for supper. The meal was a meager affair; I felt much too sleepy to bother with a fire in the stove, though when I'd finished and cleaned up, something drew me down to the upper edge of the meadow to gloat over my domain.

The spell of mountain peace was deep within me. This was what I had come seeking, and I was content to sit in the last few sunlit minutes midst the alpenglow, watching a vivid sunset bathe earth and sky alike in flaming brilliance, then pass from the plains up my mountain and be gone.

A small pack of coyotes, resenting my intruding spoor, sat on their haunches low in my meadow and voiced their sentiments in discordant outcries to the sky. I love to hear them, too, whether on the desert where the wind makes eerie cadences with their lament, or in the strangely echoing depths of a forest. Many a night I've lain in bed at the Grand Canyon and heard a pack in full tilt after a fawn. The portent of the dead silence following the last anticipatory bark always made me shiver a little in sympathy with the poor doomed thing. Tonight I was meeting them on their own ground, and all they were bold enough to do was to protest pettishly from a safe distance.

It was good to snuggle deep down into my bedroll and relax every tired muscle on the sweet-scented boughs. One blissful sigh and even the wind was quiet. At least, the next thing I heard was a sassy squirrel on my roof scolding a timid but curious deer at the edge of the clearing. It was morning, and in no time I was up. Outside in the tingling air I could see the long triangular shadow of the mountain spread out for miles into the sunny forests to the west. With the shadow drawing shorter and near all the time, I realized this delicious coolness would soon be simmering heat, and so I got under way. It wasn't much after eight when, with lunch in kerchief and canteen on belt, I started up behind the clearing for the top of Agassiz Peak.

No trail at all leads up the slope and from the cabin. The skiers who utilize the cabin in winter go down from there, not up, and but few trampers seem to use this route even in summer. I found out that the only thing to do was to pick the path of least resistance up. And up it was, practically a hand-and-foot proposition over malpais rock and slippery forest floor. An hour of puffing and scrambling brought me to the timberline, that storm-battered borderland of tortured and twisted spruce that must resist the yearly round of spring gales, summer lightning, and winter blizzards.

As it was impossible to force a way through the stunted trees, I had either to crawl beneath them or detour around the interwoven clumps in order to reach the final and toughest stretch, the talus of naked rock heaped in promiscuous ridges up to the cone rim at Agassiz Peak (12,340 feet).[27] Here it was necessary to take great care with each step lest any of the many precariously balanced boulders be carelessly sent careening and start a whole slope moving with it. More than once a lichen-covered slab that looked settled would teeter violently underfoot and slide a few feet down as I'd wildly lurch off to another "solid" rock.

Another hour, however, found me on the pinpoint summit, where I promptly forgot all my puffing and sweaty discomfort. There before my wind-blurred eyes was spread the whole of north-central Arizona. Inside the broken circle of the mountain rim, the concave slopes dip in a smoothly steep talus arc from cinder-crusted crest to meadowed crater floor, 2,000 feet of sweeping drop. On the outside slopes, which are visible for a hundred miles or more, the convex flanks fall in symmetrical forested folds to the Coconino Plateau, 5,000 feet below my peak. Clustered groups of ranch buildings with their squares of tilled fields and pasture land dot the distant fertile flats.

Like pilgrims kneeling at their shrine, more than three hundred red cinder hills, blowholes, and small craters cluster close around the mountain base. Pink-lipped Sunset Crater and the granite bulk of Elden Mountain stand out among them, but they all blend smoothly into the cleared flats and rolling sweep of forest. This in turn recedes from the axis of the mountain in every direction and is broken only by the edge of the plateau's irregular rim circling the peaks fifty miles away. Just visible beyond the eastern border of the plateau at Canyon Diablo is the circular splash of Meteor Crater, its ridged rim but slight relief on the rolling barren plains extending past it to the

---

[27] The U.S. Geological Survey now lists the official elevation of Agassiz Peak as 12,323 feet.—Editor

New Mexican border. The Painted Desert's streaked and vivid wastes bound the plateau to the east and north.

Emerging from the northern edge of peach-colored haze, a thousand-foot ribbon of cliff winds first south then west through the Kaibab Forest and disappears into the plains toward Boulder Dam. That wide white band of sandstone is the North Rim of the Grand Canyon of the Colorado River, spectacular even when viewed from my remote promontory. The canyon always dominates every scene of which it forms a part; each new phase in which I encounter it is one to be treasured.

Suddenly in the midst of my daydreaming, the ominous rumblings of local showers gathering in on every side of the mountain grew more persistent and sent a cool wind up across the peak. I came to with a start. Before getting rained off the heights or enveloped by clouds, I wanted to make the circuit of the rim a mile around to Humphreys Peak, the true summit of the mountain (12,794 feet).[28] As the crow flies it is north of Agassiz. My route though seemed to lead in every direction but north. Loose cinders and clinkers, jagged pinnacles of harder rock, and little saddles full of dirty, granular snow all conspired to delay progress, though at times, when I could find it, I followed a slight trace of trail circling around just off the outside edge of the rim.

A passing cloud spat down on me as I clambered up the last nubble to the highest point in all Arizona. Only those who have heard the call of mountain peaks and glory in the struggle of ascent can know the thrill I felt standing completely alone on the very cap of the state, a spot trod by but few of the hordes passing by.

The wind was now strong and sharp with impending rain. Looking around for shelter from the elements about to burst upon me, I found that some persevering climbers had built a three-sided windbreak of rough stone slabs just inside the lip of the rim away from the prevailing winds. By anchoring a few broken boards from the cairn across the top of one corner, I made a cozy, protected nook and curled up inside for warmth. Lying there, I watched a few strands of cloud veer across the open side. A beetle clumsily

---

[28] The U.S. Geological Survey now lists the official elevation of Humphreys Peak as 12,621 feet.—Editor

and laboriously crawling over one boot fell on his back with legs flailing. Then my eyes closed.

I had a comfortable little doze, relaxing just on the borderland of consciousness while I listened to the rain patter and the wind howl around me. In half an hour the storm was over, and a wide ray of sun shone tentatively on the glistening rocks and rivulets. For a while I just stood there and watched the storm dissipate while I deliberated on which route to take back to the cabin. Though there were still several hours till suppertime, other showers were gathering all the while, and it seemed advisable to get down into timber before another deluge hit. The ski lodge, trails, and practice slopes are at the bottom of the fanned-out bowl between the main ridges of Agassiz and Humphrey, and so I decided to hit right off down the flanks of Humphrey and cross over to see the skiing setup before climbing up through the meadows toward my cabin. Down I tore at a running schuss over sliding scree and almost vertical fields of clumpy grass, bouncing, balancing, and braking first to one side and then to the other in a series of christies and tempo turns, flying into the floor of the bowl on pogo sticks instead of skis. Partway down the slope a slight shower made me retreat to the lee of a Douglas fir, where I settled myself comfortably and very thoroughly on a big gooey blob of pitch. I just took my seat of pine needles with me when I started off again, and from then on until I had a chance to change trousers I had to scrape myself clear of everything I sat on.

The ski club trail crew have built a short tow on their main practice slope, the only one I know of in the state. Arizonans are not spoiled as New Englanders are. The lodge itself is a sumptuous, new log-cabin mansion built down where the aspens and meadows level out into the valley.

Going up the wooded ridge toward camp, the windfall was so heavy that I found it easiest to jump from log to log, running up the length of one and crossing to another, working up the slope all the time without even touching the ground. It was good to see my tin roof shining among the trees. Not that I was so very tired or hungry; no, it was just good to feel that this was home and where I belonged.

MANLESS ASCENT OF DEVILS TOWER

Jan Conn

1952

Jan Conn (1924–) might have been called a hippie if she had been born a genera-tion later. Just after World War II, she and her husband, Herb, eschewed most expectations Americans might have had of two educated Easterners when they altered an old panel truck into a moving residence. They drove around the country looking for cliffs to climb.

Jan grew up in Maryland and first climbed mountains as a child while vis-iting her grandparents in the White Mountains of New Hampshire. She and Herb were married in 1944. They had no children. Their work life served their climbing and, later, their exploring of caves (they discovered about sixty-five miles' worth of routes in South Dakota's Jewel Cave). For pay, they did things like fill cracks in Mount Rushmore's presidential sculptures (Herb) and assemble venetian blinds (Jan).

The spire this essay covers, Devils Tower, was the chief attraction of South Dakota for the Conns. After the couple climbed it, Jan lured climbing friend Jane Showacre from the East to put to rest any notions pushy tourists held that Jan had succeeded the first time only because Herb had hauled her up. As you will see, the women were equal to the task. In true early Appalachia fashion, Conn deflected the doubt and worry she might have felt by joking about their quirky food habits. She ate Clark Bars for energy, and Showacre took "enough food for six."

Herb Conn died in 2012, and Jan continues to live in South Dakota, occasion-ally visiting a school classroom, where she talks about her nonconformist life.

*I*T ALL STARTED FOUR YEARS AGO WHEN HERB AND I WERE coming triumphantly into camp after climbing Devils Tower. It had been an excellent climb on good firm rock, and we had that tired, satisfied feeling one always has after such a climb. I was feeling particularly smug because I was the first woman to climb the tower without the aid of the old ladder, which had long been out of use.

My self-satisfaction was short lived. Curious tourists had gathered around us asking questions and staring at our ropes and hardware. After looking at me with what I assumed were awe and respect, a brawny Minnesotan turned to Herb and asked, "How does it work? Do you climb up to a ledge somewhere and then haul her up?" Herb's careful explanation was lost to me as I fumed inwardly at the stupidity of the human race and the quirk of fate which made me look like a pudgy schoolgirl instead of a tall, strapping Amazon.

At that moment I took a solemn vow that someday I would climb Devils Tower with someone who couldn't possibly "haul me up," someone who wouldn't get all the credit for my straining muscles. If I could find another girl. . . .

Girl rock climbers who lead and are willing to assume equal responsibility for an ascent are fairly rare, but the climbing group in Washington, D.C., has turned out more than its share. They have developed female climbers who don't seem to have heard that men are physically superior to women. They not only do their share of backpacking in the high mountains, they hold their own on the severe practice climbs along the Potomac River.

I had seen Jane Showacre do some superb practice climbing on the Potomac cliffs, and I knew she had spent several seasons in the mountains of western Canada. Pim and Ken Karcher, who had been in the high mountains with her, found her to be a camera fiend and reported that her greatest fault was her insistence that, "If you stand out to the right of that foothold and lean back just a little more, it will make a better picture." Also, they said, she consumed more food than anyone they knew.

Well, I have my own peculiarities, and I could certainly put up with hers if she could stand mine. Herb has long teased me about my dependence on a Clark Bar for quick energy, sometimes even in the middle of a pitch.

Jan Conn, left, and Jane Showacre beamed after they made the first ascent without men of Devils Tower in South Dakota.

By our standards, a "two Clark Bar climb" is a real humdinger. I get scared sometimes, not when I am leading, but only when I have a secure upper belay. Also, I am allergic to carrying a pack.

In spite of all these things, Jane and I decided we would give Devils Tower a try. So at 4:30 A.M., July 16, 1952, the two of us crept out of the

Devils Tower campground carrying rope, hardware, a camera, and food enough (including Clark Bars) for six people.

As I was panting up the talus and wondering why the active life I lead doesn't make me lose weight, Jane was bobbing along behind munching a plum.

I was elected to lead the first pitch because it required a long reach, and being one and three-quarters inch over five feet I was three-quarters of an inch taller than Jane. The pitch required balance and the use of small holds. Jane coming up under our tremendous pack was not happy. Therefore we decided to haul it up the next pitch, the Durrance Crack.

I led again, taking well over half an hour on the 80-foot pitch. I didn't expect to lead the whole distance. For the last twenty feet I was just looking for a piton crack so I could climb down with an upper belay and let Jane lead the rest. We had so much trouble hauling up the pack that we ate some of the lunch (just to lighten the load, of course) before going on.

Thus fortified, Jane took the lead. She jammed into a narrow chimney above, where I could hear her pounding in a piton. It didn't sound to me as if it were in far, and I heard Jane remark as she snapped her rope through it, "It might not hold some six-foot muscle man, but it's good enough for us." Jane weighed only 109 pounds.

As I shouldered the pack to follow Jane, I felt grim determination. Once jammed into the chimney with the pack, I seemed utterly unable to move. But with enough heaving, grunting, and pushing, I slowly inched my way upward. Jane's face looked concerned as my head finally emerged from the crack. She said, "Golly, I hope the oranges didn't get squashed."

The next pitch was a high-angle inside corner with an overhanging bulge at the top. Pitons had been left in this pitch. Someone had placed them at arm's reach to protect each tricky spot. Jane, as leader, discovered that in each case she had to take the difficult step before she was high enough to reach the piton which was to have protected it. Being short does have its disadvantages. Nevertheless, she reached the overhand in short order and pulled over onto the belay ledge.

It is almost impossible to climb Devils Tower without gathering a large audience of inquisitive tourists. We could see them all grouped below and could catch occasional remarks such as, "Does someone pay them to do that?" and the emphatic answer, "I don't know, but you couldn't pay me to do it."

Jane and I grinned at each other. It seems to be impossible for people who haven't tried it to understand just why climbing rocks is such fun.

Jane's last lead had brought us up to the start of the traverse to the large bushy ledge, where the serious climbing would be over. Soon we were following the crude trail made by the 75 or so people who have climbed Devils Tower since 1937, when [Fritz] Wiessner made the first ascent of the rock not using the old ladder.

Beyond the ledge 200 feet of easy scrambling brought us to the large rounded summit and the flying ants. One would think that with all of Wyoming to choose from that swarm of ants would find a spot more to their liking than the top of Devils Tower. But there they stay to pester any stray climbers who are foolish enough to invade their personal domain.

After gleefully signing the register as the first manless ascent, Jane and I retreated to the edge of the summit for a bite of something besides flying ants. We had spent six hours on the ascent, and we used two hours more on the summit, exploring, taking pictures, and eating most of the food we had brought.

By the time we started down, it was really hot, and we found ourselves collapsing in every piece of shade on that sunny face. We had not brought a rappel rope, so we had to climb down to the top of the Durrance Crack. Here we had left an extra climbing rope, and by joining the two ropes we managed a rappel.

At the base there was much picture taking and staring, and I was feeling wonderful. No one could possibly think that Jane had pulled me up or vice versa. I looked too chubby to haul anyone, even Jane, and she looked so small that it was hard to picture her doing anything much more strenuous than playing shuffleboard.

But of course the blow had to fall. As a couple turned to leave the crowd that had gathered around us, I heard the man remark, "That climb must not be very hard—if *they* can do it."

FREE FALL ON THE DENT BLANCHE

Philip D. Levin
1964

Philip Dane Levin could be called the man who saved Appalachia. *The lawyer and former* Appalachia *editor started the journal's poetry department and served on the journal's committee for eighteen years (1970–1988), including four years as editor and chairman. He also served in the former capacity of councilor of publications. Levin's own writing, and the work he did to keep the journal from folding, showed his dedication to its serving a wider purpose than the journal of record for the Appalachian Mountain Club.*

In the 1970s, when the club considered ceasing the publication of Appalachia, *Levin negotiated a new arrangement that would require readers to pay for separate subscriptions rather than receiving it free as part of membership. Although that decision was controversial, it did keep the journal alive. As W. Kent Olson wrote in a memorial essay in 2010, "He contributed long, thoughtful essays on wilderness ethics, peakbagging, overdevelopment of the backcountry, nuclear energy, equal access to wildlands by minorities, and other environmental themes. The often-controversial subjects generated wonderful debates within and outside AMC. He respected and thrived on good argument, even—especially—if it contradicted his own."*

This piece predates all of that. It was one of the first Levin wrote for Appalachia, *about the event that ended his technical climbing.*

I N THE CABLE CAR FROM ZERMATT TO FURI, ON OUR WAY TO CLIMB the Dent Blanche, an American couple stared at our gear and my fingers, which were taped to protect some frostbite blisters. They turned out to be old acquaintances from Boston, whom I had not seen for years. A very hard-working businessman, he had allotted a day for the Alps and its evening for the cool and Matterhorn-dark Schwarzsee to see the nightly passion play of light on the strange-named great snow peaks five miles away across the ten glaciers. He was profoundly stirred. There seemed to be in these 24 hours an agony of missed experience, half-stifled far within him. I never saw him again. Shortly afterwards, still young, he died of his first heart attack.

Edgar[29] and I left the *téléférique* at Furi. The condensed light of the late sun was everywhere. A little too intent on making time, we hurried up along the Zmutt Valley to the Staffel Alp Hotel, from which the last travelers had returned to Zermatt for the night. Just beyond Staffel were the terminal mo-raines of the Zmutt Glacier and a construction project designed, we were told, to bring pipelines through the trunk of the Matterhorn itself. An open cart-like affair mounted on its trolley on an overhead cable and used for carrying tools, material, and occasionally construction workers crossed the Zmutt Glacier to the base of the Hohwänghorn at the height of about two hundred feet. In this unprotected open box, at most four by eight feet, we rode suspended noncommittally between the darkening ice and detritus of the glacier and the burning granite towers far overhead.

Disembarking, we found that the trail winding from the moraine past a large construction shelter along the lowest slopes of the Hohwänghorn to the Schönbühl Hut closely resembled those precipitous ramps which always lead to fabulous castles in children's literature.

Far down the winding path towards the moraine we saw Hermann Brün-ner and his cousin Christian[30] from Saas Fee. It was Christian with whom I had been climbing. We waited for them and together entered the newly renovated Schönbühl Hut.

---

[29] Edgar Frey, Levin's climbing companion from Dortmund.—Editor
[30] Levin noted that he altered some biographical details about the guides.—Editor

That night I had an unsettling dream. I had killed my brother and was standing around studying my parents' reactions, when I woke up. Being sleepy, I managed to doze off till the official rising at 3:30. Then I was really bothered and lost in preoccupation while we got our boots on and took our soup, hot chocolate, bread, and cheese. I had never had such a dream. But by the end of breakfast, I had come up with a reassuring explanation. The last words of my mother before my departure, in her continual fear over my climbing, had been for me to take great care, since she could not bear losing any of her sons. Words of caution about conditions on the Viereselsgrat must have recalled her words to me subconsciously.

Outside the night was moonless. The warm winds that had prevailed at supper had vanished into a cold, clear sky. But the scene lacked the gaunt space and dimensions of real mountains; there was something in it of the claustrophobic human beauty of the stage and the starlight of the poets.

When we arrived at the Schönbühl Glacier, we planned to make three ropes of two: Hermann with a climber from Paris; Christian with myself; Edgar with a third guide from Zermatt. We moved methodically about the lateral moraines of the Schönbühl Glacier, which merge with the slopes behind the Hohwänghorn and Aebihorn before giving out into the widened basin of the glacier. The Schönbühl flows due south and briefly southeast before joining the Zmutt; once on the glacier, we were moving practically due north towards the Zinal Valley, from which, however, we were cut off by the Point de Zinal to the northeast and the Dent Blanche before us to the northwest. The south ridge of the latter, rising on our left with unbelievable gradualness from the Col d'Hérens, turned towards us the long dark barrier of the Wandflue. This is the *gewöhnlicher Weg* or "ordinary route." Eastwards, we were encompassed by the south and north ridges of the Pointe de Zinal, terminating northward in the Col de Zinal. From this col the Viereselsgrat moved at first northwest and then due west across the head of the basin to join the south ridge at the summit of the Dent Blanche.

As we threaded northwards across the ice towards the Col de Zinal, the snow-tipped cutting edge of the great south ridge to westward went slowly from magenta into yellow above the huge black facets of the Wandflue. The closer we came to the Dent Blanche, the more it broke up into a chaotic brown and glacier-dappled mass of granite in the businesslike illumination of the rising sun. As always, the attractive features which first recommended the mountain to us dwindled into shapelessness the nearer we came to our objective and had either to be taken for granted as we climbed or else relegated to afterthought for reminiscences in the tea gardens of Zermatt.

Hermann tested snow bridges. They were all firm at this early hour. At about 5:30 A.M. we came to the northern end of the glacier, rising now at an increasing angle to meet its bergschrund. Here began the outer zone of rockfalls, which, though nonexistent at this hour, soon started and continued incessantly throughout the day. We crossed the narrow bergschrund in a routine fashion and traversed diagonally upwards on the 50-degree ice slope above its upper lip to where the rock of the Viereselsgrat began.

Some easy crag work brought us to the ridge proper, which sharpened to a knife-edge and began to shoot upwards in steep surges. We kept to the slabs over the southeast face just below the ridge. Climbing at this stage consisted mainly of slab work and opposition of forces on the blade edges. The rock throughout the climb was frequently of friable quality, as we had been warned, and moderately exposed. At times we thanked the ice and verglas which had congealed in the darkness into a sort of cement. The first of the day's rockfalls came past us, some of them whirring at high velocity. Daily thaw and nocturnal frost had rotted much of the rock, as is the case generally

Philip D. Levin gave up technical climbing after the episode he describes in this essay. This photo on an unidentified peak reveals his love of the sport.

with east ridges in this region, although they deceptively retain the sharp outlines and high exposure of better rock.

We were now filled with the exhilarating tension and airy sensation of climbing, heightened by a sense of escape from the glacier's large but enclosed amphitheater. The rock dropped precipitously now to the Schönbühl and Durand glaciers on either side, and a view opened eastward to the Arbenhorn at the southwest extremity of a chain of spectacular peaks.

Suddenly we stood on a snowy saddle where the ridge briefly flattened to support a tongue of snow protruding from a hanging snowfield on the southeast face. Here we had a "mid-morning" snack at about 6 A.M. and looked for the vaunted double cornices ahead. There was little to see, however, but the sharp upsweep of rock resuming beyond our resting place.

Moments later we were looking down from the north face upon the pleasant snow patch where we had breakfasted. Mealtime had involved a dispute over whether the next buttress went from the south or north side; whereas the preliminary part of the route generally lay on the southeast side of the ridge, immediately ahead was rotten, precipitous rock situated in the full blast of the sun. The north side was still congealed in ice, and that decided it. For rockfalls were beginning to open up with a degree of regularity, fortunately still whining and buzzing at some distance out from the face.

We crossed again to the southeast face for the final stretch before retuning to the ridge above its sharply rising steps. The climbing up to now had certainly not been difficult. This final stretch of face was a little different, consisting of a traverse on a 90-degree wall with plenty of holds available on the eroding rock, which was in turn followed by an easy chimney. Edgar and his guide moved slowly out, one at a time, the guide, in European fashion, unbelayed. Christian went next, also unbelayed. From the ridge where I stood, an effective belay could be had. Once the entire rope was out on the traverse, however, there was no holding of a fall.

Christian reached a ledge, and I moved out. I tested a handhold Christian had used and was not a little dismayed to watch it and a portion of the surrounding rock come out and head off to the glacier 1,000 feet below. While I was studying the revised topography of the face, which I had just created, there came a hard lateral tug on the rope, and I nearly came off. Instantly, I looked towards Christian. He signaled that he had tugged; he indicated that I should move smartly over the little pitch which was in fact no longer there.

Out came my choicest expletives in several tongues. He got the idea. I made the traverse and joined him.

We came to a commodious ledge at the foot of a vertical chimney. Christian started up. I waited until he moved out of sight to the left above me in order to avoid rocks which he might dislodge. Then I started up. We were climbing continuously over the easy, broken surfaces. Edgar's rope had disappeared off the face and back onto the ridge. Christian must have been about thirty feet below the crest, but I still could not see him.

Suddenly there was a single cry of "Oh!", and the clatter of a large rock breaking up in the chimney and coming down. I braced and looked up. A few pebbles followed by the first of the rocks shot out from the leftwards-rising branch of the chimney and began caroming towards me. The irregularities of the chimney held back their acceleration, but we heard the crash of many large rocks following.

I started to the left rib of the chimney, hoping to get out of the fall line, but I knew I was going to be hit. Suddenly I froze—there was Christian twenty feet off to my left! He was upright, back towards the face of the rock, which was five feet away from him, legs together, arms spread horizontally—beautiful grace and control—in his familiar guide sweater, red with its chestband of blue, the enameling of the Swiss Alpine Club guide pin glittering in the sunlight—symbols of safety without belay. As abruptly as he had appeared, he plummeted from sight.

I felt ridiculously gauche and unprepared for this new dimension of seriousness. I leaped back into the chimney directly under the rockfall to wedge and brace myself as well as possible. No time to gather rope or throw on a belay—the first rocks were already striking my head and shoulders. My eyes were shut. I hoped I would remain conscious. My mind began to race and seemed to be at a great physical distance from where the rocks were striking me. I felt an overpowering loneliness followed by a vague guilt and nostalgia—the return of the emotions of my dream, all inchoate. Would we fall straight or would we bounce? I knew I couldn't hold such a fall without a belay. I couldn't understand what was taking so long. Finally came the pull. It seemed incredibly gentle, and I felt as if I were literally floating down, rocks still impacting all over my upper body.

Suddenly came a universal sensation of arrested sound and motion—only the percussions of a final rock in the chimney and the delivery, somewhat anticlimactically, of a final blow on the head. I opened my eyes and was most surprised to find that I was still in the chimney. I had been dragged down twenty feet or so, bracing and clawing. The gloves which I had been wearing on the easy spots to protect my frostbite were hanging from a crack above me where I'd planted my hands initially. I thought later, a bit ironically, how many rescue searches had ended with similar evidence of disaster. The rope had evidently caught on the rib of the chimney. I was wedged again. I touched my head. Blood was coming down my face, my wrist was cut, and the parka torn. Faces appeared over the ridge asking for Christian—the rope disappeared below into space. Hermann came flying across the traverse dragging the Frenchman and crying out for Christian. Christian's father had been killed several years before near the Aletsch Glacier—now Christian?

I was still dazed, couldn't believe I was bleeding. Hermann began directing operations. Christian was alive, it appeared, and I was not to move. Christian was evidently dangling under an overhang with nothing but 1,000 feet of air between him and the glacier. Not seriously injured, he swung in. As Hermann pointed out hidden handholds to him, he reached the platform at the foot of the chimney. When they were squared away, I warned them off the ledge and let slide a 50-pound rock which had glanced off my shoulder in falling and come to rest on an outcropping of rock and my braced thigh. It clattered out into space, where by all odds we should have gone, and would have but for a happy combination of circumstances.

The fall had come indirectly off to one side, and the rope between us had fallen over some rocks in the rib of the chimney. Instead of flying hopelessly off the face, I was able to arrest Christian by means of the rudimentary and lucky rock belay which had resulted. Then I had come off as a result of the shock but not badly, remaining in the chimney and clawing my way down its many protuberances. As I fell, the rope between us held to the rib, and we became counterweights to each other. Hitting the next large ledges in spread-eagle position, I had stopped and wedged firmly. Christian had fallen free for perhaps 120 vertical feet before the initial pull on the rope; it is difficult to say exactly since he was hidden from me during at least half the fall, both at its beginning and end. The entire ledge on which he had been standing had given way, dumped him into space, smashed itself to pieces in the chimney, and come down on me. This occurred on one of the easiest pitches we had encountered. Three minutes sooner or later could have meant another story.

All ropes assembled in the lower chimney and on the platform ledge immediately beneath. Christian had bruised his ankle and his ribs, the latter from the rope catching him up. My cuts fortunately turned out to be less alarming than the process of acquiring them. We were, however, still stunned. Christian mumbled about giving up climbing. I doubt that he did, although he did refrain for what little remained of that season. I wanted to complete the climb, but as a rope of four, and then descend the easier south ridge (rocks were hurtling downwards regularly now along our former route of ascent). Edgar and Hermann did in fact rope into us to make a foursome, but the decision, wisely enough, was for retreat by the way we had come. The Parisian tied into Edgar's guide, and they continued up. But the Frenchman was so shaken by our close call that they did not reach the Schönbühl Hut till eight that evening, hours behind schedule, and the cause of new consternation in the hut.

The four of us moved rapidly down, Christian and I still tense and shaken. We ran down the final slope below the bergschrund onto the level glacier just beyond the outer zone of rockfall. Here we took a break. The Brünners stated laconically that our numbers just had not in fact come up. I had not decided exactly how to look at the matter, but their outlook did not seem wholly satisfying at the time. At all events, I divided what would have been the tariff for the climb between the Catholic and English churches in the village. I thought then of how I had admired the exquisite locations of their little cemeteries and the moving epitaphs of those who had been cut off by the peaks. I remembered being asked as a compatriot during a previous summer to attend the burial of a young American killed on the Matterhorn during his honeymoon; for his distraught young bride had to return home before his body was recovered.

The rest of my vacation there I spent with Edgar exploring the marvelous little byways out of Zermatt which I had so long neglected. Perhaps I should have continued climbing; frights have a way of hardening into fears unless they are purged. To some extent this was so with our accident on the Dent Blanche.

CLIMBING THE FOUR THOUSAND FOOTERS IN WINTER

Miriam Underhill
1967

Miriam Underhill (1898–1977) was in her late 60s and living in Randolph, New Hampshire, with her climber husband, Robert Underhill, when she wrote this article about a game she'd invented—climbing all 48 of New Hampshire's mountains above 4,000 feet of elevation during the calendar winter. Underhill was a groundbreaking climber whose exploits starting in the 1920s in the Alps and the western United States broke records. Her autobiography, Give Me the Hills, *appeared first in Britain and was published in the United States in 1971.*

Underhill, born Miriam E. O'Brien, first climbed in the Alps as a teenager. She grew up in Maryland, earned her bachelor's degree in math and physics in 1920 and her master's in psychology in 1921 from Bryn Mawr College. She did advanced work in physics at Johns Hopkins University and worked for several years at the Massachusetts Eye and Ear Infirmary. She got serious about mountaineering in her mid-20s, when she returned to the Alps. Sir Arnold Lunn called her "undoubtedly the greatest lady climber the United States has produced." The mountains defined her, bringing out the bold and witty side of her personality. She never bragged about her climbs. In her writing in Appalachia—*such as the article, "Without Men: Some Considerations on the Theory and Practice of Manless Climbing"[31]—the joke was usually on her.*

The route up the south wall of the Torre Grande, one of the most difficult in the Pinnacles, which she did with a guide, was named Via Miriam because she was the first amateur climber to do it. She did the first "manless" and guideless

---

[31] *Appalachia* 19, no. 2 (1932).

climb of the Aiguille du Grépon in 1929 and the Matterhorn in 1932, the year before her marriage.

Underhill's many articles for Appalachia *included climbing reports; the wonderful essay pondering how women could become climbing leaders, "Without Men"; and short fiction like the story, "Where the Birds Can Go."³² In her 70s, she edited a volume on alpine flowers for the Appalachian Mountain Club.*

*I*T DID SEEM TO US, MY HUSBAND, ROBERT AND ME, CHARTER members of the Four Thousand Footer Club, that climbing the New Hampshire Four Thousand Footers in winter would present an even more sporting challenge than ambling up the well-trodden trails in summer. In winter there is no footpath visible under the snow, and, particularly in open hardwoods, finding the route may be a puzzle. Winter is colder; you can take only the briefest of rests, no more of those sybaritic siestas, stretched out on the warm, soft ground. Days are shorter. The rucksack is heavier with all those extra clothes, not to mention the crampons clanking away and the ice ax. Then there's the business of finding water, which is more of a problem than in summer, with the rills trickling around here and there. At first it may seem strange but dehydration is a more serious concern in the winter. Every breath you exhale carries away a lot of good moisture which the inhaled air, cold and so dry, cannot replace. Add to this the fact that the water in your canteen, as well as the sandwiches in your pack, are all too likely to be frozen rock-hard. Unless, that is, you have been careful to carry them under your outer garments, close to your body, where they will be tangled up with your camera and films. And these do not like to get too cold either. Most of all, the real work of breaking trail in deep or heavy snow, or kicking steps up steep slopes, is often considerable.

All these may sound like splendid arguments for staying home, but not to us. We were old winter climbers from way back, thanks to the good old Bemis Crew.

---

³² *Appalachia* 30, no. 2 (1954).

The Bemis Crew, initiated in 1923 (I joined in 1926), was a group of tough and experienced mountaineers who met for a week of climbing in February. Many of them were veterans of the Alps, and in a later year we found, upon a check, that more than half the members had climbed the Matterhorn. They knew how to handle snowshoes, snowshoe creepers, crampons, ice axes, compasses, and maps. Tough jaunts some of those jokers led. On that first year of my acquaintance with them we ranged over the Presidentials and Carters unaware, as we reached the summits of 4,000-foot peaks, that more than thirty years later these ascents would give us points in a game, the game of climbing the Four Thousand Footers in winter.

This game was an offshoot, of course, of that very popular game of the Appalachian Mountain Club, climbing the Four Thousanders, which was set in motion, and such vigorous and enthusiastic motion, in 1958. Our game—"ours" because we were the first to play it—followed right along. As the initiators, we set the rules, which concerned the definition of "winter." "Snow on the ground" and other namby-pamby criteria definitely did not count. "Winter" was to be measured exclusively by the calendar. In 1960, for instance, winter began at 3:27 P.M. on Wednesday, December 21, too late to get up to Crag Camp by daylight.

———————

The one-day climbs, or those which would pass as one-dayers in summer, were naturally the easiest, although we did not, by any means, always get up them in one day. Weather, snow conditions, and manpower were limiting factors. We did very well with manpower, having lots of friends. Of course, when the breaking is heavy, the more manpower the more miles.

But often there was time, in the short winter days, to go only partway, and before we could get back again heavy snow would have come down once more. Even in that case we had still gained something, for though you cannot see the tracks you made yesterday your feet can feel the firm under-pinning. Quite decisive is the plunge into deep powder when you step off the old tracks. When Robert and I were climbing alone we broke what we could; the day after we broke out again the part we had done earlier, and perhaps a mile or so more; and so on. Surprisingly, sometimes we got to the top, just the two of us.

Miriam Underhill looked east as she sat on the summit of Mount Hale. The date was February 12, 1961.

OSCEOLA

Strict as our rules were on the definition of "winter" they said nothing against taking advantage of a lucky break, and our chance came on the first day of winter in December 1959. Earlier in the season snow had fallen, but in the valleys it had now pretty much melted away. Well aware of the great advantage of attacking Osceola while the Tripoli Road was still open, Merle Whitcomb, Robert, and I hurried down there. The ground we had been looking at, at North Woodstock, was bare, and we felt that even though snowshoes might be needed for a short distance at the top, it was a bother to carry them. Anyway, we did not mind a little wading through snow. We got all we cared for. It never occurred to us to take crampons. It never occurred to us, either, that the trail would be so icy that we should have to bushwhack along its edges. But on the road, as we approached the height-of-land, we came upon untracked snow, some six inches deep, which had apparently softened, become more compact, and then refrozen. With the jeep in four-wheel drive, low range, we laboriously and so slowly crunched along up. Occasionally we had to back off and get a running start to drive through a heavy place.

On the summit of Osceola we looked at our watches with consternation. But it would be only a mile to Osceola East. It turned out, however, not to be one of those rapidly covered miles, what with hard ice on the steep slopes and deep snow wherever it could lie. I remember a particularly uninviting north sidehill slope on the approach to the summit of Osceola East where, in stamping vigorously through the crust in order to stay on the slope at all, we were rewarded by plunging into the snow above our knees.

As we started down from the main peak on our return the snow under our feet glowed red from the sunset, and across the red snow the dark parallel shadows of the tall trees reached way down into the valley. Through the woods near the bottom, as we felt our way along by hand, we met many more large boulders in the trail that we had remembered. But we were buoyed up by Merle's cheerful thought: "Every day now," she observed, "the days are getting longer and longer."

ISOLATION

For the weekend of January 16, 1960, Bob Collin was leading a one-night camping trip up Mount Isolation by way of Rocky Branch Shelter No. 2. From the shelter to the Montalban Ridge above, with its Davis Path, was a bushwhack, but one which Robert and I had done in summer and found fairly innocuous. We were, of course, going on the trip, too. On the preceding Tuesday afternoon Robert and I broke out the trail towards the shelter for a short distance and on Thursday, after a new snowfall, Robert, Merle, and I broke it out again up to the height-of-land, where we cached our tents and some other gear. On Saturday, although we drove down to see the others off, my two comrades preferred to chicken out. Their trifling excuse was merely the vicious weather. Now, in the fall of 1967, I have checked up on that weather, and I find the following in the official records: "January 16, 1960, 19 degrees maximum, -12 degrees minimum, wind WNW, 79 miles per hour average, 123 peak." This was on the summit of Mount Washington, and our friends were not too far away from there when they got up on the Montalban Ridge. A wind of 123 miles per hour, even just a gust, has considerable cooling power. The records from Pinkham Notch, in the valley only a few miles away, include the notation: "High winds, snow flurries."

The other party later reported more than scheduled frills to their trip, and I quote: "Intense cold, winds of gale force. Collapse of only one tent [this was Chris Goetze's; he continued to use the tent as a bedspread]. Frostbitten cheeks were evident. One climber was picked up and literally blown to the summit." Merle's diary adds the report: "Dave Sanderson broke his snowshoe into three pieces."

On Monday, however, after our friends had gone home with their frozen cheeks, the weather turned magnificent. I even have a photograph of Merle and Robert, sitting on the bench in front of the Rocky Branch Shelter, holding their teacups with bare hands. Still, it wasn't warm enough to take off their down jackets.

Beside us roared the river. Thin edges of ice bordered the open patches of swift water. As we strolled around in the sunshine we admired for some time the lacy patterns which these ice edges assumed. When the afternoon was well along, Merle and I decided to go up the mountain right away. Robert would put up the two tents and get dinner ready, and we would all three climb Isolation again the following morning. The views from the summit in the limpid evening air were breathtaking, even though they were composed more of shadow than of sunlight. We were back at the shelter in good time, for it is entirely possible to run downhill on snowshoes, and a fortunate thing that is.

That night, snuggled in our down sleeping bags, Robert and I awoke to find a snowstorm of considerable determination raging outside. Climbing Isolation was of course out of the question, said Robert. At the first inkling of daylight he would like to start for home.

Merle ought to hear about this change in the weather, and since we felt that we should look after our little friend, so much younger than we, we woke her up. "Merle," we called, "it's snowing." "It's been snowing for two hours," she called back.

Soon we heard inexplicable sounds from Merle's tent. What could she be doing in the middle of a cold, black night? Rolling up her sleeping bag, that's what she was doing. Speechless, Robert and I crawled a little deeper down into ours. Merle was all slept out, she explained, and with her flashlight she was going to start breaking trail up the mountain. Robert must get up Isolation, even though yesterday's tracks would not show under the new snow. And that was that! Of course a storm is never so bad as it looks from a place of shelter and warmth. And it is never so bad, anyway, when you are dressed for it. When we reached the summit we gave a quick glance around, in the driving snow, and rushed back to the shelter, ready now, all three of us, to start home traveling light and fast. We left the heavier pieces of our equipment neatly piled (Merle must have done that) in the northeast corner of the shelter. For we lived nearby and would come back again soon. It was most unlikely that anyone else would go in there in the meantime.

As it happened, we did not come back soon and when we did it was to follow the tracks of other people. We pondered, of course, the likelihood of our finding anything still there in that corner. When we did, when everything turned up apparently untouched, I expressed my gratitude to those unknown men of integrity by doing a very thorough cleaning job around the shelter and its environs.

SOUTH TWIN AND THE BONDS

The day we moved to Galehead Hut was the day before the start of some winter weather. Twenty-one inches of snow came down that next day on Mount Washington, and Galehead was near enough to have about the same. Actually it seemed to us like a great deal more! The following day some additional snow appeared; the day after that, only a small amount, but there were clouds enough to keep everything covered.

For untold hours of our incarceration we sat around in our cramped quarters, now and then venturing out to find and cut up a few more dead trees for the stove. Fortunately we discovered a group of these at a little distance from the hut. The ladies were quite proud when they succeeded in cutting down six trees in a couple of hours. We then timed Robert who finished off twelve trees in fifteen minutes! So the ladies specialized in dragging the trees to the hut and cutting them into stove lengths. We had no sawhorse but discovered a way to hold the tree braced between two uprights of the hut. Two of us held while the third sawed.

Also in the stove—in the oven, that is—we parked some opened cans of food. It was the only way to keep the contents soft enough to get a spoon into them from time to time. We had no definite meal hours; anyone ate what he liked, when he liked. But now, at last, Merle's predilection for getting up early really paid off. She felt just as she did down below, all slept-out long before the rest of us. No one but the unflinching Merle would have pulled herself out of a warm sleeping bag, in that icy hut, to get the fire started. Merle did it every morning. And one morning she brought us all hot orange juice in bed. She explained that she had got herself winterized.

All this time our thoughts kept reaching out ahead. We had plans for those post-storm days and they all started with South Twin. If we could keep the trail broken out for those first 1,126 feet of elevation, and that certainly does not sound like much of a job, it would be a help on the start of our projected walk. Though the deep snow was working against us, and the wind as we got higher, at least we kept track of where the trail lay.

Late one afternoon Merle and I, who happened to be outside Galehead Hut, noticed a glimmer of clearing. Off we dashed to make a final check of our job. As I cowered behind the summit cairn of South Twin, most ornately decorated with enormous frost feathers, I looked down on a new, fresh immaculate world. But a chilly one.

The following morning all of us were off well before sunrise. Every twig of every bush and tree was coated thick with snow and frost feathers. And standing around were a few of those fantastic gnomes, small trees completely covered with snow, in sparkling white like everything else. As we neared the summit of South Twin, climbing over the hard, molded, and wind-packed ripples, ridges, and small dikes, we had to rely strongly on the crampons attached underneath our snowshoes.

One glance over to the east of the Twin Range and I realized that not everyone was considering this the glorious day that we were finding it. The summits of the Presidential Range stood out strongly but the intervening valley regions were filled with thick masses of clouds. On these clouds, way off to the northeast, floated a fire tower on a tiny island of snow, Cherry Mountain.

I cherish the memory of that day's walk from Galehead to South Twin to Guyot, to West Bond, to Bond, and then back to Galehead. The sunshine on the snow, the sparkling air, the chance to stretch our legs after sitting still so long gave me a fine feeling of exhilaration. And I liked knowing that for so many miles nobody had stepped on that new layer of snow except a large wildcat, who paced us for most of the way between South Twin and Guyot.

When we reached Guyot and looked over to the south towards that broad col below Bond I was astonished to see many fewer trees than usual, and much smaller ones. Where had the trees gone? Buried, most of them, and some merely shortened, by the snow. The general effect was of a snowfield, not a forest as in summer. And everywhere the snow was furrowed and grooved with parallel lines which looked like glacial striations, only much deeper and more irregular. For a while the going was easier, for we did not sink far into the wind slab, except of course now and then, and that deeply.

But there was never anything very easy about getting to West Bond in those days before a trail existed. As we went up towards Bond, and particularly as we turned off for the bushwhack to West Bond, we found traces of Bob Collin's party, who had come up the day before from the Zealand side. In this area the extremely thick vegetation, vertical and horizontal, had protected the snow from the wind. It was still light and fluffy and very deep. One of the hazards of winter climbing is stepping near a buried coniferous tree. When snow falls on ordinary ground it either packs down or not, in any case more or less evenly. But when it falls on evergreens it had great difficulty in getting in underneath the branches, with the result that near the trunk of the tree there is just empty space. If you cannot see the tops of the trees, and if you happen to step near one, you are headed for trouble. Even snowshoes will not save you. It's a helpless feeling to drop suddenly into snow not any more solid than a cloud, and thrash about with nothing to grip. I know, for it happens often. I remember one time, when I fell in, that Al Robertson called, "I'm coming Miriam, I'll be there in just a minute." So he was, but he came too close and fell into a hole of his own. Another man came to rescue us both, with the same result. And so there we were, three in a row, all down in holes. I don't wonder that we looked funny to the two remaining men, who finally got us out. Then there was the time when Ken Turner, on falling into a hole, stretched his arms up above his head. All we could see was just the fingertips of two pairs of mittens waving for help. And a faint voice from faraway said, "Get me out of here, it's cold." Of course, you understand, pictures always come first in cases like these.

But to come back to West Bond. Merle's diary said that "the whole area was pockmarked with holes where Collin's party had fallen through. But Miriam said to lie down on our stomachs and crawl. We did just that and it worked fine except for the huge blocks of snow which crashed down on our heads from every overhead branch which we disturbed."

The winter view from West Bond was extraordinarily fine, with the white summit of Mount Washington in the distance looking like Cho Oyu (only I didn't know it then).

As we finally looked down once more on Galehead Hut from the summit of South Twin, heavy, dark, most unattractive clouds were pouring in.

Was this a bad omen for the second trip which we had hoped to make from Galehead? By the following day we had to admit that the one wonderful day which we had already enjoyed was all the good weather we were going to get. After quite a trip down into the valley of the Gale River through deep and fluffy powder snow we reached the logging camp and the jeep. Here we learned that "those two rangers were just here, looking for you. They've been here every day." We telephoned as soon as we could.

Now that I think of it, how would the AMC have felt about having a signal fire built on the roof of their Galehead Hut?

OWL'S HEAD

Robert and I, on a Thursday, pulled our toboggan from the dam above Lincoln, the head of jeep navigation at that time (the Kancamagus Highway was not plowed or paved), to a beautiful brand-new shelter,[33] and left some supplies there. The snow was wet and sticky after a storm on Wednesday. By Saturday Merle had arrived and we three went in again to the shelter, arriving in plenty of time for lunch. In the afternoon Merle and I strolled around the countryside, but did not chance to follow the old logging railroad, now the Wilderness Trail, to the east. A few miles in lay Dr. Miller's plane,[34] which had not yet been found. I suppose it was distantly possible, but unlikely, that at the time one doctor was still alive.

We spent the night in our open shelter. Inside my large down sleeping bag I wore a down jacket, down undershirt, and down underpants besides, of course, regular climbing clothes and fur hat. I felt just wonderful. I never mind hardship as long as I am perfectly comfortable. Robert offered to lend me his air mattress, since I had not brought any, but with all that resilient down underneath I didn't need one and so was not put to the inconvenience of sliding off slippery nylon. Boots are the only things that

---

[33] Camp 9 Shelter.—Editor

[34] On February 21, 1959, Drs. Ralph Miller, age 60, and Robert Quinn, 32, crashed in their small Piper Comanche during a snowstorm. They'd been trying to return to the Lebanon, New Hampshire, airport following medical calls in the Lincoln area. Rescue teams finally found their bodies at the wreckage site two months later. Underhill's reference here refers to the fact that the bodies had not been found when she went through this area that year, probably a few weeks after the crash. According to notes the doctors left behind at the wreckage site, the men had lived for four days, during which time they made crude snowshoes and tried to hike out, but could not find their way.—Editor

I take off at night and, since I prefer to keep my boots outside my sleeping bag, by morning they are frozen rigid and it is impossible to get socks and feet inside. But I have got this contingency licked. I put the boots on with just one thin pair of socks. With feet inside they soon thaw out enough to accept the regular outfit: one medium thick pair and one very thick. From Merle's diary I can add the information that it took me from 6 to 7 P.M. to help Robert get into his sleeping bag. The diary says that when I urged him to try to inch down a little farther he replied he could not move a millimeter.

Sunday morning we left the shelter at 7:10 in nippy air of zero degrees and were soon removing extra clothing as it became too hot. Each removed piece we hung on some trailside tree to the entertainment of Bob Collin's party when they returned that afternoon. I have a picture of Robert changing clothes, sitting on top of the National Forest signs which directed walkers to the Franconia Brook Trail and the Lincoln Brook Trail. The signs projected above the snow just enough to make a very comfortable seat.

To find the summit of Owl's Head in the Pemigewassett, the real highest point, is a puzzling job. When we first walked over this long, level, thickly wooded ridge one summer day our two sons, Bob and Brian, were with us. One of them would climb a tall tree now and then and peer in both directions. It was most difficult to make out whether another elevation ahead or behind was a few feet higher. We ended up by walking this pathless ridge along its full length, being careful to stay on the high points: and was that a chore, shoving our way through the frightful blowdowns and tangles. We then deduced that we must, at some moment, have been on the top. Finally, Al Robertson's Four Thousand Footer Club found and marked a tree which, by decree, was appointed the official summit.

I told Bob Collin about this tree. I said there was no difficulty in finding it, since we had again been up there the summer before and tied on some guiding red rags. The standard method of marking a route through wilderness has long been a quick chop with the ax, "blazing" or "spotting." The AMC trail-making pioneers ran a line of string through the woods. But to mark a tough bushwhack we like red rags, one of our better innovations!

We tied the rags as far up as we could reach, often pulling down a branch with an ice ax. Even so, high in the mountains snow is deeper and, come winter, there may be no rags in sight. I remember a trip up Cabot in 1959 when the area around the cliffs was more open than it is today. No rags were to be seen. Finally somebody discovered one underneath the snow. Sure enough, that's where they all were. Our party spread out, and with ice axes and canes beating the snow we uncovered enough of the row to guide us.

On Owl's Head the slide was a crampon job, with snowshoes dangling behind the back. When we were partway up we met the others coming back down, sinking in well above their knees with their snowshoes over their arms. (Nobody likes to keep shifting back and forth, snowshoes to crampons and vice versa.) We congratulated them warmly on having done this outstanding climb, the first "sporting" winter ascent of Owl's Head. We put in "sporting," for who knows whether some logger of the old days hadn't gone up there timber cruising? (If he'd gone for fun, he'd been making a mistake.) They replied that we, too, were members of the party who had made this ascent and entitled to the same congratulations. Not so, we insisted. Even disregarding the fact that we had not been there yet, we still would not have been the "first" party. But they were determined, as well as courteous, gentlemen and would have it no other way.

We followed their tracks to the marked tree, and then, not having to be at the office desk the following morning, we spent a delectable hour and half wandering here and there along the ridge, particularly fascinated by the wide views. For in the summer, according to the AMC guidebook,[35] "The views are restricted." I should amend that to say that the views are restricted right down to the point of not being there at all. No views. But in winter the leaves are off the deciduous trees and the snow was so high that we could look over many of the others. At one moment, to our surprise, we found ourselves walking uphill and a little farther along, somewhat off to the side, walking uphill again. We got together and examined every step carefully. There was no doubt about it, we had found a point perhaps six feet higher. This was startling. And it was also the time we began to feel that perhaps after all we did belong to the group who had made the first winter ascent!

---

[35] Very likely the *AMC White Mountain Guide*, 18th edition, published by the club in 1966.—Editor

We decided not to tell. The difference was so slight, it really did not matter. Then so many people in the summer had trustingly patted the marked tree and added Owl's Head to their list of Four Thousand Footers. And finally, it was I who had told Bob Collin that the marked tree was the summit, and perhaps prevented him from looking around for himself. All my fault!

Later, down in Boston, we got together, those who had been on the winter climbs, to look at each other's slides. When some of mine, taken on Owl's Head, came on they met a chorus of exclamations. "How did you get those pictures? We saw nothing like that," and, straight out from the shoulder. "Did you find a higher place?" Not being a quick thinker, all I did was hesitate just a second and I did not need to say anything. They knew.

I believe that the Four Thousand Footer Club gives credit for Owl's Head to those who reached the marked tree before the higher point was discovered, which is certainly fair enough. But the Collin group went back another year and repeated the climb.

JEFFERSON

You'd think that Jefferson, practically in our own front yard, would have been one of the earliest climbed instead of the very last. We did make gestures toward it. Between December 20, 1959, and March 21, 1960, accompanied sometimes by Merle, by Iris and Bill Baird, or by Klaus and Erika Goetze, we four times got well above timberline, only to become enveloped in clouds or battered by wind. I am not counting a couple times when we merely spent the night at the Log Cabin (with little ermines dashing around in the dark), ready, to no avail, to storm up the peak the next morning. The worst defeat was one when Robert and I, alone, got to Edmands Col, whereupon clouds came in. Too small a party, we thought, to go higher, when we couldn't see. And suppose one of us had broken a leg? All this time we kept our crampons at timberline, hidden between two rocks in a gray, rock-colored bag which we had great trouble finding again ourselves. We were a little surprised and chagrined to reach the end of winter in March 1960, with every peak over 4,000 feet climbed except Jefferson.

But winter rolled around again the following December and in the meantime Bill Baird had made some plans for us. The Log Cabin, said Bill, was too low. Crag Camp, although farther away from our goal, was higher and should be our base, to take quick advantage of any spot of good weather. We ought to live there. They would see that Crag was kept stocked with provisions and gasoline for the whole winter if necessary. And they would come up to bring us fresh food every weekend! Although I am not sure that the entire program would have been carried out as sketched, we at least started in on schedule. In October we cached a large stock of supplies, carried up mostly by the Bairds and John Nadeau, between two large boulders near certain trees on the trail just below Crag Camp.

December 22 was the starting day. Our son, Bob, was going to leave college a day early in order to be present at this historic event: the Fall of the Last Winter Four Thousander. In Harvard Square he ran into Chris Goetze, who came along, too. George Hamilton also joined the party, with instructions from Brud Warren of the Berlin *Reporter* not to come home without pictures. These were powerful reinforcements.

We all went up to Crag on December 22. Along the trail where we thought we had left our cache there were no boulders at all in sight or anywhere within reach. Nobody could recognize the trees. I lay on my stomach on the snow and plunged my mittens in here and there. Finally I brought up a branch which had been cut. Although I couldn't remember having cut any, it proved that human beings had been there and gave me new strength and longer arms to burrow farther. Finally, of course, we found everything.

We left Crag Camp the next morning with a gorgeous red sunrise over Gorham. It was lovely, but "Red in the morning, sailors take warning." Sure enough as we approached Edmands Col wisps of cloud started blowing rapidly by. What did we care? We sat for a minute or two, for a bite to eat, in the lee of the emergency shelter on the col. George had been having trouble that winter with the coffee in his canteen freezing. He didn't like that. This time he was going to outsmart the elements; he would leave the coffee at home and put in something which would stay liquid—namely, sherry. On opening the canteen at Edmands Col he found a solid block of ice in the middle and, sloshing around outside of it, pure alcohol. "Who would think a thing like that would happen?" inquired someone, to which a more knowledgeable friend replied that it was one of the recognized methods of obtaining pure alcohol.

We did not stay long. The official weather records for that day on the summit of Mount Washington, and Jefferson is close enough to use the same, were: high, -7 degrees; low, -18 degrees; wind, 72 miles per hour. When somebody wanted a string tied I removed a mitten for not more than a couple of seconds and felt a little crackling in two fingertips. Frostbite. I was interested to learn that it would take place so quickly. We left our snowshoes at the col and traveled up the cone on crampons. Chris, who had recently been up Jefferson, recommended that we avoid the summer route, now pretty icy. (Firm snow, which gives the crampon points something to bite into, provides easier going.) Chris led by a good route: a snow slope, traverse left, then straight up hard snow again. In an hour or less we were all on top, now in thick clouds. And such wind! Nobody stayed any longer than was necessary to climb, or just touch, the summit cairn. Chris stood by nonchalantly swinging his own thermometer. This read -8 degrees on Jefferson, -11 degrees on Adams— whither Chris and Merle took a little side trip because she had not done it in winter—and -1 degree inside Crag Camp when we got back there. These temperatures, with a wind of 72 miles per hour, make for cold weather.

LOST ON MOUNT CRESCENT

Ruth M. Dadourian
1976

Ruth Dadourian's escapade happened many years before her rueful recollection here. The story rides on the perspective of that double-narrator: Dadourian as an older woman remembers how Dadourian felt as a younger woman. Appalachia would not have published such a story right after it happened, but a half-century later, readers had to admit that this woman and her husband were unflappable. They got themselves out of a situation that, by the time she retold this, would have undone many a walker. Dadourian (c. 1891–1983) and her husband, the Trinity College physics and mathematics professor Haroutune Mugurditch Dadourian, coauthored mathematics textbooks. She was deeply involved in the women's suffrage movement in Connecticut, where they lived most of the year.

To those who know Mount Crescent, this title is a contradiction. If anyone had told us, that afternoon in late August of 1925, that we of all people could be so completely lost on Crescent, we would have thought him crazy.

That summer we had rented a cottage on Randolph Hill in Coos County, New Hampshire. Our "cottage" was really a cabin, lacking even the basic comforts available in the early 1920s: it had cold running water, a small iron stove, a bathtub, and a toilet. The large room had a big fieldstone fireplace, two cots, two big tables, kerosene lamps, and candles. Since we were both

Friendly and gentle though it is, Mount Crescent in Randolph, New Hampshire—seen here in a 1925 snapshot—was a daunting wilderness for Ruth and Haroutune Dadourian, who lost their way while trying to mark a new trail as the sun set.

working, we spoiled ourselves by taking our meals at the Mount Crescent House, a quarter-mile down the lane.

It had rained for three days and heavy clouds blanketed the summits. The ceiling was so low that familiar landmarks were obliterated. On the third day of the downpour, the rain let up in the afternoon. We stoked the stove, filled the kettle and the pots, changed to woolens, and set off up the lane. Soon we were squdging through soaked grass under rain-laden branches. That summer my husband had been exploring the region south of Crescent in order to lay out a trail from Carleton Notch south to Lookout Ledge. There was just enough time to hurry to the Notch, do a little scouting, and get back before dark.

The Crescent Range lies across the valley from the Northern Peaks. Arriving at Carleton Notch (2,700 feet) we automatically turned south, or left. The first hundred feet were well trodden. Then we began to scout, marking the way with broken twigs, following a southerly course. Absorbed in the job, we had not noticed that it was growing dark. We retraced our steps, arrived at Carleton Notch, and prepared to turn east, toward home, for a quick bath and supper. The path had vanished. We did all the things we knew better than to do. We milled around, sure that the path was underfoot but unable to see anything.

"Here it is!" I shouted. A clear path led downhill; after 100 feet, I knew it led in the wrong direction and would take us northwest to the Pond of Safety. Now I had only to return to the notch and keep on east. Only there was no trail. . . . Once more I thought I had it, until an enormous lichen on a beech tree reminded me that I had seen it before. We stood in the notch in deepening gloom. What to do?

The Pond of Safety lies in a swampy area between the Crescent and the Pilot ranges. It got its name from a time during the Revolution when some Continental soldiers who "differed with the authorities about the terms of their enlistment" hid out in this isolated region. The pond forms the head-waters of the Upper Ammonoosuc, and for years it has been marked by an enormous pile of sawdust covering an acre, visible from the summits across the valley. The region is swampy and crisscrossed by old logging roads, rust-ing railroad tracks, and animal trails. No place for us on a black night.

We stood in the notch discussing the alternatives. Soaked as we were, to sit on the wet ground and wait for morning was impossible. We had left for a short walk without knapsack, extra sweater or socks, first-aid kit, matches, hatchet, or even a pocketknife. We seemed unable to go back the way we had come. It was impractical to head downhill and east on the chance of hitting the end of the Hill Road, for the whole mountainside had been recently logged and was knee-deep in slash. The most reasonable thing to do in the dark seemed to be to follow the range over Mount Randolph and then turn south, going down into the valley to intersect the Valley Road.

As we stood there, that loneliest of all sounds—a train whistle—pen-etrated the fog far away. "Whoo-whoo, hoo-hoo." That would be the cross-ing at the foot of Gorham Hill. We waited. Nearer, the crossing of the Dolly Copp Road at Randolph Station. "Whoo-whoo, hoo-hoo." Appalachia, a flag station at the foot of Mount Adams, due south. On to Bowman, then only a faint echo: the Boy Mountain crossing at Jefferson Highlands. The 6 o'clock freight carrying pulp from Berlin to the St. Johnsbury mills. We had the time and the direction. We started.

Again we felt the soft mosses underfoot. Ferns swept our ankles. With outstretched hands and straining eyes we felt our way from tree to tree. Branches swept our faces, leaves dripped down our necks. If we seemed to be dropping off on either side, we corrected our course. At first there were few problems, but then we struck an area where every third tree was

The woods of Randolph in 1910—like Mossy Glen, above—seemed too verdant and calm for danger.

blown down. Should we go through the branches, over the trunk or around the end? We found that walking with eyes closed relieved the strain and sharpened other senses. The fragrance of those wet woods was wonderful. Hour after monotonous hour passed. The silence was complete. Raccoons and porcupines and bears would be in the valley raiding garbage cans and the town dump. We spoke only now and then. "Don't come this way, better go over the trunk." "Wow! Here's a big one—maple? Beech?" "This must have just come down. Try the root end; I'll wait here until you get around." Dry branches cracked under foot, broke under our arms. Hard work, hour after hour after hour. It must have been well after midnight when a change came—the air seemed dryer, lighter. By looking up, we could see a few stars against the black sky.

My husband said, "Come back here, I want you behind me." "I *am* behind you." "I could have sworn you were in front." Later: "Damn! There's a ledge here. I went down about six feet. Sit down. Now where's your foot? Give me your hand; let yourself go, I'll catch you." We had to be especially careful to avoid Lookout Ledge, the last point on the Crescent Range. From it there is a beautiful view into the floor of King Ravine, but also a sheer drop of some forty feet.

It was a long night and we should have been tired and hungry. But no. We were too busy to guess the hour. All at once, through a break in the trees we saw lights in the valley far below. They must be at Lowe's Cabins. We were right on target, well to the west of the ledge. At last, the sound of running water. We followed the brook until it turned too far west. Then a rocky, dry streambed, probably a freshet in spring. Here, for safety, we went backward on all fours. For the first time, we could talk; we could discuss whether to tell about our misadventure or keep quiet. We decided to keep quiet for the present. This would involve our appearance for breakfast at the hotel; otherwise someone would organize a search party, and we wanted none of that.

The dry streambed led to a wood road. It was gray dawn. We skirted a farm house, dark and silent. A muddy Ford stood in the dooryard; a cat jumped from the seat and curled herself around my ankles. As we ran down into the highway, a faint light showed in the east. Looking across the valley to the summits, it was apparent we had two miles to go to the Ravine House where we should turn up through the woods to the hill. It was glorious to stretch our legs and feel solid ground under foot. Cottages and farms along the way were dark; no smoke came from the chimneys; no dog barked.

The rising sun raced down the shoulder of Madison, lighted the west wall of King Ravine, and at last burst over the horizon. I have seen sunrise from the summit of Mount Washington with a sea of clouds below and the faint blue line of the Atlantic 100 miles away. I have seen the sun rise on the snow-capped peak of Ararat turning it rose before the day-long cloud cover closed in. I have seen the sun rise on Mount Olympus, home of the gods, and on the ice-capped peaks of the Caucasus. None of these lives in my memory like the moment when the sun poured its light and warmth over the valley, turning the grass to sparkling jewels and the rocky summits to gold.

We skirted the silent Ravine House, found the half-buried boulder that marks the beeline through the woods, took a ritual drink at Carleton Brook, and swung into the needle-carpeted path to the hill. The morning was fragrant with rain-drenched balsam and hemlock. Chickadees chattered as we passed. After a mile, the path leads into Grassy Lane, and this to the Hill Road. We were home.

A cold bath is not a cheerful prospect, but there was no time to build a fire. We shuddered, dried, set the alarm, and hurried under the blankets. When the alarm rang, we dressed, ran to breakfast (two cups of coffee, two eggs, griddle cakes, and maple syrup), and then went back to sleep until noon. Not until the official opening of the Crescent Ridge Trail did we tell the story.

The Mount Crescent House and the Ravine House are gone, victims of the motor and motel age. Many of those who ate their lunch with us that day at the spring below Mount Randolph are gone. But the Crescent Ridge Trail is still used summer and winter, up Crescent by the new east side trail, down the new trail to Carleton Notch, over Mount Randolph, down to Lookout Ledge, and back to Randolph Hill—a round-trip of seven miles, all maintained by volunteers of the Randolph Mountain Club.

AVALANCHE!

Robert D. Hall Jr.
1978

The December 1978 Appalachia *published this story of an avalanche that swept New Hampshire's Willey Slide in 1970. Although it reads like a short story, told in the third person, it is the tale of its author, a credit union chief executive officer from Needham, Massachusetts, who had taken up rock climbing when he was 41, in 1968, and who was 51 when he wrote this. Presumably he told the story this way, eight years after the accident, because he made no claim that his memory was completely accurate. At the time of publication, Hall resided in Northfield, Massachusetts.*

$\mathcal{H}$E HAD JUST PUT THE BAG OF GORP BACK INTO HIS pack. A last charge of energy before moving out onto the ice face where Jack was stamping around to get the feel of his crampons. The man did not hear a thing except Jack's warning shout:

"Avalanche!"

He had always thought that avalanches roared. Instinctively his hand moved toward the ice ax he had stuck in the snow. At the same time he glanced back and saw the avalanching snow wave dash against the prow of a granite outcropping behind and to his right.

The ice ax actually belonged to his son. It had been the man's Christmas gift to his boy a scant six weeks ago.

As the mountaineer packed that Friday night for the weekend of ice climbing in New Hampshire with his friend, Jack, he thought how odd it felt to be getting ready for a climbing trip without his son. Always before, he and his son had packed their camping and climbing gear in a ritual of togetherness. But, for the first time, the boy wasn't going. A newly turned fifteen, he had developed his own interests and had made other plans for this weekend. And they did not include his father.

"Rightly so," the man thought. "After all, climbing's my sport. Mike always came along mostly because I wanted his company. Now that he's older, he's got more important things to do with his weekends than to keep his old man company on an ice mountain."

He sorted out their two sets of climbing gear and then put the boy's back in storage with the rest of their camping and climbing supplies. They had accumulated quite a store over the past seven years.

At first he thought he could stand up against that onrushing silent white wave, so he braced his legs and back against it. (He hadn't been able to reach the ice ax in time.) The force of the snow mass was incredible. It engulfed him. It plucked him from beside the granite. It encased him in darkness. It started him on an express ride down the mountain.

He seemed to be breathing normally although wrapped completely in that icy blanket. Hadn't he read somewhere that avalanche victims were suffocated by breathing in snow and ice crystals? (Days later he was to find out that those caught in an avalanche frequently were able to breathe because of air pockets that formed about them.)

It was dark inside the wave. Somehow he expected everything to be white and bright like the surface snow. Instead, it was more like being suspended inside a mass of chocolate ice cream.

DIGGING ME OUT OF AVALANCHE NOTE BOOT HEEL - BROKEN LEFT LEG - FOOT COMPLETELY TURNED - MY HEAD IS AT THIS END SPIRAL FRACTURE OF LEG BONE

Robert D. Hall lay partially covered in this photo he saved of rescuers digging him out of the avalanche on the Willey Slide. The turned boot that appears under the rescuer's legs at bottom left is that of Hall's broken leg.

It was still dark when he parked his car that morning. Willey Slide, the New Hampshire mountain where they were planning to do their ice climbing, was 194 miles to the north. Jack would spell him during the four-hour drive. But in just a few more months Mike would be old enough to get his automobile learner's permit. Then his son could spell him on those long trips they frequently took to climbing areas all over New England and New York State. Someday maybe they would drive to the West and do some real climbing in the Rockies, the Tetons, Yosemite, all the famous climbing areas he and his son knew by name and reputation but had never been able to know firsthand. Someday maybe he would be able to get three or four weeks' vacation all at once so they could try themselves on the big ones.

He remembered the warning instructions about bending his knees. "Keep your crampons up so they won't get caught and break your legs." The Appalachian Mountain Club instructors had been very explicit about the ways to save yourself from harm when ice climbing accidents occurred. When he had first learned the techniques of ice climbing under the tutelage of the AMC two years ago, they made him practice self-arrests for hours. How to stop yourself with your ice ax if you fell on a snow or ice slope and started sliding down on your back, on your front, feet first, head first, sideways. And they always warned about the crampons on your feet: "Keep your knees bent and your feet up!"

He remembered all they had taught him—and he tried—but he could not bend his knees. The chocolate ice cream snow that engulfed him was too thick and heavy for him to move his legs. Its weight was actually pushing his legs down and out. They were thrust forward, straight and brittle, like two wooden matchsticks. He was still the captive of the snowslide, a helpless victim rocketing along with it down the face of the mountain.

When he had made up his pack on Friday night, he stocked it with all the things he expected he would want or need for the two days of camping and ice climbing which lay ahead. Clothes: not much to go into the pack because he would be wearing most everything he would need. All that went into the pack were one set of "long-john" underwear and four handkerchiefs. These four were backups for the two he carried in his pockets. (The cold always made his nose run.) Plus a change of socks, one pair of Raggs to absorb moisture and to be worn under the two pairs of woolen ones he also carried. A windshirt. A poncho. A sweater. That was his spare wardrobe.

He put each of his planned meals into separate food bags, each marked to identify both the day and the meal. "Saturday Lunch": a wedge of cheese, a small can of Spam, a bulkie roll. He planned to wash it all down with a bottle of tea and honey, which he stored deep in his pack after wrapping it in a pair of the woolen socks to help keep it from freezing. Into other bags he stuffed Saturday's supper and Sunday's meals.

The pack also held an aluminum bottle of gasoline, his Optimus stove, and a small funnel, all carefully wrapped in a plastic garbage bag. A sleeping bag was the only other major item he carried. The balance of the pack's contents were the same small but essential things that had been in there ever since the day he and Mike first hiked together into the woods and onto the mountains seven years ago. Wooden matches with wax-coated heads in a waterproof container. Sewing kit. Survival handbook. A first-aid kit his family doctor had helped put together so it was custom designed to meet almost every medical emergency one might encounter while camping. Benzedrine in case somebody needed a stimulant to dash through rugged terrain for help. Toothache remedy. Poison antidote. Calcium pills to combat muscle cramps. Darvon, a lot better than aspirin in the event of real pain.

He had broken his leg, snapped it in two just like that. The crampon on his left foot had struck against something and stuck. He was held fast against the pressure of the sliding snow. The snow spun him around, and the bones in his foot and leg snapped and popped as he was pulled up to the top of the chocolate mass where it miraculously changed to vanilla and he found himself in the bright daylight again. Just his head was out of the snow. He looked up at the sky as a few last snow trailings skittered across his face. Somewhere down underneath—he did not know quite where—his left leg began an agonizing throb.

"Is everybody OK?" . . . "Anybody missing?" . . . "Who got caught?"

The other climbers were shouting as they came down off the ice face and headed in his direction. He found his voice: "Over here! I think I've broken my leg!"

They approached him with caution and circled him. The snow where he lay buried could start sliding again, so they moved with great care. They terraced out a platform just below him and braced it with snowshoes. Just like Chinese farmers terracing a hill. Then some of the climbers tramped down the snow to one side of him to make a firm spot on which they could work.

Gear was sticking out of the snow all around the area. Snowshoes. Clothing. Knapsacks. All the things the climbers had left in the supposedly safe bivouac area. Now, together with the man, these were captives of the avalanche.

One of the climbers carefully approached him and asked him to describe the approximate locations of his arms and legs. All the climbers were wearing crampons and if, inadvertently, they stepped on his legs or arms or hands, the trauma to human bone and tissue from crampon spikes would be enormous.

The man indicated that both his arms were pressed alongside his body. His right leg was extended straight out at a right angle from his hip, but he couldn't quite figure out where his left leg was located. It seemed to be twisted and turned underneath him and yet off to the side. Anatomically, it made no sense. It hurt like a searing fire. They dug him out with their hands and snowshoes. In a few minutes they had freed his entire body from the snow. His right leg was unhurt.

His left leg was swiveled down from the socket in his pelvis, and his knee was bent. From there, at a level about two feet below his trunk, his lower left leg and then his foot were both twisted about at peculiar angles. It was obvious to the climbers who had dug him out that his left leg was a mass of compound fractures.

Although the man could not see his leg because of his position, he knew it was broken from the throbbing pain he felt. He looked at his watch: 9:40 A.M. It had been less than an hour ago that he and Jack had left the car, strapped on their snowshoes, and begun their hike 2,000 feet up the trail to the bivouac area.

One of the climbers put himself in command of the rescue operation and ordered two men down the mountain to the parking area with instructions to bring up the litter and first-aid kit that had been left there for emergencies. The injured man realized that the trip down and back would take at least an hour. In the meantime he could use the Darvon in his first-aid kit.

"Has anyone found a red Kelty pack yet? I've got a first-aid kit in it. So, if you can, find it . . . please." They found it and gave him two of the three Darvon he had in the kit. He washed the painkillers down with a swig of "Saturday Lunch" tea. The self-appointed leader kept the third capsule to show to the doctors when they finally got the injured man to the hospital. No one knew the exact potency of the drug they had administered him.

Some of the climbers removed their down vests and down jackets and covered the victim. But these failed to warm him and keep him from shivering. He was lying on the wet snow and getting colder by the minute. Because of the condition of his leg, they did not dare to lift his body to put anything under his back. So he shivered. "Shock," someone said.

While they waited for the litter to come up, they probed for and gathered up the scattered gear. The man's concern became centered on his son's ice ax. "Has anyone found an ice ax? It's an 80-centimeter Stubai. It's not mine. See if you can find it, please."

Then someone pulled the tie line he had fashioned to secure the ice ax to his arm when he climbed. They pulled on the cord and unearthed the Stubai several feet down and just off to his right, slightly above the spot where his head rested. The ax had been following right behind him in the snow slide. "Thank God it stopped when I did," he thought. They stuck the ax in the snow just in front of his left foot as a marker to warn the other climbers of where his broken leg was positioned.

Every once in a while someone would come over to him and ask how he felt, or offer him a piece of orange or a sip of water. As they waited for the litter to be brought up, they milled around him searching for lost equipment. They probed into the snow with ice axes, dug around with snowshoes, kicked with their crampons. All of them darted frequent glances at the injured man shivering under the mound of down clothing.

Except for Jack, he didn't know any of the climbers. They were all young men. "Probably most of them are students," he thought. "Kind of strange, isn't it? I'm the only one hurt and obviously the oldest person here. Maybe my wife is right: 'Climbing is best left to the young.'"

Eventually, the two climbers came back with a litter and first-aid kit. The leader took the kit and knelt down by the ax marker. The injured man could not see what the leader was doing, but he could feel competent hands at work on his damaged leg. First, his gaiter was unsnapped and pushed up over the top of his boot. Then the crampon was unstrapped and the bootlace untied. As the leader worked, the injured man grimaced and grunted whenever he was hit with the searing pain. It came with every movement of his foot or leg. At last the winter climbing boot was removed from his foot (it had been necessary to cut the laces and then the gaiter to make their removal easier and less painful). His socks were left on. Next an inflatable plastic splint was placed around his leg and zipped up. The leader blew through the valve. Gradually, as the air pressure began to hold and support the broken bones in his leg, the pain abated and the leg was straightened out with a minimum of discomfort and difficulty.

They lined the bottom of the litter with some of the down jackets. Four men were positioned on each side of him and at a signal from the leader, they smartly lifted him up from the snow then slowly and carefully lowered him into the litter.

He had practiced this rescue routine three or four times with the Appalachian Mountain Club, so he followed their actions with professional interest. "Strap the head so it cannot move. Strap each foot, but be gentle with the left one. Tie down the legs, the arms, the torso. Make certain the victim is totally immobile." At those AMC practice sessions, the classic demonstration was to turn the litter on end with the "victim" trussed inside, feet up and head down. As the instructors had said, "You just don't go no place, even if we drop you." He had a gag snapshot Jack had taken of Mike and him during one of the practice sessions. The boy was upside down in the litter. The man stood beside it with a silly grin on his face, looking for all the world like a fisherman standing beside a sailfish which had been trussed up by its tail.

Thoughtfully, these climbers did not test their ties by turning his litter on end. They organized themselves into four three-man teams. Two teams got on opposite sides of the litter and lifted it. One team led off in front to guide and break the trail down. The other team walked behind, ready to relieve when needed. As one team tired of carrying and put the litter down, the men shifted positions with either the front or rear group, then they all went on. The man in the litter did not know how many times they shifted this way. He did know that it took them well over an hour to get down the mountain, while the usual trip with just a backpack to carry took about fifteen or twenty minutes. But they were hampered severely by the weight of the litter and the fact that they couldn't wear their snowshoes, which would have kept them on top of the snow. Instead, they had to wear crampons to keep themselves from slipping on the downslope. Also, had they worn snowshoes, they would have been stepping all over each other as they carried the litter. Consequently, every bearer found himself frequently sinking into snow up to his knees or hips. Yet the litter seldom pitched, despite the sinkings, because the other bearers immediately took up the slack.

He wished he knew the names of these young men, where they were from. He wanted to thank each for his help and concern. Physically they were knocking themselves out to help someone they did not even know.

"How do you say 'Thanks'?" he wondered. "Maybe Jack can get their names and addresses so I can write each of them a letter and tell them how much I appreciate what they're doing for me. Wonder where Jack is."

They didn't say much on the drive up. Their small talk with each other was infrequent. Perhaps that was why they had become climbing partners. Neither man liked to talk on about unimportant things. The man recalled how he and Jack and Mike had gone on a winter campout two years earlier. They had been together in Tuckerman Ravine when the temperature had fallen to -32 degrees Fahrenheit not including the wind chill factor. On that occasion, the only conversation between him and Jack had occurred at the point when his feet became frostbitten and he told Jack to look out for the boy while he snowshoed back down to the AMC lodge at the base of Mount Washington, where he would find medical treatment. That was his last misadventure. He hoped that all would go well with them on this trip, although for some strange reason he had feelings of apprehension during the entire drive up. He was grateful that his son was not with him but didn't know why he felt that way.

He had glimpsed Jack gathering up equipment while he was still lying on the snow awaiting the arrival of the litter. At one point during that long wait, Jack at last had approached him and, after inquiring how he felt, asked for the car key, which the man gave him. At that point, he spoke a few brief words with Jack, asking him to be sure to take charge of Mike's ice ax and to be sure that the boy got it back when Jack returned home.

They finally got down the mountainside and out to the road. A yellow Ford Econoline van which had been converted into a camper had been pulled up beside a snowbank at the bottom of the trail. They opened its door and carefully slid him inside. In addition to the driver and the leader who sat in front, there were two other young men in the back of the van with him. He did not know them either. They immediately began tending to him. One brewed hot cocoa while the other covered him with blankets to replace the down jackets that had covered him on the trip down the mountain. He complained that his right foot was cold. It had lost its circulation and grown numb. They stripped off his boot and socks and massaged his foot until the circulation returned. Then they eased his foot into a down bootie.

He was feeling drowsy. The van owner had tied slings attached to carabiners to the roof struts so they resembled subway straps. As they drove, the straps rocked rhythmically back and forth. He dozed.

As they pulled into the hospital grounds, one of the climbers removed the Joe Brown climbing helmet from the sleeping man's head. Then they started to take off the snow goggles which sat on the beak of his woolen balaclava. "Leave his goggles on," the leader said as he looked back. "He looks more like a mountaineer that way." A mountaineer with a borrowed ice ax.

THELAY SAGAR:
PARADISE AND DISILLUSIONMENT

Jonathan Waterman
1980

This essay about an attempt on Thelay Sagar, like much of Jonathan Waterman's writing about mountain exploration, goes deeper than mere adventure into ethical and moral territory. It captures the gulf that can develop between team members as they struggle against fatigue and altitude.

Waterman grew up in suburban Boston and worked as an Appalachian Mountain Club hut croo member from 1974 to 1979—learning, as he says, "the art of suffering quietly under heavy packs for low pay." He then worked as a ranger on Mount McKinley, which he came to know intimately, climbing it by the Cassin Ridge in winter. One of his most influential books is Surviving Denali: A Study of Accidents on Mount McKinley 1903–1990 *(American Alpine Club, 1991).*

Waterman's many expeditions include his solo crossing of the Northwest Passage mostly in a kayak, a 2,200-mile trip recounted in his book Arctic Crossing *(Lyons Press, 2002). He won a National Endowment for the Arts Literary Fellowship. He has researched climate change in the Arctic and on rivers in the Southwest and has paddled 1,450 miles from source to sea down the Colorado River, writing two books about the river. In recent years his journalistic interests have turned to plastics pollution in the Pacific Ocean. Waterman, who calls himself an accidental filmmaker, has also made a half dozen films that have played on TV and at festivals and won awards. He has received the Banff Mountain Center's Best Adventure Book award three times. His latest book is* Northern Exposures: An Adventuring Career in Stories and Images

(University of Alaska Press, 2013). He splits his time living with his two sons in Colorado and South Carolina.

Waterman made some corrections and changes to his original piece prior to its inclusion in this anthology.

1
WOKE AT FIRST LIGHT AND THE MORAINE SEEMED TO BE tumbling down onto the meadows of our 19,900-foot camp. High above the glacier, the unclimbed Thelay Sagar (22,651 feet) caught the first rays of the sun, then cloaked itself in clouds and drew everything, including us, like a great magnetic force. An amur falcon soared down the river, while a herd of deer grazed high in the green meadows. The Kedar Ganga Gorge was a mountaineer's vision of loveliness; I had regrets about leaving our base camp paradise for the comparative sterility of the glacier.

Dr. Peter Thexton barked, "Let's get on with it chaps!" John Thackray, who had painstakingly organized the expedition, got up and began searching for the coffee; Roy Kligfield moaned and burrowed deeper into his bag.

That afternoon at 15,500 feet we trudged up knee-sucking snow around the icefall. Thelay Sagar shone magnificently above, and I had a stiff neck from craning my head back to inspect the North Face, its startlingly golden and yellow hues of compact granite rimmed with rotten black shale. I was glad we had the good sense to leave that route for someone else. We pitched our tents behind a huge crevasse, which, in theory, would absorb the avalanche from above.

There was an ominous silence amongst us as the sunlight faded from the tip of our jewel, 6,500 feet above. I tried to fathom the foreshortening in the multicolored rock wall. From down below, the mountain made sense, it had proportion, it was a conceivable climb. But up here, I felt detached from reality, as if I were in a dream, and the once inanimate mountain seemed alive. Maybe it was the altitude, or maybe the holy man who hosted us at the ashram in the nearby village of Gangotri—with his pronouncements of Hindu goddesses being transformed into mountains—had me shaken with new possibilities. My logical brain told me that I simply couldn't reconcile my fear of climbing a mountain that was so big and so very beautiful. Sleep was a welcome refuge.

*Climbing began for me with my friend Ed Webster. We read
inspiring accounts of enigmatic mountaineering figures, then
started fingertip pullups, followed by climbing the walls on one
another's houses. We ran to high school together on our toes,
shunning jackets and gloves in the tradition of Herman Buhl
and Reinhold Messner. We were pretty anxious then.*

John Thackray's alarm interrupted our reverie, and we stumbled upwards
in the dark toward the bergschrund at the start of the couloir. We were a
restless Anglo-American foursome, charged with apprehensive energy by
Thelay's shadow looming over us.

Roy, formerly from New York, worked in Zurich as a research geologist.
The English alpinist, Dr. Peter Thexton, was impatiently put off by his three
less-experienced companions, but his talent was balanced by John's humor
and warmth. John, a Scotsman, was old enough to be my father, but he was
also my trusted friend.

Although I knew John from winter climbing in New England, New Hampshire, and Scotland, I hadn't met Roy or Peter until the expedition began. I
dreamed of being a writer like John, but mostly I worked for Outward Bound
and cleaned swimming pools to pay for the transcontinental plane fare. We
were probably the most diverse lot of mountaineers ever assembled in India.

*Between classes at school Ed would accost me with his in-
fectious grin, stretch his orangutan arms, and re-enact his latest
bouldering find somewhere down by the field house. Our friendship was cemented by the rope we held for one another at the
"Canyon," a forty-foot band of abandoned highway of blasted
rotten rock that seemed as big as El Capitan. We dreamed of
following in the footsteps of the "hard men" we read about in
the mountaineering journals.*

At Thelay Sagar's cold bergschrund, dawn lit the sky. We traversed
across hard snow and water ice into the couloir. The ice, though moderately
angled, made us feel like we were climbing vertical waterfalls, 60-pound
loads slowing us beneath seracs that could roar down the couloir and engulf us. There was no escape from the game we were playing, no refuge

in daydreaming, no rests anywhere. The climbing was intensified by my pounding headache and the heat of the reflected sun and the thin air. At the end of a dawn-to-dusk day, I chopped a ledge in mid-couloir, nauseated and too numb to speak.

I opted for my bivy bag on the ledge, while the others hacked out a tent platform. We silently eyed the seracs above, until darkness colored the flame of our stove, sputtering at the pot of freeze-dried gruel. John handed me dinner and with Roy inside the cramped tent, began unloading his pack. Then I heard John fumble something, gasp, then swear just once—and loudly—as Roy's sleeping bag shot into the depths below. We gave him extra clothes and my inner sleeping bag.

The spindrift woke me when I couldn't breathe from its weight on top of me and I dug myself out at regular intervals, imagining how cozy the tent would be. As night blended into morning, we started moving quickly up névé and ice. In our pile suits, the heat became unbearable as we climbed higher on the steepening ice. Each rope length consumed mind and body.

After a harrowing descent, Jonathan Waterman's fellow climbers return to base camp beneath the dramatic face of Thelay Sagar.

At first I thought I heard rocks whistling past. Soon enough, the mischievous alpine choughs revealed themselves: dive-bombing past us, then pulling out their wings and swooping away from the couloir in spectacular, whistling arcs. The black-as-raven choughs had never seen people here before. I envied their wings. The birds made me go dreamy headed, and desperate to escape this labor, I dredged up more pleasant memories.

> *Ed and I weren't the same after Bonnington's Annapurna lecture in Boston. I was stunned by the pictures of the Himalaya; Ed's deep blue eyes glowed with a new intensity. My partner was better than I: on the ice floe at the "Canyon" he would dance on his frontpoints while I swung my ax with an intensity that I mistook for grace.*

Thelay Sagar's ice steepened to 60 degrees and Peter and I pushed on in the ensuing twilight, vying for the top of the couloir. Even at 20,000 feet this was something I knew: splay one foot, tap the other in, and plant my ax with a calculated swing. Then step up with the other foot splayed and so on up the ice. Contortion, rhythm, power, but always in balance. We were floodlit by the soft alpenglow of the Garwhal Himalaya and moved swiftly, surely, out of breath, but never out of control, racing the sunset and looking for a suitable bivy.

But we couldn't reach the couloir's top. So we tied ourselves into a piton, sat on a sloping rock and exchanged pleasantries about the verdant and misted valley feeding the holiest of all rivers below: the Ganga. We dismissed drinks or dinner since there was no flat place to set the stove. A rope length above, John and Roy chopped a ledge, showered us with ice, then profanities as they dropped a mitten and a freeze-dried dinner packet—I tied my boots around my shoulders, fearing they would share a similar fate.

Peter's sleeping pills did nothing but blur our minds and distract us from our lack of comforts. Sleep was an elusive luxury, curtailed by sliding off the ledge. Each time I dozed off I'd stop bracing myself and slide down until the sling tensioned the crotch strap of my harness, abruptly disrupting my sleep. I'd hang half-awake in misery for a minute or two, then pull back up a few feet to our eyrie and repeat the cycle: falling back into dreamland for another precious few moments.

In Ed's basement we straightened rusty pitons and used the grinder wheel on two pair of old axes and crampons we borrowed from our Explorer post. We slept fitfully at Ed's house and hoofed it down to the highway at 5 A.M. for the hitchhike to New Hampshire's Mount Washington, where we planned to climb an ice gully in Huntington Ravine.

The high-altitude bivouac regressed into a warped, wretched dehydration and sickness, which would hold me in its grip for three days. That day John and Peter led, fixing rope, while Roy and I inched along in a disembodied state up the blue ice. I spent the day reeling along, 40 feet at a time, oblivious to the seriousness of the situation, drunk on too much thin air and lack of sleep.

Every 40 feet or so I'd doze off into Himalayan high-altitude wonderland, slumped over my jumars, until someone shouted and woke me up. Forty feet seemed like an eternity, swaying almost backwards over the abyss with each racheting upward movement.

Huntington Ravine was a walk-in blast freezer of rimed krumholtz and black rocks—Damnation, Yale, and Pinnacle gullies showing between wind gusts. Armed with pitons, antiquated axes, and goldline, we reassured ourselves: this was what we liked.

Once we gained the Jogin Ridge leading to Thelay's summit cone, Roy pitched the tent and invited me to sleep in the sagging half, hanging down the couloir. The next morning I held my head and staggered off in John and Peter's footprints, not really sure where I was.

Frost clung to our eyelashes, blocking our vision, as we clambered up boulders toward a blue bulge of ice. At the base of Yale Gully two climbers retreated down and we abandoned the rope, since speed was of the essence in this foul weather. Ed started up.

Peter and John were somewhere ahead, looking for a place to set a final camp. Behind me Roy nearly lost his crampon, which fluttered off his left foot by a single strap. I was too wasted to help him.

After a relatively comfortable evening on a flat snowfield at the high camp, I was still sick. John fixed me cups of tea, then deduced they would have to go to the summit without me. As I lay flat on my back, Dr. Thexton aptly diagnosed my symptoms as high-altitude mountain sickness; he dismissed pulmonary or cerebral edema. In other words, I probably wouldn't die, but since I couldn't walk heel to toe, I was no candidate for the summit. "Let's get on with it chaps," said Peter.

Whacking in my ax beside Ed, I stepped onto Mount Washington ice and we moved spastically up the gully, gripping our axes tighter when the wind threatened to pluck us off. Suddenly my ax popped out and Ed looked concerned as I slid, just out of his reach, and self-arrested in the brittle ice—the ax pick caught solid, my shoulder dislocated from the momentum, and I continued sliding down the ice clawing desperately, seconds stretching into long minutes of clarity, everything appearing in slow motion: the boulder field getting closer, Ed's horrified expression, my crampon catching on the ice, and the dull snap as my leg broke, cartwheeling me to a stop on soft snow before the boulders.

The sun set on the seventh evening just as the exhausted trio settled down for a bivy on Thelay Sagar's summit. Eighteen hundred feet below them, I watched great bolts of lightning flash across the sky and wondered if my oxygen-deprived brain had devised an illusion or if it was real.

The next morning boulders thudded into the snow 40 yards away, as the three cautiously rappelled down from the summit through execrable rock. Shouting congratulations, I fixed sweet tea for their arrival. John looked ten years older, while Peter consoled me with a story of his sickness and failure on Latok I in the Karakoram. But there was no time for disappointment— we still needed to find a way off the mountain, without enough hardware to rappel back down the couloir.

I wanted to tell Ed I was OK, but I couldn't stand up. My demise seemed a just end for our brash attitude towards our first major ice climb. We balked at the idea of a rescue and decided it was our own problem to deal with. Ed would grab me by my good

arm, drop me over a boulder, then I'd hobble to the next boulder,
and we'd repeat the process. At the bottom of the boulder field I
alternately began limping and crawling down the trail. When we
heard other climbers approaching, Ed would prop me up against
a tree and I'd pretend all was well—anything to avoid the indig-
nity or shame of a rescue. Once we reached the Harvard Cabin,
we told the snow rangers in their Thikol that I sprained my ankle
and needed a ride the last two miles down to Pinkham Notch.

On our ninth night we ran out of food while descending the Jogin Ridge and the next morning discovered that we faced a thousand-foot descent of running water and vertical, crumbling rock. I started down the first rappel and, in the middle of it, like a sickening slow-motion film, a huge shale flake creakily detached seconds after I touched it with my boot and had moved below it. I closed my eyes thinking this was the end but the ten-ton missile only grazed my jacket shoulder and whooshed past as I spun round in space on the overhanging cliff. I opened up and watched the boulder hit the ropes below and bounce me up and down like a yo-yo—I closed my eyes shut again, my hands gripping the rope like vises. It took courage to rappel past the obviously frayed section of rope, but I had no choice—the time it would take to climb up the rope would only expose me to more rockfall.

Ed and I then began the three-hour hitchhike home. De-
spite my groans in back, our driver bypassed the North Con-
way hospital, but allowed a short stop at the Concord Hospital,
where I had my leg casted and my dislocated shoulder reduced.
In the weeks that followed, Ed was apologetic though, of course,
he had no need to be. My ever-wise mother, driving home a life-
long lesson about the dangers of unroped climbing, made me
limp-walk a mile to school every day.

We reached the bottom of the first rappel but no one said a word when we realized that the ropes had been cut halfway through. We couldn't see the bottom through the mists. In desperation we tied together 600 feet of single ropes and Peter followed it down. I was last and felt a horrible loneliness on the ledge, listening to Roy and John's distant shouts as they got stuck on the knot and hit by rockfall. The wet single 8-millimeter [about ⅓-inch] rope stretched dangerously thin under my weight and the grit running down the rope in a waterfall wore grooves in my descender ring. One more double-rope rappel put us over the bergschrund. We thanked our luck as we ran out away from falling rocks that pockmarked the snow. Then we sat like ship-wrecked sailors: washed ashore, hungry, but very happy as avalanches roared with the regularity of surf on either side of us while we waited for the snow to harden. Thelay Sagar dominated our thoughts and I stared at it as though the goddess within had been malevolent, but ultimately merciful.

Back at base camp we bathed in the cold spring and slept in the lovely green meadows beneath the timid deer. But Thelay wouldn't leave me alone—she was haunting me, always watching from higher above the gla-cier, still beckoning like the Hindu goddess of truth and deceit, Bagalamukhi. According to legend—and much like the multicolored jewel rising above us—this goddess is usually depicted in yellow, on a golden throne, and sur-rounded by yellow lotuses. In one hand, or so I imagined, she held the high-altitude club and in the other, the tongue of a rotten black-shaled demon.

Early the next morning John and I left Roy and Peter at base camp to hire porters at Gangotri. The flowers were blooming in the green gorge below, and I picked wild rhubarb. In the village, we drank chai and laughed with the children as they peered through my camera—we were the first Westerners allowed here in twenty-five years. Our liaison officer brought the porters up to base camp, then John and I headed toward Delhi.

We walked down trails on sore, nerve-shattered feet and sat on buses, sick, with drivers playing Mario Andretti around single-lane hairpin turns, seemingly forever down alongside the raging Ganga torrent, where current-propelled boulders crashed downriver like thunder. Down, down, down to the ravaged, hungry hordes in the lowlands, down into the devilish heat and humidity that is India.

To ward off my disillusionment, John and I plotted other expeditions to-gether. As true devotees, our lives would continue to revolve around rocks or mountains. Of course we didn't know that we would both pursue successful writing careers, that Roy would accept a geology professorship at the Uni-versity of Colorado, or that we would all lose partners, including Peter, who died—lungs rattling with pulmonary edema—while lying flat on his back in a tent high on another Himalayan peak.

LIKE HAY IN THE WIND:
TRAGEDY ON MOUNT WASHINGTON

Christopher Hardiman, Ali Kashkooli, William Moss, Thomas Murri,
Albie Pokrob, Douglass Teschner, and Michael Torrey
Compiled by Douglass Teschner
1984

Most stories with seven narrators would seem jarring. This one unfolds naturally as it tells this story of a fall, death, rescue of the survivor, and carry-out of the dead. Douglass Teschner of Pike, New Hampshire, was 33 when he found himself initiating the rescue and recovery operation. Afterwards, he convinced the others to tell their stories, and he edited their accounts.

The ordeal took place on Thursday, March 24, 1983. Ken Hokenson, age 23, and Heidar Ali Kashkooli, 30, were knocked down by a sudden gust of wind, upwards of 80 miles per hour, just after they started down from the edge of the Mount Washington summit parking lot. They slid approximately 2,400 feet (or 800 vertical feet) to the Alpine Garden. The pair, who had been on the mountain for four days, could not stop themselves in the unusually thick ice that formed when intense cold followed a period of heavy rains. Hokenson, who resided in Scotia, New York, suffered head injuries and was killed. Kashkooli, an Iranian national, survived and told part of the story here.

Twenty years later, we heard from some of these men. Teschner, a native of Massachusetts, climber since high school, and holder of advanced degrees in forestry, biology, and education, spent much of his career in the Peace Corps and in 2013 was working as Peace Corps director in Ukraine. He served for twelve years as a New Hampshire state legislator and for four years as director of legislative strengthening projects for the Rwanda and Morocco parliaments through the U.S. Agency for International Development. Doug and his wife, Martha, are parents of two grown sons. "I had thought the excitement of that March 1983 day would be doing my first solo ice climb on Mount Washington," Teschner wrote to us. "I unexpectedly found myself in the midst of a life-and-death struggle that seemed to focus like a laser everything I had ever learned. I still think of that day as perhaps the most defining moment of my life, knowing that it profoundly shaped who I am today."

A few months after helping with this ordeal in the mountains, Chris Hardiman earned his PhD in chemistry from the University of Massachusetts. In 2013 he was living in Farmington, Connecticut, with his wife, Pamela, and their three sons and working as director of technology for Kuo Elastomers, which is the largest producer of synthetic rubber in Latin America. He is an inventor on 24 United States patents.

Albie Pokrob worked as a backcountry caretaker in the White Mountains. He also worked for the Mount Washington Observatory and hiked long-distance routes including the entire Appalachian Trail in the mid-1980s. Pokrob now lives in Ashland, Oregon, where he coaches his two daughters' basketball, volleyball, and softball teams and explores the Trinity Alps.

Ali Kashkooli begins the tale:

W HEN I WAS A SMALL BOY IN IRAN, MY FAMILY SPENT THE summer in our country home (and sometimes in tents) in the Zagros Mountains. I often climbed the nearby peaks, where I would sit all day and lose myself in fantasy. I looked out to where the grass that surrounded the mountains gave way to sand, where the desert gave way to the horizon—the end of the world, the great abyss (a scary thought).

As I grew older, the world expanded and lost its edges. It also lost its innocence, becoming filled with hatred, wickedness, and greed. I sought the mountains where the peace of nature enabled me to transcend the turmoil and mundane; this was the world as it was meant to be. A mysterious force continues to draw me to the peaks where I feel one with the world below and the world beyond.

When I came to study in the United States, I sought out the New England mountains and went on numerous trips with my new friends from the University of Maine. Among the most memorable was in January 1983, when Ken Hokenson, three others, and I spent a week in Baxter State Park. The day we climbed Katahdin was most unusual: the sky was jade blue, the wind totally absent, and the temperature mild. We were overwhelmed by the serene calm and brilliant reflections off the snow-covered peaks. On our descent back to Chimney Pond, we witnessed a spectacular night scene, when the streaks of the Northern Lights extended in every direction. It was at Baxter that Ken and I first discussed a spring trip to the White Mountains.

Everyone who knew Ken enjoyed his company. He seemed to be at total peace with himself and others, was easygoing and always ready to help. For his college major he chose surveying—he could not bear to be indoors for very long.

The day we started our expedition into the Whites, the weather turned sour. A few days prior it had rained and then became very cold. Consequently, above the timberline we traveled on solid ice. The visibility was near zero most of the time. We spent Monday night (March 21) at the Hermit Lake shelters and Tuesday and Wednesday at Lakes of the Clouds. We had planned to spend a week traversing the mountains, but, when the conditions of Thursday (March 24) continued to be poor, decided to end our trip prematurely. We elected, however, to climb to the summit of Mount Washington en route to Pinkham Notch.

At noon we reached the top, and the clouds suddenly dispersed for the first time on the trip. All the surrounding peaks were visible. Although the winds were very strong, we felt a great calm and sense of peace. Ken was as jubilant as I had ever seen him, and he delighted in naming every mountain he recognized. He probably loved the White Mountains more than anywhere else in the world and commented that this special moment made the entire trip worthwhile.

Moments later, as we began our descent, I was knocked off my feet by a large and powerful gust of wind. Before I could even react, I was sliding down the mountain at a tremendous speed. Although conscious, I did not feel my left glove and both crampons being ripped off. I felt a total nothingness: I was like hay in the wind, without will, at the mercy of an enormous force.

Finally I came to rest and lay on the mountainside, unable to move and in a state of total shock and disorientation. I tried to get up but fell back down.

Where is Ken? I thought. *He should be coming to help me.* As I tried to move again, I saw him lying motionless about thirty feet away. A feeling of utter despair, grief, and fear overwhelmed me. I never saw him fall. Had he, too, been knocked over by the wind, or had he fallen in an attempt to stop me? I will never know the answer. I feel that I did not come into contact with him, although perhaps I did and just cannot remember.

I looked at my uncovered left hand—it was white as snow and frozen stiff. But somehow I got Ken's pack off and tried some CPR (cardiopulmonary resuscitation), but it was to no avail. In total desperation I cried to God for help, a cry that came from every cell and part of my body. I could not imagine or accept that Ken was dead and decided to put him in his sleeping bag. This task was very difficult, as Ken was a very big man. When I took off my right mitten in order to pull open the zipper, the wind took it. Now both of my hands were frozen. At one point we both started sliding, but I did not let go. Using my teeth, arms, and frozen hands, I managed to get him in the bag.

I had no strength left in me and wanted to lie down next to him and just go to sleep. Then I thought of my mother and family, whom I have not seen in many years, and I knew I had to visit my home again. A voice from inside told me that I had to make it down and send help for Ken.

I felt cold, terribly cold. My clothes were torn, the pants shredded into many pieces. As the wind blew, I felt as though my skin was being cut by a sharp edge. My nose felt broken, and my face and clothes were covered with blood. Frozen blood glued my beard and mustache together, making it difficult to breathe.

I headed across the Alpine Garden, walking, falling, and sliding. The ground was as slick as glass, and I had lost my ice ax and crampons. The ligaments were torn in my right knee and ankle, and my lower leg felt like it was moving sideways. Walking was difficult, but I had to go on.

I struggled to take off my pack, and as I did so, it slid off down the mountain. Eventually I reached the top of the Lion Head. Looking down the steep drop, I knew that I could not safely descend without an ice ax and crampons, even if I had been in perfect health. Once again I cried with my heart and soul to God for help.

Just as I was about to force myself to start down the frightening drop, I turned my head and saw a man approaching.

Doug Teschner writes:

I used to invest a major amount of my energy in mountaineering, but my knees began to resist, and priorities shifted. I still enjoy an occasional adventure, however, and by mid-March had done a few ice climbs. But when my partner suddenly dropped out the next week, I decided to do a solo ascent of Huntington Ravine's Central Gully. The high wind forecast for Wednesday favored Thursday, March 24.

Thursday dawned beautifully, but the heavy cloud cap on the Presidentials confirmed my fear of continued high winds. I apprehensively set out for Huntington Ravine, wondering if I might be pushing too hard, trying to make something take place that simply wasn't slated to be. Gradually I relaxed and enjoyed the hike, just being on Mount Washington for the first time in over two years.

Except for one climber I met descending, the ravine was mine alone on this midweek day. In a place of usual deep powder snow, the Fan was perfect, hard névé, which made for easy cramponing. Fortunately, Central Gully, an easy climb, was protected from the greatest thrust of the southwest winds. I could enjoy the excitement and empowerment of the technical climbing without fear of being blown off the mountain.

Still, I was very aware that the consequence of a fall would almost certainly be death, and the word *vigilance* reverberated through my mind. *Vigilance . . . freedom . . . life lived fully has meaning. . . .* I concentrated intently on the details of the climbing but was having fun.

At 12:30 P.M., I topped out onto the Alpine Garden and down Lion Head.

After only seconds in the cold wind, I felt chilled. Shortly I observed a figure that acted a little strange, about one-quarter-mile ahead. He seemed to be tottering in the wind, and I thought I saw him throw down his pack that appeared to slide off down the mountain. I wondered if perhaps the wind was too much for him, and since I was going in the same direction, decided to follow in case he needed a hand.

When I reached the place where I first spotted him, I found a pack. Fifteen feet away was what I took to be a small tent or bivouac sack. *Someone is camping here,* I thought, despite all the rational evidence that this was preposterous in these severe conditions.

Only when I stood next to the "tent" did I realize I had come upon a body. It was stuffed three-quarters into a sleeping bag, its arms drawn across

A rescue crew, circa 1980, makes its way downslope with a snow vehicle similar to that used in the 1977 recovery.

the head and bare hands exposed to the biting wind. Thin whitish-blue fingers were stiff with frostbite, presenting a macabre perfect image of my personal vision of death.

Fear of the greatest intensity imaginable overwhelmed me, but I forced myself to make a closer examination. I forced his arms apart to find a head coated with blood, with the remnants of sunglasses dangling from it as if in a piece of surreal art. It was a man, clearly not breathing. I fumbled and took off my mitten (which immediately blew off down the mountain) and attempted to get a pulse. After merely seconds of exposure, my fingers were very cold, and I could reach no definite conclusion. I bravely reached inside his shirt and placed my hand on his stomach. It was still warm. Clearly this accident had happened only minutes before.

What to do? What next? I felt terrified but tried to come to terms with my strong feelings of wanting to get out of there to safety. *Is it simply impossible for me to do anything?* Or was I afraid to act, without confidence in my ability to help? I was alone with a corpse half stuffed into a bag in a featureless windswept mountainscape.

I struggled to cover the man with more of the sleeping bag. When I looked at his face again, the first eye was open and stared back at me. This terrified me. I knelt down next to him in fear and doubt and yelled through the consuming wind, "ARE YOU ALL RIGHT?" into his face. There was no response.

At that point I made a conscious decision not to begin CPR and went into my pack for my second pair of mittens. After one last look I turned and walked toward Lion Head, possessed by renewed vigor and clarity of purpose.

I came upon the man whom I had seen from a distance seated in the rocks atop Lion Head, looking southward, unaware of my impending arrival. Unsure of what to say, I settled upon a tentative, "Hello!?" He turned in surprise, and stammered, "Where did you come from?" Whatever his expression, it was hidden behind a mask of blood. Red icicles hung from his nose and moustache. His clothes were in tatters—shreds of gaiters, windpants, wool pants, and even long-johns flapped about in the gale. Heavily abraded skin was exposed through the multiple layers of ripped clothing. His hands were bare and bone-white with frostbite, little better in appearance than those of his companion. He had neither ice ax nor crampons. I thought the men ill-equipped at the time.

My initial reaction to the sight of Ali was a powerful sense of connectedness, almost a spiritual tie. I felt almost instantaneous bonding to him, due to the intensity of the situation, my encounter with the body, and my great sense of mutual need. The discovery of the physical remnant of a person had shocked me but was put aside now, as I recognized the cry for help that this other person in desperate need was unable to utter.

Everything in me, all of my powers became focused on this event before me, as a personal sense of power welled up simply because it was necessary—and because the mountains are a source of power for me. All my years of experience there and personal failures and triumphs fed into that moment.

Internally I shouted, *It's you and me buddy until we get off this mountain!* . . . I had no doubt in my mind that we would somehow make it. I fought with the wind to put my fiberfill vest and Dachstein mitts on Ali, to ready us for the descent to safety.

Just then, two men appeared on the trail a few yards below us. Not wanting to discuss the situation in front of Ali, I left him briefly and set out to meet the others.

Tom Murri continues:

Chris Hardiman and I had planned our annual Mount Washington trip several times during the winter, only to cancel at the last moment due to the weather. I convinced my wife, Kathy, to give me my crampons, which she often keeps hidden during the winter. (She always turns them over when asked, but seems to find comfort in knowing that I cannot go climbing without her consent.) We planned to depart on Tuesday evening, March 22, but—when Kathy became ill—we postponed again. In the morning she was feeling better, so Chris and I piled our gear in my car and headed north.

At Pinkham, we tramped up the trail to Hermit Lake. I stepped outside the shelter several times to look at the spectacularly clear sky, Boott Spur, and the walls of the ravine. The wind had come up and strong gusts swirled around me.

We walked quite comfortably the next day up the Lion Head Trail, soon passing the treeline and becoming increasingly exposed to the powerful winds. We reveled in some of the finest views I have ever seen in the Whites. Somewhat below the Lion Head, I slowed my pace and readjusted my balaclava, scarf, hood, and frosted goggles. Several minutes later, I saw Chris ahead waving his arms, motioning to me to hurry and join him and another climber. When I arrived, I sensed that something was wrong. Then I felt numb as the other climber, Doug, told me that he had "a couple guys up here; one of them's dead and the other one is in pretty bad shape."

I climbed to the top of the rocks to find a person half sitting and half lying, his face bloody and expressionless, clothing torn, one leg badly injured, and hands frostbitten. He was clearly only minutes from succumbing to exposure. I sat down next to him and put my arm around him, trying to lend some comfort and encouragement. But at that moment I was afraid we would soon watch helplessly as he died.

He told me that his name was Ali and about his long slide over rocks and ice and that his friend had hit his head very badly and needed help. Ali said that he would have died for sure if we had not come along.

Chris Hardiman continues:

I offered to go down and inform authorities of the accident. Doug wanted to send a note with me, but his initial attempt to write one on a roll of toilet paper was unsuccessful. I offered the inside cover of a Gideon Bible, which I rather superstitiously carry with my survival supplies. (My rationale for carrying it is that if circumstances should cause me to lie dying, then my mind—freed from all distractions other than my immediate demise—could compress spiritual development and understanding into a very short period of time.) As I was about to disappear down the slope I turned and saw the three silhouetted figures of Doug, Ali, and Tom proceeding down the trail.

Doug Teschner continues:
My recollection of the next hour (or two or more?) is largely a blur. I remember Ali's arms over Tom's and my shoulders, and the slow, tedious clambering down the mountain, and the numerous rest stops, during which Ali hunched forward between us. I agonized briefly over our decision—whether to take the winter trail (steeper, but it would get us quickly into the trees and out of the wind) or the summer one (gentler, but more exposed and with a potentially dangerous traverse of some avalanche scars)—and decided on the latter. But mostly the descent was a calm, flowing—even enjoyable—experience. The wind seemed more a nuisance than a danger. I felt content, at peace with myself and the mountains. Whatever doubts I might have had about leaving the body behind were distant and subdued.

I had been trained as a rescuer to keep a patient talking, and the questions about Ali's background (but not the accident) flowed freely. Although interesting, the merging facts and events of the past were insignificant. The universe was the present moment and the immediate space—three people on the side of Lion Head. Clarity of purpose precluded the relevance of a larger context.

Tom Murri continues:
All I thought of as we moved along was the young man lying on the ice high above us. My feeling were of helplessness, tragedy, and uselessness; of horror at Ali's personal agony as his friend lay dead, zipped into a sleeping bag. These feelings at once overwhelmed me and yet left me numb. I felt no rush of excitement, no surge of adrenaline. Time seemed to pass neither quickly nor slowly. I felt oddly detached from all that was happening and all that I was doing.

Doug Teschner continues:
Tom's presence was a tremendous boost. It almost seemed as if we had known each other all our lives and had been trained to work together. At

One of the rescuers, Tom Murri, as he looked in the 1970s.

one point I tripped and fell. I sheepishly looked up from the ground at Tom powerfully, steadily supporting Ali.

At one point Ali asked, "Did you see my friend? Is he dead?" I replied that I did not know, that as soon as we took care of him we would do our best for his companion.

Treeline was a blessing, a relief from the wind—such a significant factor before. As Ali was unable to use his frostbitten hands, I broke away the blood icicles that blocked his mouth and plopped in bits of cheese, chocolate-covered raisins, and prunes.

A brief comic interlude provided additional relief. After Ali had sipped some lemonade, Tom—not noticing the bloody canteen—requested a swig. I tried to nonverbally communicate to Tom that he did not want to drink from that bottle. Just as Tom got the message, Ali commented, "Yes, have some lemonade, Tom." Thinking quickly, Tom responded, "No, I think it would be best if we saved the lemonade for you. I'll have some water instead." Our transition to the subtleties of valley life, after the simplicity of survival on the summit cone, was under way.

Our next obstacles were the two avalanche scars that we had to traverse. Tom did most of the work, with Ali bear-hugging him from behind while I traversed just below, helping Ali place his feet in the steps. Farther down we came upon a short, steep patch of water ice. I climbed down on my knees and crampon points while Ali grasped me around the waist, his back against the ice and legs out to either side. Shortly afterward we met the first wave of the rescue team: Peter Crane from Tuckerman's, Rob Taylor (whose book *The Breach* describes his own epic accident and rescue on Mount Kilimanjaro), and Jim Hebert, who was dragging a Thompson litter.

Bill Moss writes:

It was my first visit to the mountain since November—an opportunity to check the snow cover and assess my ski equipment, left over the winter in our Mount Washington Volunteer Ski Patrol building at Hermit Lake. My wife, Ann, and I wandered over to enjoy the warmth of the caretaker hut, and Peter Crane invited us in for tea. Our friend Rob Taylor and his friend Jim Hebert also happened to be on the mountain; it felt like a mini-reunion.

But just as we were starting to relax, a person with a blank stare and frozen glasses [Chris Hardiman] ran in saying that there was an accident. One dead, one injured. Internally, the concept of one person being dead did not register or want to be accepted. During that initial instant, it felt like a dream.

Chris produced a Bible with the message, ". . . 99.9% sure dead body in Alpine Garden. I'm descending with second—frostbite and sprained knee. Need litter for #1, heavy guy. . . . Doug Teschner." The note had been written by another friend of ours, surprisingly. Peter grabbed the phone to notify Pinkham. He loaded fresh batteries into the radio and packed necessary gear. From the Forest Service building we got a Thompson litter, climbing ropes, backboard, and associated gear. Peter, Rob, and Jim departed for the scene. Ann maintained a log while I monitored the telephone. Despite a strong urge to go up, I thought it was the most useful thing for me to do.

Mike Torrey writes:

AMC Huts Manager Dave Warren and I were at a meeting at the Forest Service's Androscoggin Ranger Station when I received notification of the accident. As it was my day on the Notch Watch, I returned to Pinkham to coordinate the rescue. I had been a permanent staff member for just over a month and had never been seriously tested as a rescue coordinator. In past situations, more experienced personnel had taken over, and I was forced to stand close by and try to learn by observation, instead of action. But this time I was determined to get some experience and was given the chance. I took my assigned seat at the radio.

During previous rescues my heart had pounded with anxiety during my involvement. But this time, for some reason I was calm and in control. For one thing, the rescue was already under way. Jack Corbin had notified Fish and Game, and experienced people were at the scene. Later, when the pressure built again, my body proved acclimatized to the pace and adjusted to the strain without notice.

We decided to send a group from Tuckerman (Crane, Taylor, and Hebert) up Lion Head to meet Teschner and the survivor (whose name at that time was unknown). In the meantime we contacted the Mount Washington Observatory and observer Albie Pokrob started down from the summit to locate the body. We also alerted Rick Wilcox, owner of International Mountain Equipment in North Conway and director of Mountain Rescue Service (a volunteer technical rescue group), that we might be in need of MRS services.

Tom Murri continues:

When we met the stretcher party, I knew that Chris was safe. We conferred briefly and it was decided that Rob and I would continue down with Ali, and Doug would reascend with Peter and Jim to help locate the body. It was a relief to reach the Tuck Trail, but the final little rise to the caretaker's hut sapped my remaining strength and exposed us to a blast of wind. Finally Rob and I carried Ali into the cabin, our crampons gouging the floor, and delivered him to warmth, rest, and medical attention. I was happy to be reunited with Chris, and we sat and shuffled about while Ali was treated.

Bill Moss continues:
After managing the phone awhile I headed up the trail and soon met Rob, Tom, and Ali. They were managing quite well, so I retraced my steps to the caretaker's hut and notified Pinkham that their arrival at Hermit Lake was imminent and requested that the Forest Service Thiokol start up the mountain. When the group arrived, we prepared tea and washed the frozen blood from Ali's face. We put a mattress on the floor and made Ali comfortable. I undertook a survey of his condition. The facial injuries appeared minor, although we could not rule out a possible concussion. His frostbitten left hand was badly swollen, and his fingers were blue. He had lacerations on his exposed right buttock, and his right leg was in a splint that the stretcher party had taken with them.

When the Thiokol arrived, we put Ali in a pre-warmed sleeping bag and blankets and placed him in a Stokes litter. Word came over the radio that Doug Teschner was descending the Raymond Cataract, and Rob set out to meet him. The trip down was slow; every time the Thiokol slipped on the ice, we were thrown about and bounced on the deck. It was all we could do at times to hold on and keep the litter steady.

Finally we reached Pinkham and were met by State Police, Fish and Game, AMC personnel, and the ambulance crew. [*Kashkooli was transported by ambulance to Androscoggin Valley hospital in Berlin, where he was admitted to the intensive care unit.*]

Ann and I loaded our car and headed home. The mountains still looked pretty—but different. I knew that there was someone up there, someone I would never meet but still felt close to. A body so cold and quiet and lifeless in the wind and snow. So sad, so alone. Does he have a mother? A brother? Will people cry?

I thought about Ali, now en route to the hospital. We simply packed up and left and it was over. But for him, maybe the worst was yet to come. Later, the body would be retrieved and it would be over for the other rescuers. But for Ali, it might never end.

Tom Murri continues:

After the Thiokol headed down the mountain, Chris and I walked down to Pinkham Notch. Without further information, we loaded the car and began the long drive home. Intervals of conversation were followed by long periods of silence. We failed to produce a neat philosophical accommodation to the events of the day.

Doug Teschner continues:

Although tired, I felt surprising reserves of energy on the return climb with Peter and Jim. But somehow I had failed to remember the intensity of the wind; when we passed the treeline, I felt its cold cut right through me. Unfortunately, the wind also caused the sleeping bag attached to the sled Jim was dragging to blow off down the mountain. Peter and Jim dropped packs and the radio to run down after the bag.

Since finding Ali, I had felt remarkably energized, focused, and in control while making decisions and methodically employing rescue techniques I had practiced numerous times before. But when I was suddenly alone again on the windswept mountainside, I began to feel physically, emotionally, and intellectually drained—the antithesis of what I had felt just minutes earlier.

The radio did not work properly; we could receive but not transmit. While I was waiting, a request came over that we attempt to answer yes/no questions by one versus two clicks. But when the speaker at base (Mike Torrey, I later learned) asked the question, "It this an emergency?" I did not answer. I knew Mike was really asking if there was any chance we might find a live patient instead of a body: if we should continue or retreat until the next day. Whatever I knew in my heart, I guess I did not want to be the one to make that very final decision. But I also knew that whatever remote possibility there might have been for Ken Hokenson to survive when I had first seen him, several more hours of exposure to this weather had certainly sealed his fate.

By the time Peter and Jim returned, I was very cold. Albie Pokrob, who had just descended from the observatory to assist, reported that he had not seen the body on the Alpine Garden and had descended the upper section of Raymond Cataract before traversing to meet us. We decided to check the ravine for a pack Albie had noticed, since the wind might have blown Hokenson downhill, before continuing up to the Alpine Garden. En route I happened to look at the fingers of my right hand; two were white and my thumb was a waxy gray. I calmly acknowledged the frostbite and decided to go no farther up the mountain.

At the flat area atop the cataract we found the pack about a half-mile below the accident site. I thought (correctly, as it turned out) that this was not the same one I had seen next to the body, which suggested that Hokenson was still somewhere on the Alpine Garden.

I told Albie, Peter, and Jim that I would descend the cataract, and Albie radioed a request that someone meet me at its base. The trio set off up the mountain as I descended the waterfall carefully and slowly, much like I had ascended Central Gully earlier in the day. The sight of Rob Taylor at the base proved reassuring, although, in reality, there was nothing he could have done to prevent me from falling.

I descended alone to Pinkham in impending darkness. The fire trail was unusually "homey." It seemed flat, and the large trees cut virtually all of the wind. The two-mile walk at twilight brought me not only down out of the harsh reality of the summit cone and the biting, cold light of death but also into the murkiness of doubt and fragility. My composure of the moment up on the mountain was a clinical response to extreme circumstances. People—Ali, Chris, and the others—had been empowered by events to call forth reserves of strength and control and compassion in order to do what had to be done.

Now, the wind only moved treetops far above me. I plodded in the darkness down the trail, feeling very mortal. The clarity of action up high evaporated; the body and battered Ali began to emerge as people like me and the others, with dreams and joy and families. As I approached Pinkham and the valley, with the sound of cars on the road and lights just ahead, I felt much less a calm, rational rescuer than a participant in a complex of events that briefly bound many people's lives together at an amazingly intimate level. My role was finished, and my previously repressed emotions came to the fore.

It was dark and after 6 P.M. when I arrived at Pinkham. My first impression of the world of the office was of the new word processor, upon which a press release was being composed.

At this point I just wanted to sit down and have someone take care of me. Although the staff were very busy amid the details of the rescue operation, they quickly offered support. Huts Manager and friend Dave Warren acted the part of a kind nurse, and prepared a 105-degree Fahrenheit bath to rewarm my thumb, and later warmed up my car. Bob Vashaw of Fish and Game assured me that my medical bills would be covered under a new state law that provides Workmen's Compensation benefits to organized rescue personnel, an outgrowth of the tragic death of rescuer Albert Dow the previous winter. Before leaving I gave Mike Torrey a factual account of what had happened and calmly called my wife Marte to tell her that I would be home after a stop at the Littleton hospital.

But at 7 P.M., when I drove away from Pinkham, north between mountains that seemed so big and dark, I suddenly felt very alone, almost overwhelmed. I stopped at the first phone booth in Gorham and, asking Marte to meet me in Littleton, broke out sobbing in a deluge of tears.

Albie Pokrob writes:
After Doug descended, Peter, Jim, and I continued searching. At 5 P.M., about thirty yards above the Alpine Garden Trail near the right spur of Raymond's, I spotted the sleeping bag. A dismal feeling set in; all my philosophic acceptance of death abandoned me as I neared the probable corpse. I checked for respiration and pulse. Neither was present.

Mike Torrey continues:
The dynamics of the office during a major rescue had always been a source of wonder for me. Pinkham employees and senior staff constantly circulated through to ask if they could assist—handling press releases and press calls, going for food, giving advice (usually insightful), and hushing every time the radio keyed. Although we often joked, to take the edge off, it was clear that those I had previously thought most callous were indeed very caring. I was moved by the unstated order of events, how even the most senior staff yielded to the collective opinions of the group. I was also struck by the role played by Fish and Game personnel; although they have ultimate responsibility for all search-and-rescue activity in the state, they also yielded to group opinion.

Although I was challenged and awed by the seriousness of the situation, the operation was no more complicated than orchestrating hut operations. The difference was that a human life hung in the balance. The tension was further accentuated by recognition that the lives of the rescuers were also in jeopardy.

At 5 P.M., when the three located the body, we decided that we could not in good conscience abandon it—especially since no one person with advanced medical training had declared Hokenson dead. It was a difficult decision. Although we were as sure as any nonprofessionals could be that there was no possibility of recovery (and aware that others' lives were on the line), we decided we had to take that responsibility and risk. We all could see that under other circumstances in other times, it could easily have been any one of us.

Mountain Rescue Service was called at 6 P.M. to handle the evacuation. As we waited for Rick Wilcox and his team to arrive, I occasionally radioed the three rescuers. I heard the howl of the wind in the background and felt strange sitting in the office near the woodstove. I dared not think about the arriving MRS volunteers, and the risk they willingly took. I preferred not to consider the possible consequences of another slip or a loose crampon strap.

Albie Pokrob continues:
The winds died down, and a bright moon lit the Alpine Garden as Jim, Peter, and I huddled together for two and one-half hours. Peter occasionally asked how our feet were and Jim offered gorp now and then. Not much else was said. Each of us was lost in his own thoughts.

At 9:15, we saw the welcome sight of headlamps approaching. The Observatory's Ken Rancourt and Danny Theibolt and brought nine MRS volunteers to the seven-mile mark on the Auto Road in television Channel 8's snow machine. Six others rode up with Guy Gosselin in the observatory's vehicle. It took merely 45 minutes to sled the body back to the road, and by 10 P.M. the loaded snow machines were headed down.

Mike Torrey reflects:
An EMT in the group made his report that the victim was deceased, a conclusion which was subsequently confirmed at the Androscoggin Valley Hospital.

After all the rescuers were down, I was left alone in the office with Hokenson's pack. The scars of the slide were imprinted along its length, and one pocket and one shoulder strap were ripped off. As requested by Fish and Game, I went through it looking for identification. In the process I came to appreciate how well these guys had been prepared. The contents included sewing and first-aid kits, a novel for long layovers, crampon guards (proof that they had crampons, later verified by Kashkooli), clothing for extreme conditions, stove, cooking pots, even what appeared to be homework from school.

Finally I located a wallet and license. Looking at his picture gave me a chill; it put a face on all that had occurred. It felt so real that I had a flash thought that his pack was his body. It was the sense that the body had been a means of transporting something useful and—its purpose fulfilled—was no longer viable or even relevant to that which had been before. Standing in the warm office, alone with Ken Hokenson's pack, I felt a brotherhood with him. I was somehow now his friend, and I suddenly felt a great sadness at the loss.

Throughout the rescue effort I had been a technician, and only afterward did I find myself suffering a delayed reaction to the horror of those long falls down the summit cone. Although I had never left the office, I was consumed by a clear, unrelenting vision of the accident—the pressing wind, the initial falls, the quick acceleration (although my mind played it in slow motion, I knew it was fast), the jerking of battered limbs, bumps, and obstacles tossing the two men in the air only to crash and tumble harder when they hit ice again. I saw the awesome violence of the elements that impaired Kashkooli's attempts to assist Ken and felt his horror and sadness and fear and pain as he tried to help his friend and then set off to try to save himself. I saw Teschner rising out of the Huntington Ravine and his own surprise and reaction; Chris Hardiman and Tom Murri appearing at the perfect time; Rob Taylor—who had barely survived his own injury on Kilimanjaro—being there and helping out; my own involvement and that occurrence and discovery, escape and rescue—and, in subsequent conversations with others, appreciated the full importance of the brief event to those of us who participated.

When Ken Hokenson's family came to Pinkham to collect his things, I felt completely inadequate. His mother and friends were silent as we showed a photograph of the summit cone and described the accident. We pointed out that although the mountain is dangerous, Ken and Ali's degree of preparedness normally provided an adequate margin of safety. It was on this point that they sought clarification—whether the two should have been on the mountain that day—and I suppose that our words were reassuring. But when our explanation ended, there seemed much to express but little to say. An awkward silence ensued as the family continued to stand in a semicircle staring at the photograph. Finally Mrs. Hokenson said that it was time to go.

After a final glance of disbelief, they turned and slowly walked out, tottering slightly under the weight of the pack.

Albie Pokrob reflects:
Three days later we had another sliding fatality associated with record icing conditions on the summit cone. Arriving at the scene, I met a woman who was very upset. She had organized the Boston University trip and said it would be her last. Why and how could a life end so quickly, she asked. Although unable to answer her question, I told her that I hoped she would continue to share the beauty of the outdoors with others. For it is the quality of life one lives that matters most. How many people have been enriched by hiking in the mountains?

Since these accidents some people have suggested winter hiking restrictions. Not only would these be impossible to enforce, but I am also opposed philosophically. As Leo Buscaglia wrote in *Living, Loving and Learning*:

> *To hope is to risk despair, and to try is to risk failure. But risks must be taken, because the greatest risk in life is to risk nothing. The person who risks nothing . . . may avoid suffering and sorrow, but he simply cannot learn and feel and change and grow and love and live. Chained by his certitudes, he's a slave. . . . Only the person who risks is truly free.*

Some people view death as a time of celebration, an opportunity to meet the creator of this miraculous planet. In his book *Illusions: The Adventures of a Reluctant Messiah*, Richard Bach writes:

> *The mark of your ignorance is the depth of your belief in injustice and tragedy. What a caterpillar calls the end of the world, the master calls a butterfly.*

Chris Hardiman reflects:
With time, a proper solemnity has taken hold of me and the romanticism I associated with death on a mountain has vanished. Death on Mount Washington is just as mean as it is anywhere else. I know that people grieve for Ken Hokenson. I now truly appreciate my relatives' pleading for sense when I undertake some risk-taking adventure. Logic is served when loved ones try

to prevent a potential grievous loss. And yet, those people have not seen that other world of rime ice or the jagged alpine flora clinging to a rocky rubble of scarred land, so their appeals fall far short of convincing me to always remain within the supposed safety of home.

Tom Murri reflects:
As I write this five months later, I think of the odd twists of fate that brought us all together at that place and time. But I discount the suggestion that these events were destined to occur, or that we were deliberately brought together for some higher purpose. I do not want to search for the meaning in the death of a young man but rather hope that Ken Hokenson's family and friends find meaning in the life that he lived.

I felt good about the part I played in helping out but don't feel that I risked much personally or did anything that anyone else would not have under the same circumstances.

As the vividness of the incident fades, I am left feeling much as I did on the mountain. The exhilaration that I could not feel (but that must have been there) combines with the despair and leaves me oddly detached. In some way I am changed, and yet I am at a loss to explain how.

Doug Teschner reflects:
Fortunately I suffered no tissue damage to my thumb or fingers. But, at another level, my life was very changed by the accident and rescue. In the past it seemed that too often I looked at things from a negative perspective. It would be easy to criticize the rescue effort: I never should have lost my mitten, nor should the sleeping bag have blown off the litter or the radio have failed. But to focus at this level is to miss the essence: the wonderful way everyone involved responded, pulled together, gave their very best. Ali's effort to get his friend into a sleeping bag was an especially remarkable act of courage.

In my own case, I am able to vividly recall the special power I experienced on the mountain, the way it flowed out of me intuitively and unconsciously. But where did it come from?

On the one hand, I have come to appreciate the gift of human capability— our instinctive desire to do the very best. The trait of heroism is inherent in every one of us, waiting (even begging) to be tapped. But if this is true, I wonder why had I failed so miserably the first time I was on a mountain rescue?

That accident had happened some fifteen years earlier, curiously enough on the very same date—March 24. I had huddled through the bitter night at the base of Odell's Gully in Huntington Ravine, waiting for the patient to be lowered to my position. If heroism had indeed been one of my traits, why had I lost control of the litter (empty, fortunately), which took off like a freight train down Huntington Ravine's Fan, barely missing several other rescuers? The authors of "Accident and Rescue in the Odell Gully," *Appalachia*, December 1968,[36] were kind enough not to specifically credit me with this serious, if ultimately inconsequential, blunder.

A team rescues an injured climber on Mount Washington, circa 1980s; the operation recalled in this essay would have looked something like this.

When I recently reread that account, I relived the moment: once again I was 18 years old. I realized that the source of my different responses to similar situations derived from the gift of intervening experiences—fifteen years of climbing and living and risking. I began to appreciate that any failings I suffer as a human being derive from the lack of an appropriate experiential base and not from any innate negative characteristics. Even when I had dropped the litter it had been my very best effort at that moment in time.

---

[36] Jeff Damp, et al., *Appalachia* 37.

Despite impressions to the contrary, helping on the mountainside is relatively easy: when a person is battered and bloody, the need is very clear. Perhaps now my real goal is to hold onto that special power—believing, hoping, trusting—amid the complexities of everyday life. The real challenge is to bring the energy of the mountain down into the valleys, where it is needed the most.

Lastly, despite lingering (indeed necessary) doubts, my decision to leave Ken Hokenson behind continues to pass the test of unbounded internal analysis.

Ali Kashkooli reflects:
I spent six days at the hospital and twelve more at the University of Maine infirmary. Somehow I suffered no major injuries other than frostbite on my hands and some ligament damage to my leg. My hands are much better, except for two fingers on the left hand, which are still kept bandaged. In order to help prevent infection, I had to stay out of the water during a hot summer.

But the heat has not been as consuming as the guilt I feel for not having written to the many kind people who helped me survive this painful ordeal. I am probably thought of as forgetful, ungrateful, or thoughtless. In truth, not a day or night passes without my being reminded of the accident and especially the people involved. I have tried to write but feel betrayed by the pen, which seems incapable of expressing all that is going on inside me.

I miss Ken. He had been planning to spend the summer here in Orono and we had talked about taking canoe, bike, and hiking trips. At the time it looked as though this would be a great summer for both of us. But instead, it was a summer he never lived to see and one in which I have lived with much pain. Sometimes when I walk down the street, I expect to run into Ken. On the nice, sunny days I ask myself why he cannot be here to enjoy them. But I believe what his mother said when she visited me at the hospital: "God resides on the mountaintops, and it was His will."

At one time, I had wanted to work in the United States for a couple of years, save some money, and travel around the world. But since the accident, my priorities have changed. Right after the fall, the thought of home and my mother gave me the strength to walk. Now I want to return home as soon as possible. Then I don't care if I die.

PAINE AND SUFFERING IN PATAGONIA

Todd Swain
1988

Todd Swain of Joshua Tree, California, is a veteran climber whose writing makes readers feel as if they are right next to him. In his many articles, including several for Appalachia *journal, Swain has covered topics like climbing routes ("Diary of a New Route Addict"),[37] a lost Peace Corps volunteer ("The Search for Walter Poirier"),[38] and his almost 40-year climbing career ("1.5 Score and 7,000 Routes Ago").[39] His guidebooks include* The Gunks Guide *(FalconGuides, 2004) and a guide to Red Rock National Conservation Area near Las Vegas, Nevada.*

SOON AFTER MY FIRST CLIMBING EXPERIENCE TWELVE years ago, I started to devour every climbing book and magazine I could find. It didn't take me long to realize that the tip of South America harbored some of the most impressive peaks in the world and that I wanted to climb them.

In high school, my friends and I drove to the White Mountains, Green Mountains, and the Shawangunks to climb. During our outings we encountered all sorts of obstacles and had many vertical epics. Some were

---

[37] *Appalachia* 46, no. 3 (1987).
[38] *Appalachia* 59, no. 2 (2008).
[39] *Appalachia* 60, no. 2 (2009).

as simple as rappelling off the ends of our rope; others involved surviving huge winter storms. We always overcame them and considered them "training for Patagonia."

We had an insatiable appetite for climbing and were convinced that real climbers climbed in any weather and always went for it (consequently, I didn't expect to live to be twenty). My first lead climb (Pete's Tree 5.5, at Pawtuckaway State Park in New Hampshire) resulted in a twenty-footer, followed by a 100-foot slider to the ground the next year (off-route on Mistaken Identity 5.6, at the Whitehorse Ledge in North Conway, New Hampshire). Such were my humble beginnings.

December 1986 found Tad Welch and me packing for our first trip to Patagonia. Tad lives in the Adirondacks, and we had climbed together extensively in the Northeast. We also took part in an expedition to a remote mountain range in Colombia, and we had been on separate winter climbing trips to Scotland. We felt confident climbing together; I trusted his judgment, he trusted mine. Tad and I were now going to Chile, to the Paine region (pronounced "pie-neigh") of Patagonia. We had no firm objective in mind, planning to spend only a month in the area since Tad had commitments at home.

Six meals worth of flying time put us in the city of Punta Arenas on the Strait of Magellan. A marathon food-shopping spree and two bus rides later, we reached the Towers of Paine National Park. Here we arranged with local gauchos to horsepack our mound of gear twenty miles from the nearest road to our base camp in the Rio Frances Valley. The rim of the valley is festooned with beautiful granite spires, and there we found our goal—a striking spire called the Sword, high on the eastern rim of the valley.

On January 10 we organized our new home—a lean-to in the base of the valley (about 2,000-feet elevation). We sorted and hung out two duffel bags of food, racked our climbing gear, and scouted a route up through the trees to the talus slope (and eventually, the spire). The weather was excellent—60 degrees Fahrenheit and sunny, with a light breeze. We were ready to climb, and with weather like this, Patagonia seemed tame.

The alarm went off at 4 A.M.; we had already been awake for hours. Our lean-to was being pounded by the worst rain and windstorm either of us had ever seen. The sound of the wind could be likened to standing on an airport runway while jets take off. It was 35 degrees Fahrenheit, and outside was what we were to call a horrential (horizontal/torrential) downpour. That day we stayed in our sleeping bags eating and reading. This was to become a typical Patagonian occurrence.

Four days later, in the first "good" weather (cloudy, 15-mile-per-hour wind, 40 degrees Farenheit), we made the three-hour trudge up to the base of the tower. We hiked up a boulder field twice the size of Cannon Cliff's talus slope and continued to climb up through a gully and snowfield similar in size and steepness to two Central Gullies in Huntington Ravine. Upon arrival, we decided to attempt a new route up the west arête of the Sword.

This particular spire had been climbed only once before, by a seven-man South African team over eight days in 1971. We planned to climb the route alpine style (using no fixed ropes), with one bivouac.

We climbed the first four pitches in about two hours, with mostly 5.7–5.8 free climbing. As the spire steepened to vertical, we had to resort to more aid climbing, which slowed the pace. At about the same time, the temperature dropped from the mid-40s to the 30s, and it began to rain. We pressed on, encountering two pitches of A2 nailing, hanging belays, and incredible exposure. The cracks in the rock became parallel; we were forced to leapfrog the few identically sized nuts and pitons we had brought with us.

This increased the fear factor and decreased speed, because we had to keep descending to remove the pieces from below. As Tad had jumared to our high point he seemed shaken. With the wind, rain, and no chance of an outside rescue, he was in an unfamiliar situation in what he considered extreme conditions. I had experience leapfrogging gear from other aid climbs but was starting to get chilled from the cold and rain.

I thought we had a good chance to reach the summit, but since this was our first attempt, I agreed to play it safe and submit to the weather. I felt confident that we could regain our high point quicker on the next try and make the summit. Twelve rappels later (we had only brought one rope on this attempt in an effort to save weight), we were at the base of the spire. The retreat down the snow and talus was a blur of wind and rain. We arrived back at the lean-to soaked and exhausted.

The days that followed included storms that plastered the spire in rime and snow. We immersed ourselves in novels and tried to improve our culinary skills over an open fire. Tad seemed at ease with our remote situation and did a fantastic job of enduring the grim living accommodations and me.

It was ten days before the weather gave us another chance. This "good" day was windy, with temperatures in the teens. Our second try ended before it really began. What had been easy rock climbing turned into difficult

Todd Swain climbs on one of the Towers in Paine National Park, Patagonia, in 1986.

grade-5 mixed climbing. Each crack and ledge was backed with rock-hard snow that had to be hacked clear before we could advance. Despite our best efforts, we only made it up three pitches by 4 P.M. We fixed our ropes and rappelled off. That time, Tad climbed brilliantly and showed no sign of the anxiety that had been apparent on the previous attempt. Another stint of forced lethargy followed. Our initial theory that Patagonian weather had been exaggerated was swept away in the winds. Our time was running out, and we realized that we might not reach the top.

The alarm rang at 4 A.M.; it was calm and clear. In the darkness we dressed and wolfed down some food. The approach to the tower was silent and lonely, and the possibility of failure was in both our minds. Neither of us wanted to fail, but the weather and living conditions had lowered our morale. I was determined to give my all, since this was the last attempt. Arriving at the base of the spire, we immediately started jumaring up the fixed ropes. The rock above our ropes was still encrusted with rime, making progress slow. Eventually we regained our high point and I set myself up at the belay. We had been swapping leads on the route, and it was now Tad's turn to go first.

Until this point, we had been following the same crack system. Above our hanging belay the crack ended, but ten feet to the right and even with us, another corner led upward toward the summit. The rock between the two corners was blank and offered no nut or piton placements. It was too steep to tension into the other corner, and since the crack started even with us, penduluming was also out of the question.

Tad explored every option, and after twenty minutes of debate I convinced him to place a cliff hanger, drill a bolt, and then swing into the corner. He gingerly top-stepped in his etriers on his first hook placement and started drilling the bolt. With the hole only half the proper depth, he decided to drive in the bolt and try nailing upwards.

Tad top-stepped on the bolt and placed a knife blade. Suddenly, he was falling. I looked up in horror—the only piece of protection between my hanging belay and Tad was the poorly secured bolt. Luckily, the bolt held the ensuing ten-foot fall. After Tad caught his breath, I convinced him to swing into the corner off the bolt. He placed a couple of pegs in the corner, and then refused to go on. The fall changed everything.

Tad returned to the relative safety of the belay and wanted to go down. With the weather holding and time running out, I desperately wanted the summit. Tad pointed out that the cracks above were parallel sided, and we would obviously be forced to leapfrog gear again. I argued that we were in Patagonia, and that if there was ever a place to "go for it", this was it. He was convinced we had neither the time nor the gear to make a successful summit bid. Eventually I convinced him to let me lead the next pitch.

After switching places at the belay, I swung off the bolt in the corner and began nailing upward. A few awkward A3 placements brought me to a sloping ledge at the base of a huge dihedral. From here, it appeared to be one or two more aid pitches, and then easier free climbing to the top. I set up a belay and called down to Tad to follow. He refused. He wanted to retreat.

I tried to encourage him into following and when that failed, tried to bully him. After a few minutes of silence, I admitted defeat and rappelled down. Six rappels later, we safely arrived at the base of the spire. I stayed near Tad down the snowfields and then set off down the talus alone. The weather was still decent, climbing was possible, and I felt betrayed.

There was tension in the air that night at the lean-to. While I realized that Tad had been subjected to something far more extreme than he had wanted to experience, it was still difficult for me to accept failure on something that I felt in control on. I couldn't bring myself to talk with Tad about this, so we ate in relative silence and then went to bed.

As I lay there in my sleeping bag, I thought about what had happened. For years I had been obsessed with climbing and had on numerous occasions risked death for a particular route. It's not that I was suicidal; climbing was simply the most important thing in my life. Regardless of the consequences, I was totally committed to reaching the summit of the Sword that day. Because I had climbed extensively with Tad, I just *assumed* he shared the same level of commitment. Until you are put in extreme conditions with someone, you never really know what his reactions are going to be or what his priorities are. By trying to convince and then bully him to go on, I was forcing him to decide on the spot if he was willing to risk it all for one route.

During the night the worst storm of our trip engulfed us. For the next 36 hours the winds roared and snow fell. For the first time snow even accumulated on the valley floor. Had I persuaded Tad to continue toward the summit, we would have surely been caught in the tempest. I doubt we would have survived.

A LEG UP:
ONE PERSON'S ACCIDENT

Doug Mayer
1990

This essay combines an accident with an adventure. It shows how staying calm and flexible, the key to a good mountaineering adventure, can also save your life. Doug Mayer grew up in New York City with long stretches in Sandwich, New Hampshire, and he has lived in Randolph, New Hampshire, for many years. Mayer worked for the Mount Washington Observatory as a search-and-rescue and trails volunteer, and as a volunteer trails chairman for the Randolph Mountain Club. In his professional life, he is a producer for the National Public Radio show, "Car Talk." He manages Run the Alps, a Swiss Alps trail running vacation service. Mayer and Rebecca Oreskes coauthored Mountain Voices: Stories of Life and Adventure in the White Mountains and Beyond *(AMC Books, 2012).*

> "Two are better than one . . . for if they fail, the one will
> lift up his fellow; but woe to him that is alone when he
> falleth, for he hath not another to help him up."
> —Ecclesiastes 4:9–10, quoted in Oliver Sacks, *A Leg to Stand On*

*D*ECEMBER 1, 1989 WAS A VERY COLD DAY IN NEW Hampshire. At the observatory on the summit of Mount Washington, Peter Crane reported on the WBNC morning weather show that the current conditions were -15 degrees with a 72-mile-per-hour northwest wind. The summit forecast predicted a warming to -10 and winds averaging 50 to 70 miles per hour with high gusts.

For a few days I had wanted to get out for a good winter hike: maybe a summit or two, with a swing by the Randolph Mountain Club's new Gray Knob cabin on the side of Mount Adams. The night before, I filled my pack with all the usuals: sweater, shell, pile pants and jacket, Dachsteins, overmitts, balaclava, crampons, bivvy sac, two-way radio and spare batteries, headlamp, map, compass, food. The radio was a leftover from my summers spent working in the White Mountains, when I often hiked alone for miles at a time. Several times the radio had proven useful, and I did not begrudge the extra weight. I also tossed in a large pack of toilet paper, for Paul, caretaking at the Knob. We had joked a week or so earlier about his running short. Finally, I left behind a description of my intended route. I was planning to hike up the Valley Way, loop over Madison and Adams and down to Gray Knob.

> *Valley Way–Watson Path–Madison Hut Adams via*
> *Airline–Lowes Path–Gray Knob–Appalachia, back before*
> *9 p.m.—Doug.*

I arrived at Appalachia around 9:30 A.M. and headed right out, dressed in polypro, pile pants, and double plastic boots. About 11 or so I was getting near treeline. The trail was slippery, with not quite enough snow to cover the ice. In many respects, though, it was a perfect winter hike: a cold, clear, and windy December day, no one else on any of the trails. No signs of anyone having been through, either. Near the Watson Path, I stopped for some hot chocolate. It was evident that the above-treeline hiking was going to be a classic winter experience with lots of ice, lots of high winds, and bitter cold. On most days, I would get keyed up for such an adventure, stopping just below the treeline to get "suited up" and ready for entry into the acrtic scene above. Today, though, I somehow just didn't seem into it. I have rarely, if ever, found myself with such a feeling. So I packed up and turned around. *Don't force it, you're up here to enjoy yourself,* I thought.

Fifty feet later, I tripped on a rock. I heard a snap and a soft crack as I fell. Before I landed, I knew it. The thought that went through my mind was very simple and objective: *So, that's what it's like to break your leg.*

Doug Mayer as he looked around the time of his fall. His dog, Barkley, posed with him here on the outlook called the Quay, on Lowe's Path in the White Mountains, around 1990.

I kidded with myself, trying to calm down. *Maybe it's just a bad bruise.* I tried, slowly, to get up. But something was different. My right leg collapsed under some of my weight and I fell again. I felt the broken bones grating against each other. *Damn.* The next few thoughts seemed beyond my control. They automatically presented themselves. I sensed that they had to be brought out into the open and answered if I wanted to work past their presence. It was the worst-case scenario. *If I don't get someone on the radio, I could be here until early morning before help comes. Zero. If it's a bad break, there might be internal bleeding, damaged nerves, or other problems. I could be in serious trouble. I could go into shock and then. . . .*

Nonsense! I pushed that last thought away. In fact, it was so unreasonable, I spoke out loud. "You've got years of outdoor experience. You're an EMT, you're just a few miles from help, you can handle a night out. Just stay cool, Mayer, and everything'll be fine."

You know, in these situations staying level headed is all that matters and the rest will fall into place. If you lose your cool, you will have beaten yourself. So don't freak out, just deal with it.

I took off my gloves and got out the radio. The Randolph Mountain Club frequency. "KAD4855, this is unit 93, to Gray Knob or Randolph, anyone around?" No answer. Again. No answer. Again. Silence. *Come on, answer!* Switch to the AMC repeater. Can't key it up—the mountains are blocking the path to the summit of Washington. *Damn!* I switched to scan—no one on any frequencies. *God damn! Bad luck, Mayer.*

At this point, my mind switched gears, effortlessly. It simply went into a new, no-nonsense level of operation without any prompting. *No one is on the radio. Forget the radio. Put the radio away, your hands are freezing already. Just forget it. No one hears you. Move on to the next step, this one is not working.*

The choice was pretty clear: I could stay and wait, trying to stay warm, or I could try to work my way down the trail. My old first-aid training reminded me of things I really did not want to know. If I moved my unsplinted leg, I risked cutting into any one of several decent-sized arteries. I could lose circulation in my leg for several hours and face a much more serious injury. I could also injure a nerve and realize permanent damage to my leg. The other choice was to wait: get on all my clothes, break out the bivvy sac, and play mind games to pass the time. But it was COLD. There also was not enough snow for a good snow cave—and I hadn't brought my stove. *Mayer, you idiot. You always bring your stove in the winter.* Hypothermia presented itself as a prospect. *No way can I sit around for twelve hours. Self-rescue is the way to go. Now is your chance to take complete responsibility for yourself. Solo hiking in winter—this is what you have to be ready to deal with. So, deal.*

I pulled myself over a few branches that were across the trail. I grabbed one and smashed it against a tree, breaking it to a four-foot length. Same process with another branch. I pulled the straps off my crampons, and tried to improvise a splint. *Too damn cold.* My fingers just didn't work at all—totally useless, completely clumsy. Couldn't tie a simple knot.

Your fingers are worthless like this. Forget the splint. Rewarm your hands. The splint idea will not work. Forget it. Move on to the next step. Your hands are freezing. Keep your warmth. Bundle up now, before you lose heat. The next step is to bundle up.

I put away the crampons and put on all my warm clothes: sweater, pile jacket, storm jacket, balaclava, mittens, overmittens. *Avoid going into shock. If I go into shock I'm in real trouble.* I took my pulse. *One hundred, seems strong at my wrist, steady.* Not bad. I took ten deep, slow breaths and drank a half a quart of hot chocolate.

I grabbed my two sticks. Time to move. Can I stand with these sticks? Can I walk?

I stood up. My right leg was nearly useless, but I could balance off of it. I could move. *Nice trick, Mayer. You must look pathetic. But you can move yourself!*

I began to move, ever so slowly, ever so gingerly. Each step was carefully selected. *What's underneath that snow? Is that a rock? Don't get snagged on that stick! Slow, slow, put your weight down slowly. OK . . . good, good. Now, what's next? OK. . . .* Any jolt to my foot sent a wicked surge of sharp pain up my leg, culminating in an involuntary yelp. *You sound like a wounded dog.* A good incentive to treat it gently. *See that tree? Your next goal—that tree. Five minutes to that tree. Here we are, great, you did it! Good job, Mayer. Good job! See that gully? Our next goal, that gully. Take it slow.*

My mind cruised along at full speed: strong, focused on the moment, no other thoughts. It was dragging an injured body out of the woods. It was on a mission, for me. *Don't think about how far you have to go. Pick easy goals, take your time, remember all those stories.* I had been doing a lot of mountaineering reading, recently. I would never have thought that those tales would be put to this kind of use. Moments of Doubt—*remember? Brad Washburn and Bob Bates in Alaska? How about* The Breach—*Rob Taylor coming off Kilimanjaro after that fall.* Touching the Void—*Joe Simpson's three days' crawl through the Andes with a shattered leg! Your situation is zero compared to those guys. This is nothing at all. Those guys could do it—you can do this little walk.*

But every now and then my mind did wander. I began to get my hopes up—perhaps someone really would come along this trail. *It's a Friday afternoon, the Valley Way's well-traveled.* I began to imagine my scenario. "*Hi, uhh, I don't mean to bother you, but I just broke my leg . . . can you give me a hand here? Boy, it's great to see you!*" Every time, though, my mind put the focus squarely back onto me. *No one will come. No one is coming up this trail today, no one at all. That's all there is to it. So get back into it and keep moving. No one will come up the Valley Way today.*

Talking out loud seemed to add some much-needed levity to the situation. "Not one of your better days, huh Mayer?" "OK, this is the last leg of your trip." "Sure would be a shame to slip and break the other one too." "Don't worry, you've got a leg up on the situation." "If I were asked, I would have to say that today really is one of my less enjoyable days."

I made pretty good progress. On the steeper sections, I would slide on my back, right leg high in the air. It would have been an odd sight, but no one was watching. *Oh, hi! Hello! Nice day, isn't it? Why this way? Well hiking just gets so damned boring sometimes. . . .*

It was 4:45 when I got out of the trailhead, just dark—a five-hour trip over two and a half miles or so. I waited at Route 2 for a car, a truck. Nothing. *This is the worst day of my life. Don't I get any luck today? None, huh? OK, to hell with it.*

I unlocked my car door, pushed my pack onto the passenger's seat, and slid the driver's seat all the way back. I got the car started, with a short jab on the accelerator. A fresh, warm burst of pain flared up my leg. *Oh, yeah, times like this you wish you'd taken that automatic they had on the lot, huh, Doug? "*Well, personally, I like the automatic because it's just so much easier to drive with a broken leg.*" I got the car into first gear, set the cruise control at 20 miles per hour, put on the flashers, and headed along the breakdown lane to Barb and Don Wilson's, two miles away. *Four thousand rpm, kind* *of revving the engine a bit high today, Doug.* Second gear just wasn't worth the effort.

Pulling into the driveway, I honked for several second and waited. *Hah! No one's coming . . . of course! Remember, you're just out of luck today. The final blow. Where now, Mayer?*

Don Wilson appeared at the door! I had been wondering for the last hour or so how he or Barb was going to handle this upcoming comment. "Umm, hi, Don. Doug Mayer. I, umm, uhh, broke my leg on the Valley Way and, uhh, need a hand." *He's going to think you're joking. He's going to think you're nuts.*

Perfect! Fabulous! Less than a minute later he was outside with an old pair of crutches, giving me a hand inside. Totally calm, very helpful. I couldn't have asked for more. *You're OK, Don. You're the best. Now I can turn this mess over to other people. I can relax.*

A phone call, then an ambulance ride to Berlin from Gorham Ambulance (*"Say hi to Mike Pelchat for me. Tell him I walked out 'cause I knew otherwise he'd be treating me and carrying me out, and you can naturally imagine how scared I was of that prospect!" A good laugh with the EMTs.*)

Others have had much more spectacular accidents. For me, December 1 was just a long and tiring day of intense emotions and pain. I may have been on the edge of a life-threatening situation, but I always managed to keep it at bay. I ended the day in surgery, with a handful of screws and a metal plate in my leg, to repair three broken bones and a few disconnected ankle ligaments. Four days later I was out of the hospital. Seven weeks later I was off crutches. In March, I was done with physical therapy. This June, I plan to join four friends on a trip up Denali's Muldrow Glacier.

If I did come away with anything from last December (barring the crutches and an endless flow of medical bills), I came to understand what I had always heard but never listened to: that such accidents are a challenge not just for the body, but also to the mind. I consider myself fortunate, for I experienced only a brief minute of fear, of fleeting, unanswerable thoughts: Will I get out? How bad is it? What will happen to me? Can I stay warm? After that, my mind took over the situation like an idle bystander coming to my rescue. Those fears, those questions I could have not answered, were pushed aside. They were subverted to the task of getting me to the trailhead. In *Woodsmoke*, the late New England outdoorsman Ross McKenny wrote: "Within the shadows of the forest I have also learned the meaning of fear—fear that is within all of us and which can turn into terror and cause embarrassment or disaster; fear that can be governed and overcome in self-reliance. . . . Have you ever given deeper thought to this hidden fear within you? What would you do in an emergency? Think it over, it's time well spent."

TRAILING DREAMS:
MAGIC ALONG THE APPALACHIAN TRAIL

Elizabeth McGowan

1993

Walking alone up the chain of the Appalachian Mountains for half a year is hard enough, but Elizabeth McGowan did it as respite from another round of cancer treatments. In 1991, she was a young woman with her life ahead of her. She believed, against some advice, that what she most needed was putting the hospital doors at her back for a period.

McGowan has forged a career in journalism and adventure since that pilgrimage. She has backpacked an assortment of trails including the Superior Hiking Trail, the Lake Tahoe Rim Trail, and the Benton MacKaye Trail. She told us that she doesn't feel fully human unless she sleeps in a tent for at least two weeks each year. Elizabeth also has bicycled far and wide. She pedaled 4,250 miles across the United States in 2000. After reporting for several daily newspapers in Wisconsin, she moved to Washington, D.C., in 2001 to pursue a career as an energy and environment reporter. A series of articles written for InsideClimate News *about this country's lack of oil pipeline safety measures earned her a Pulitzer Prize for national reporting in 2013.*

"In the spring of '27, something bright and alien flashed across the sky. A young Minnesotan (Charles Lindbergh) who seemed to have had nothing to do with his generation did a heroic thing; and for a moment people set down their glasses in country clubs and speakeasies and thought of their old best dreams."
—F. Scott Fitzgerald

$\mathcal{P}$RIORITIES. MY COWORKER'S COMMENTS IN MARCH 1991 HAD started me thinking about them. His words of two years ago still ring in my ears.

"You know how it is, Elizabeth," he told me as he shook his head. "I just couldn't give up my job. I've got bills to take care of . . . I'm making payments on the condo I just bought. Plus, I'm still paying off my truck. You understand why I could never do what you're planning. It just seems like such a sacrifice."

"Does he really believe what he is saying?" I remember thinking to myself at the time. "He seems . . . what's the word? Desperate?"

What I was planning was quitting my newspaper job, packing up the belongings in my apartment, and giving up my permanent address to strap 50 pounds on my back and hike the entire length of the Appalachian Trail.

With spring's finger beckoning, I'd be heading for the southernmost tip of the trail—Springer Mountain in the Chattahoochee National Forest of northern Georgia—and following spring and summer up through twelve eastern states. By autumn, if my knees cooperated, I'd be hiking through Maine's wilderness toward the rocky pinnacle of Katahdin in Baxter State Park, the northernmost point.

Try as I might, I couldn't fully understand what my coworker was trying to tell me. Actually, it seemed he was a little jealous that I was able to leave everything that he valued just to take what he considered to be a walk in the woods.

But I was looking at my trial as more than a six-month tromp through the woods, over rocks and streams, up and down mountains, across pavements, and into tiny towns.

For it wasn't to be just a journey of miles and obstinate terrain. It was also an opportunity to be a minimalist: to let go of the material possessions that almost everybody seems to value deeply. To think, to bond with fellow hikers, to do some emotional and perhaps physical healing, to gain insights, and to discover a few more ounces of spirituality.

Nobody was forcing me to take a hike. And my decision to put aside pens, notebooks, and word processor for a brief interlude wasn't made on the spur of the moment. Ever since college, hiking the Appalachian Trail had been a goal I kept on the proverbial "things to do" list that decorated my refrigerator. It's a trek I wanted to take when the time was right. And April 1991 was that time.

In the spring of 1991, I was feeling strong, healthy, and positive about branching out in a new direction.

But I hadn't always felt that way. While living in Vermont in 1985, I'd been diagnosed with melanoma—a type of skin cancer for which there is no known cure. I was terrified. Melanoma was the same disease that had killed my father a decade before when he was just 44 years old. I couldn't shake those hideous images of what cancer can do to the human body.

I had the lesions removed at an area hospital and tried to put the incident behind me.

I couldn't. The cancer recurred in my lymph system a year later. I was hospitalized for surgery, then underwent a year of experimental treatment. Though my energy decreased significantly, I was able to keep working, playing sports, and living a relatively normal life.

Evidently, that treatment wasn't enough. Just months after I'd moved to Wisconsin for a job as a reporter, my Wisconsin doctor discovered handfuls of suspicious-looking spots in my lungs. Unfortunately, the tumors had doubled in size over the course of the year.

A lung biopsy was necessary, my doctor informed me as I sat on the examining table. I started to shake. And couldn't stop for what felt like hours. The biopsy—which required the surgeon to go through my rib cage and cut into my right lung for a tissue sample—forced me into the hospital for a week.

And that wasn't the end of it.

The tumors were malignant. More melanoma. At that time, my journalistic instincts kicked in, and I called dozens of clinics and doctors around the country before choosing a treatment regimen. More tests. More pain. More stress. Three rounds of vicious chemotherapy stole my summer of 1989, but they gave me something I might not have had otherwise—more time on the planet.

When would all of this end?

Nobody had any definite answers. Through treatment, support from friends, family, and other cancer survivors, and my own strong will, I held the cancer in my body at bay, so to speak, until late winter in 1991.

Then, another setback. That day in February 1991 still gives me the chills. Here I was just two months away from setting foot on Springer Mountain and my doctor was telling me that more tumors had spread to more of my internal organs. I was frustrated, angry, and frightened. Mostly frightened.

It was time to make some choices. Hard ones.

My doctor gave me several chemotherapy options. I considered each of them carefully and reviewed them with other doctors who were tracking my case. Physically, I probably could have handled the side effects—nausea, hair loss, weight loss, extreme fatigue, and pain. Mentally, however, every part of me was rebelling against chemotherapy. No matter what the treatment, no cure was promised. And I knew that if I didn't believe in treatment 100 percent, my body would never accept it as a healing agent.

A week later, I told my doctor I'd decided to take my chances and start the hike that I'd been dreaming and scheming about since the mid-1980s. If I couldn't heal amid the envisioned serenity of the trail, then I wasn't sure I ever would.

I couldn't have made a better decision.

When a friend from Wisconsin dropped me off at Springer Mountain on April 13, I felt excited. But I also felt a bit nervous about the mission I'd carved out for

"At last, the adventure begins . . . " I wrote in my journal that first day.

> Sometimes I have to pinch myself to believe I'm finally here. But here I am, sitting in a shelter near Springer Mountain with four hikers I've never met before. We've already shared food and stories. My, how one's life can change in 24 hours. Yesterday at this time, I was in a house with a roof and four walls, eating a meal that didn't contain noodles. On the way to Springer Mountain today, my friend who drove me here asked several times if I wanted to turn back. "No way," I told her. "I'm committed to going and finishing." The closer we got to Springer, however, the more nervous I was. At least I never had the feeling of "Oh, my God, what am I doing here?" I figure that's a good sign. It's cold, rainy, and foggy; kind of a miserable way to start out. But the walking is splendid and therapeutic, too. Cooking with a camp stove is the worst part. Second worst part is taking down a wet tent.

Two days later I celebrated my 30th birthday on the trail in Georgia. Pure serendipity. I quenched my thirst with sweet spring water, pitched my tent on

Mother Earth's belly, and watched the stars dance over the twinkling lights of a distant southern town.

It got better.

And better.

"It's amazing how little we really need to survive," hikers would comment as they boxed up and shipped home items they had once considered necessities. The walking was simplicity at its peak. A world where your main considerations for the day were food, clothing, and shelter. Oh, and moleskin, too, of course.

I didn't earn the trail name "Blister Sister" because my feet took easily to wet socks and wetter boots. Most mornings I spent up to half an hour rinsing, taping, peeling, and doctoring my abused feet before inserting them back into the dreaded leather boots. I knew I was in the running for the trail's annual "Ugliest Feet" contest by the time I reached the Georgia–North Carolina border.

But bad feet weren't going to keep me from following through on this dream.

I had plenty to spur me on: healthy doses of trail magic, outstanding scenery, time to appreciate all that was around me, and plenty of support from friends and family.

Wildflowers poking their tiny, glorious selves through southern soil reminded me that spring was bursting forth in the colors that distinguish it from other seasons. On lucky days I'd run into a day-hiker carting a flower identification book I could borrow for a peek.

Though there were no newspapers out in the woods, trail registers—notebooks placed in shelters and hostels—provided me with reading material. What a link. They were jam-packed with tips about water sources and town stops from southbounders, hikers' laments about equipment problems, hellos from hiker friends ahead, insights about the trail, poetry, stories, sketches, perspectives, frustrations, and complaints.

Once I'd set up camp for the night, I'd try to capture highlights of the day in my own journal. Each evening I inked: mileage logged, wildlife sighted, people I met, places I saw, and stories I watched.

Hiking the trail was no trip down the Yellow Brick Road. It was a test of will, spirit, and desire. Always, I carried the words of trail guru Warren Doyle within easy reach.

Elizabeth McGowan on the frosty summit of Katahdin at the end of her 1991 Appalachian Trail thru-hike.

"Don't *fight* the trail," Doyle wrote in his handbook of advice. "You have to flow with it. The trail itself cannot be changed. You have to change.

"Don't waste any of your energy complaining about things you have no control over. Instead, look to yourself and adapt your mind, heart, body and soul to the Trail."

You don't have to have a life-threatening disease to take risks with your life, to live life on an edge. Dealing with cancer, however, made me much more aware of living in the moment. Hiking the trail wasn't something I could put off until retirement, because I wasn't sure that was an option.

Before I made a commitment to the hike, I wrestled with my own demons. What would people think about my obtuse plan? Was the whole idea foolish? Would I be throwing away many years of security? Would they think any less of me if I didn't make it to Maine? Would I ever again be welcome in the world of newspapers?

Sure, I felt selfish about pitching everything aside to focus on one goal— making it to Katahdin before the first snow fell. Anybody raised with even an iota of the Puritan work ethic probably would feel the same way. We're brought up believing that hedonism isn't healthy; that you should look out for others before you take care of your own needs.

But if I kept putting off what my heart was telling me to do, I knew I would have been safe, yet miserable. So I took a step and rearranged my priorities. Made changes. Took a step a bit closer to this edge.

It didn't hurt too much. And I didn't fall.

A certain number of folks I met before, during, and after my hike told me that hiking the trail was a goal they had always wanted to reach but never had met for some reason or another. I recall an older woman I met on the trail in North Carolina. She was out walking with a couple of friends and admiring the wave of wildflowers on a marvelous May day.

"You're hiking the *whole* trail," she said, her voice bursting with enthusiasm, admiration, and a smidgen of envy. "That's something I always wanted to do."

"But, well, you know," she added, her voice tapering off, "I just never got around to it. And now I'm too old to do something like that."

I was carrying bits and pieces of other people's hopes and dreams on my journey to Katahdin, people just like that woman. These thoughts added not a burden, but a new perspective to my hike. And they kept me going, inspired me to keep plugging away, to keep climbing mountains and fording streams, to keep following the white blazes to Maine and the brilliant autumn colors.

I have no regrets about putting my newspaper career on hold to hike the Appalachian Trail. The work world was still there when I returned. I got more out of my hike than I would've gotten out of six months at a job.

About a month after I finished my hike in the fall of 1991, I made a trip to see my oncologist. I'd been dreading the exam since I'd called for an appointment. Deep down, I felt I'd made the right decision by going with my hike, but that ever-present sliver of doubt kept me up at night imagining the worst-case scenarios.

"I'm not sure what you were doing out there for those six months, Elizabeth," he told me, "but it sure did work for you."

Yes! My medical scans indicated that my tumors were indeed in a holding pattern. Hallelujah, I could remain treatment free. I'd just have to continue going in for regular checkups. Hiking for six months—following through on the adventure of a lifetime—turned out to be just the therapy my body needed. And, oh, am I grateful for that.

When people find out about my hike they often want to know how somebody goes about walking 2,167 miles in six months, anyway.

"One step at a time," I tell them. "One step at a time. Just remember to put one foot in front of the other."

After all, that's what most everything in this world is all about, isn't it? Onward.

REMEMBERING RICK

Michael Lanza
1998

The worst nightmare of a rock climber happens in this story. In the retelling, syndicated columnist Michael Lanza heals some of the rawest psychic wounds left from this accident on the rocky cliffs of Katahdin in Maine. He also boils down the pain into an elegy of sorts for the carefree climbing life he'd led for years with his friend Rick Baron and the two women who climbed with them. But the random tragedy did not send him fleeing from mountains. As you will see here, his love of the mountains didn't wither. Lanza's attitude had clearly deepened from the more lighthearted cultural observations he had shared in his earlier Appalachia *essay, "Camp 4 Journal,"[40] in which he described the freewheeling routine of rock climbers in the Yosemite Valley's crowded encampment.*

*T*HE WHOLE SCENE SEEMED SURREAL AND CONTRADICTORY. I sat on the side of a cliff on Katahdin, gazing out at a wilderness that, even after several visits, I still looked on with wonder: the mountain's unrestrained sprawl of gray rock, an unbroken forest at its feet, the embracing quiet.

I had arrived the day before with an enthusiasm that had been building for months, since organizing the trip back in early winter. I was to spend a week around Labor Day in Maine's Baxter State Park with friends, rock

---

[40] *Appalachia* 51, no. 2 (1996)

climbing and hiking Katahdin, backpacking north of the mountain. That enthusiasm suddenly seemed as distant as the vague remnants of a dream right after awakening.

Beside me, still tied into his rope, lay the body of my friend Rick Baron. His chest no longer rose and fell with his breathing. The T-shirt I'd draped over his head hid the grisly evidence of an inexplicable tragedy. Three hours earlier, a rock slide had abruptly transformed a casual day of rock climbing into a nightmare. That brief hail of stone passed and carried with it Rick's life—but also, as I was only beginning to comprehend, it had assured powerful changes in my own life.

Trying to compose myself to help evacuate his body, I struggled against a slowly gathering eruption of grief, which in the days to come would prove more overwhelming than anything I had known in my 34 years. Over and over I replayed the morbid mental tape of what had happened; the events simply found no base in reality for me.

I recalled our mundane conversation immediately prior to the slide; then the fusillade of stones and one huge block roaring down toward the small ledge where three of my companions sat while I watched helplessly from above, sickened by the certainty that I was about to see them all killed. Somehow the slide passed right over my girlfriend, Penny, and Rick's girlfriend, Diane, leaving them without a scratch. But I vividly remembered, one rock among that torrent finding Rick's head, tearing his helmet off, flipping him violently over backward. I relived my interminable 150-foot down-climbing to the ledge, then clinging to hope despite Rick's lifeless eyes, Penny and I working to revive him as his pulse faded and grew cold in our hands.

I thought about Rick's parents and brother, whom I've known for more than twenty years, and how this wound would devastate them. I thought about my own family, the pain my nearness to death would cause them, and how this episode would forever color their perception of climbing.

But mostly I wrestled with the incongruity of it all. For me, the mountains had always been places of solace. I spend many days in mountains every year but never tire of putting a pack on and heading out again, no matter how soon after the last trip, no matter where.

Now the mountains had exacted an unreasonable toll: more grief than all the happiness I could expect from a lifetime of climbing. No measure of joy justified Rick's death. I couldn't help but wonder whether any of it was worthwhile.

After the evacuation was completed and a helicopter was on its way to Chimney Pond for Rick's body, I hiked, alone, back to Roaring Brook Campground. Beside the trail, Roaring Brook ran low in this drought year, yet it still possessed the calming power of moving water. I gave it no more than a fleeting, angry glance, however. I only wanted out. As I raced down the trail, alternately sobbing and spitting with rage, the beauty of that place seemed to mock me.

I have known the sadness of someone close dying, even people who died young. But I have never known grief that brought such a debilitating and protracted emotional and physical paralysis. For days, weeks, I couldn't concentrate on work. At times, I felt devoid of the strength to stand up or speak. I began to wonder whether this was what it's like to have a nervous breakdown.

The four of us who survived have second-guessed many of our decisions that Saturday. We switched our intended climbing route that morning—how might things be different if we had stuck with our original plan? I wish I hadn't urged Rick and Diane to join us or made the effort to arrange their visit for them. Although each of us had ample climbing experience, I've

Rick Baron died in a freak accident on this side of Katahdin, above Chimney Pond.

agonized over whether I—the most experienced and the first climber on the cliff that day—should have recognized the rockfall hazard beforehand.

We remind ourselves that this climb was well within our abilities. We had climbed routes more difficult and complicated, from New England to the Tetons to Yosemite Valley. But saying these things offers no consolation. And the grim echo that it could have been any of us does not escape us.

Before the accident we had embraced the illusion that smart climbers survive. We believed tragedy reserves itself for the climbers we see everywhere these days who don't know how to use their gear safely, or those few unfortunates for whom circumstances eclipse ambition on the world's high peaks. It's not an illogical way of thinking—we do it every day in our cars, in spite of all the accidents we pass by. We either rationalize risk and do our best to minimize it, or we hide away in our homes from the world's dangers.

The inexplicable death of someone young makes you contemplate the randomness of fate and discard assumptions about time ahead. And an accident like this one can make you rethink the dynamic relationship between risk and pleasure in the outdoors.

For weeks after the accident, our gear sat, unsorted, in my climbing pack in a closet. I didn't want to look at it, and the others did not ask for their gear. The rope Penny and I climbed on—and which I used to lower the gurney containing Rick's body down the cliff—lay in a tangled clump in a corner of our mudroom. I walked past it every day as I might pass the carcass of an animal on the roadside, glancing at it but unwilling to touch it. That rope, it occurred to me, had become a symbol for climbing and how we had all chosen to disengage from the sport, at least for a while.

Returning to the mountains—hiking, backpacking, skiing—was never in question. A few days after Rick's funeral, the three of us joined his brother and two other friends for a hike of Franconia Ridge. In this respite from overwhelming sadness, I saw one of the deep ironies of mountains: after knowing pain in them, you can turn to them for comfort.

Still, if we were unsure about rock climbing, we knew what others thought. Family, friends, and acquaintances voiced sentiments that ranged from the vocal disapproval of a small minority, to nervous acceptance of it, to outright encouragement for us to return to the cliffs.

My own feelings were less certain. Searching for an answer to that question, I found only consequences of actions. In a conversation about the accident, an acquaintance insisted to me, "You can't stop climbing." She meant well, so I didn't tell her what I thought. But my urge was to say, "Yes, actually, I could stop climbing." I don't climb out of a sense of mission, or some misguided notion that climbing is an innately ennobling activity. Frankly, a friend dying on a rope strikes me as adequate explanation for losing the desire to climb. I would miss it, but it's not the only dimension to my life. Quitting would ease my family's worrying about me, something that pains me. If only a sacrifice as small as retiring my ropes for good would bring Rick back.

Climbing inherently conjures up very powerful emotions; they rise from the universal fear of falling and the addictive high born of controlling that fear, of achieving something you might not have thought possible, whatever your level of ability. For me, the desire to climb and the pleasure it engendered had always overshadowed the fear. Suddenly, I bore a horrible association with climbing. My desire was vanquished; the pleasure had turned bitter, the fear was compounded.

The accident left me with a strong conviction. As Bill, the fifth member of our party on Katahdin, said to me, "I could never take a beginner out climbing without telling them about Rick."

I wanted to write a happy ending to this story. I wanted to say that the death of a good friend on a mountainside has not affected my love for the mountains. But that would be a distortion of the truth.

Now, the memory settles into my everyday thoughts like dust in the cracks between floorboards. A day doesn't pass without something reminding me of Rick or the accident. I read in the morning paper of someone killed in a car or plane crash and, though it strikes me as silly, I have to fight back the tears. I go to see the sort of clichéd gangster movie I've seen many times and find myself so sickened and angered by its graphic scenes of men brutally beaten about the skull—dying, in images too familiar to me, of head injuries—that I swear never again to watch a film that makes cheap entertainment of human tragedy.

Hiking a trail or driving alone, I find myself wracked with guilt over the injustice of Rick's randomly dying while I lived. I feel cheated out of a friendship I'm certain would have flourished through more shared outdoor experiences, and I wonder what our bond might have become at age 50 or 75. Just writing this makes me ache.

I do not expect to look at the mountains the same way again. I expect a heightened caution to pervade my decisions in them. Maybe that's a good thing—we should never allow ourselves to grow complacent about their dangers.

But if my friend Rick Baron's life produced a parable, it is a tale of someone who knew that no cocoon of safety exists to shield us from risk, and that life is sometimes most fully appreciated along its edges. Its moral is that grief can make that pleasure seem trivial and vain; but the same grief can also be seen as a hopeful measure of the deep caring of which we are capable, not something that erases the value of pleasure.

Rick and I shared experiences that enlarge life. We had known each other for many years but grew much closer through climbing together. Viewed from this perspective, the long emotional fall that accompanies losing such a friend becomes understandable—and, if painful, still far preferable to not having known that friendship.

If we shrink from chance out of fear of failure or pain, we reduce life to no more than a biological function. Rick Baron has reminded me that life is more valuable than that. His death has taught me something about life's fragility—and that this fragility may be its most precious quality. Denied assurance of another day, we learn to celebrate the one at hand, in the ways we enjoy most, with the people we care about.

JAPANESE CARIBOU: ALONE IN THE ALASKA RANGE—IN WINTER

Masatoshi Kuriaki

2009

In the winter of 2007, at age 34, Masatoshi Kuriaki climbed 17,400-foot Mount Foraker in the Alaska Range—alone. This was the first winter solo of the mountain and the only success among 21 attempts in that entire year. His climb was the culmination, so far, of his Alaskan mountaineering. Masatoshi fell in love with Alaska on his first visit at age 22, and, with the exception of a post-monsoon visit to Nepal in 1996 (where he sooled four 20,000-foot peaks), all of his overseas mountaineering has been in Alaska. He has been there twelve times and concentrates on solo winter climbing in the Alaska Range—arguably the most severe winter mountaineering environment on earth.

Masatoshi operates entirely alone, climbing in a modified siege style, relaying everything himself. He tried to complete each climb in calendar winter. He made the fourth winter solo ascent of Mount McKinley—Masatoshi prefers the Native American name, Denali—in 1998. Twice before 2007, he ascended Foraker alone, but he reached the summit shortly after the end of winter each time. He has spent a few years' worth of days alone in the winter Alaska mountains since his first winter climb in 1997.

Following his solo winter ascent of Denali in 1998, wishing to learn more about Alaska and its people, he made an 860-mile solo journey across Alaska from the Pacific Ocean to the Arctic Ocean—from Anchorage to Prudhoe Bay—on foot, pulling his gear in a bicycle trailer along the Glenn, Parks, and Dalton highways. For this trip, Masatoshi named himself the Japanese Caribou, recognizing the trip as similar to the wild caribou's migration.

Masatoshi's accomplishments and his modest and friendly demeanor have won him the respect and affection of Denali park rangers and staff, distinguished Alaskan climbers, and ordinary Alaskans alike. When not mountaineering in Alaska, he lives in Fukuoka with his wife and family. He is a popular mountaineering lecturer in Japan, has written a book (in Japanese) about his experiences, and maintains a website, japanescaribou.com, where he posts accounts of his mountaineering exploits, in both English and Japanese, and an album of beautiful photographs of the Alaska Range in winter.

Here, at the request of Appalachia, *Masatoshi Kuriaki describes the technique and philosophy of his unique mountaineering style, which he calls the "sourdough style" in a tribute to his Alaskan pioneer predecessors. He also discusses what motivates him.*

—Jeffery Parrette[41]

Developing My Climbing Style

MY CLIMBING BEGAN BECAUSE I WAS PROFOUNDLY impressed at age fifteen by a movie with a scene of beautiful evening clouds over the Japanese Alps. I joined the high school alpine club, and then the college alpine club. In 1995, at age 22, I began to gather information for my first overseas challenge and, unexpectedly, got more practical information about Alaska than for other countries. For example, I found the book *High Alaska* by Jonathan Waterman (American Alpine Club, 1989) through reference materials in a Japanese version of a booklet, "Mountaineering in Denali National Park and Preserve," and I had climber friends who climbed Denali in 1993. If my first experience overseas had been with Himalayan climbing, and the expedition had touched my heart, perhaps I would now repeatedly return to the Himalaya instead of Alaska.

With a partner on the summit of Denali's West Buttress in July 1995, I dreamily gazed at the 8- and 12-mile distant Hunter and Foraker, rising in

---

[41] Jeffery Parrette is the editor of *Appalachia* journal's Alpina department. Parrette's introduction appeared with the article upon its original publication. His original footnotes are also reprinted here, and are indicated with his name.—Editor

pyramidal form under the midnight sun. After returning home, I learned from *High Alaska* that the three greatest peaks in the Central Alaska Range—Denali, Foraker (Sultana), and Hunter (Begguya)—are a "family", because, in Athabascan, Denali means "high one," Sultana means "wife," and Begguya means "child." This enchanted me a great deal, and I felt the tug of destiny.

While planning my return trip to climb Hunter and Foraker in April through June of 1996, I did not want to go alone. I asked other club members at the college to go with me, but the trip meant taking time off from school, and they could not commit. I did not want to force them and, realizing my passion I decided to go solo. From April to June 1996 I attempted solo climbs of Hunter (via the east ridge) and Foraker (via the southeast ridge). I failed on both because of unstable snow conditions. These failures gave me a keen interest in winter climbs. I shifted forward my climbing seasons step by step: I climbed in the summer of 1995, spring of 1996, then winter of 1997. Despite the severe weather conditions of 50 degrees below zero Fahrenheit, 100-mile-per-hour winds, short daylight hours, and the possibility of one or two weeks of continual storms, I find joy traveling in the cold Alaskan winter, watching the sun rise and set, the moon against the dark night sky, the twinkling stars, and the Northern Lights over the mountains.

I learned from the practices and experience of other Alaskan climbers to develop my style for long, unsupported winter climbs—for example, the first winter ascent of Denali in 1967 (with 40 days' supplies) by Dave Johnston, Art Davidson, and Ray Genet. In 1986, Johnston walked alone into Denali, starting 45 miles away at his cabin at 400 feet above sea level, climbing to 13,200 feet with 50 days' supplies. I also learned from Vernon Tejas, who in 1988 was the first to ascend Denali alone in the winter and survive—and others.

Perhaps my style differs from that of most winter Alaska Range climbers because I have adopted a two-month climbing term. I have done research about the accidents to Naomi Uemura and to Noboru Yamada's team[42] in the winter Alaska Range. I believe that a violent wind was the major fac-

---

[42] The famous climber and explorer Naomi Uemura was the first man to reach the summit of Denali alone in winter on February 12, 1984. He was caught in a severe storm on the descent and his body was never found. The very experienced Noboru Yamada attempted Denali with two companions in February 1989, reaching 17,200 feet on February 20. The group attempted to reach the summit later, probably in a short break in the weather, and were caught in a storm with winds estimated at 200 miles per hour. Their frozen bodies were eventually recovered by a Japanese search party.—Jeffery Parrette

tor. So for more safety in the face of the possibility of one or two weeks of continual storms I must have the ability and enough equipment and supplies to wait for better weather. My style for the long, unsupported winter climb could be called the capsule style or really the sourdough—Alaskan pioneer—style. It falls between the alpine style and the polar expedition method (also called the siege style).

Challenges

There are three major challenges in this sourdough style: the severe cold and the very high wind (shared by all who climb in the winter Alaska Range), the crossing of crevassed glaciers alone (shared by all solo climbers), and the challenge of transporting the heavy gear and supplies required for a two-month, unsupported winter climb. My approach is to use lighter gear and supplies for more safety and more comfortable climbing and camping, and to enjoy being there on each trip. (I take it step by step.)

I like a wise saying of Edward Whymper:

> Climb if you will, but remember that courage and strength are naught without prudence, and that a momentary negligence may destroy the happiness of a lifetime. Do nothing in haste; look well to each step and from the beginning think what may be the end.[43]

Severe Cold and High Wind

My typical winter clothing is two layers of synthetic fiber underwear, tops and bottoms; two down jackets, XL and XXL size; down pants; down mittens with woolen fiber liner gloves and one layer of fiber fleece mittens; three layers of synthetic and woolen fiber socks; and down booties for camping. All this weighs about eight pounds. To keep things dry, I iron my down gear with a hot-water pot, freeze dry clothes in the sun, and use body heat in the 4.5-pound, 58-below-zero range sleeping bag.

---

[43] Masatoshi is quoting from the final words of Whymper's 1871 book *Scrambles Amongst the Alps in the Years 1860–69.* This quotation immediately follows Whymper's description of the disaster on the descent from the 1865 first ascent of the Matterhorn.
—Jeffery Parrette

I use tents and snow caves for shelter, usually camping in a tent on the glaciers and in snow caves on the ridges. I carry a kind of bivouac bag for an entrance sheet to the snow cave opening, a sleeping pad, and a sleeping bag cover. If caught by a sudden storm, I build a small emergency snow cave with a shovel, which I always carry in my emergency gear.

I have had almost no problems with hypothermia or frostbite. Strictly speaking, I had a first-stage frostbite of the tip of my left toe on Foraker in 2007. I think I know why. Preparing the descent from the high camp, I was warming the liner boot with hot water in a plastic bag. A water leak got the tip of the boot liner wet. I should have stayed at High Camp that day, even though fuel and food were on the decrease.

Crossing Crevassed Glaciers

I use a pair of fourteen-foot aluminum poles (weighing seventeen pounds) clipped into my climbing harness for my glacier travel. I use the poles crossed or parallel depending on glacier conditions. They have not always worked well. I am still thinking about longer, lightweight, and strong poles for more safety. I know that Naomi Uemura used bamboo poles and that some Alaskan soloists have used poles or a ladder for their glacier travel. For my safety, I sometimes use additional systems for crossing badly crevassed areas; ropes, anchors, and ascenders in a self-belay. I test the edges of hidden crevasses with a probe.

My biggest problem with a crevasse happened on the descent from the 1999 Foraker attempt. I was traveling without the crevasse poles and one of my skis, all previously swept away by an avalanche. I broke the snow bridge myself while probing with a ski pole. I got a bit lucky, landing on my pack at the bottom of the crevasse about fifty feet down. I had the feeling, "Oh my God!" and thought at first that my thigh was broken (actually it was only bruised). I taped it up, but I was still at the bottom of the crevasse with my sled and 120 pounds of gear. I used ice screws and webbing to climb out of the crevasse with about half the gear, which took an hour. This was one time that I could not carry everything to satisfy Leave No Trace principles.

Gear, Supplies, and Carrying Them Up the Mountain

Allowing for 70 days on the mountain (60 days plus an extra ten days if caught by storms), I start at the base camp with 330 pounds of gear and

Masatoshi Kuriaki took this image of himself during one of his solo expeditions to the Alaska Range in winter.

supplies not counting the heavy winter clothing that I wear and my climbing boots and overboots (a total of about fifteen pounds). Of course, food is a big item. I normally weigh 130 pounds. My specially effective climbing diet (on a calories per pound basis) averages 4,500 calories in about 2.3 pounds of food per day. I mostly carry freeze-dried and dried food available in normal supermarkets. The food is principally rice, noodles, or pasta with meats, fish, and vegetables. I also take butter, dry soup, energy bars, sports drink powder, jerky, and other lightweight treats to vary the diet.

On the winter climbs, all of my water comes from the melting snow using white gas stoves. I need nearly 1.6 gallons of water a day. The total weight of white gas for 70 days is 60 pounds in nine one-gallon cans. When waiting out a storm in a snow cave, my intake of food and water drops by about 20 percent, but I do not count this in planning, so my total allowance for food and white gas to melt snow is a little more than three pounds a day, 220 pounds for 70 days.

Gear includes the tent and a spare, skis to cross glaciers and a spare pair, and light for the long period of darkness. A small, lightweight LED head-lamp (2.5 ounces including a lithium battery) works well in the winter Alaska Range, although it is dangerous to move on the crevasse fields in the dark even with a high efficiency headlamp. I use the headlamp for camping, cooking, reading, and writing. I use small candles for room light in the snow cave. The candles also add a little bit of warmth. I carry a spare headlamp and an extra 0.6 ounce lithium battery per week. I use a hand-held aviation radio to communicate with bush pilots and carry a portable emergency locator transmitter (ELT) to the lower and middle camps. And, of course, I carry the usual climbing gear and ropes.

I store approximately 40 pounds of gear and ten to fourteen days' worth of food and white gas at the base camp and about twenty pounds of supplies at camp 1; the weight of the caches is less at camp 2 and higher. For example, on my last trip, the southwest ridge of Foraker in 2007, for the ascent I made six relays between Base Camp (6,450 feet) and Camp 1 (8,100 feet), five relays from Camp 1 to Camp 2 (9,780 feet), four relays from Camp 2 to Camp 3 (11,300 feet), and two relays from Camp 3 to Camp 4 (which I called High Camp, 13,400 feet). On the descent, I made a total of seven relays. I spent eleven days in camps waiting for high winds to drop. I put in nine fixed-line pitches for relaying at steep sections (60–80 degrees on snow or ice) on the ridge, using two 60-meter [196-foot] dynamic ropes.

I find my route of ascent by map and compass and mark the way by red-flagged wands. Again taking my 2007 Foraker climb as an example, if I could climb summer alpine-style without all the relaying of gear, it would be a vertical gain of 10,900 feet (from the base of the ridge to the summit) and about five climbing miles one-way. The total vertical distance in my sourdough style was about 38,700 feet and fifteen climbing miles, more or less. Thus, my total vertical gain was 3.55 times longer than for the alpine style. Relaying plays a less important part on the descent, but because I follow the Leave No Trace ethic, I must strip the mountain of all my gear and garbage and carry it down.

Leave No Trace

I hope that I will leave my field for mountaineering, Denali Park and Preserve, as the pristine natural environment that it is. If I keep everything picked up and leave no trace, I will leave it great for the next person, who might be on the next trip. The weight involved can sometimes be considerable. I follow the National Park Service guidelines for disposing of human waste. That is, to use biodegradable bags and crevasse all human waste in winter climbs. If no crevasses are available, I carry the bag until I find a suitable crevasse. In January through March 2002, I attempted Foraker by the southeast ridge but achieved only 8,540 feet at Camp 2. There were no suitable crevasse fields. I spent 56 days on the mountain and carried down all of my garbage (ten pounds) and human waste (28 pounds). According to the National Park Service, this is the longest reported trip into the Alaska Range in which all human waste was packed out. The weight of garbage to be carried out has been getting less lately.

Waiting Out a Storm

When I am waiting out a storm in a snow cave, I must spend four to six hours per day cooking food, melting snow, shoveling out the entrance and probing the roof of the cave to form a chimney for ventilation. Particularly when I use the stove in a snow cave, I must check for oxygen depletion—which could cause the stove to produce carbon monoxide—by trying a gas lighter at the cave roof. Irregular flame or failure to light indicates a lack of oxygen. I pass the rest of the time with haiku, thought, sleep, reading a paperback book, and listening to my tiny radio (I could hear 51 radio stations at the High Camp on Foraker in 2007). Even if the storm goes on for days, I have no other choice. If I go out before the weather has improved, I risk death, being blown away, being flash-frozen, or losing my route. I always base my actions on getting back on my own, not on getting forward. The decision to go back or to stay in place is much more difficult and important than the decision to keep going up the mountain. Perhaps I have learned patience from my wife, and the severe environment of the winter Alaska Range and the lifestyle of Alaskan people who are friends of mind have taught me to "go with the flow."

The Family

I have had the ambition to climb "the Family" of Denali, Foraker, and Hunter solo in calendar winter since 1998. This ambition is my alpinism. I believe that if you ask 100 different climbers they will have 100 different personal alpinisms, personal climbing goals. This is mine.

In 1997, I failed in my first winter solo attempt on Denali, "the high one," but in 1998, I reached the top on March 8—alone, the fourth man to do so and the third to descend safely. I tried Foraker, "the wife," alone in the winters of 1999, 2001, and 2002—either reaching the top after the end of calendar winter or failing to reach the summit. In winter 2007, I became the first man to climb Foraker alone in calendar winter.

I attempted Hunter, "the child," in the winters of 2003, 2004, and 2005. I never reached the summit—my greatest height was about 9,000 feet. I plan to return to "my child" in the winter of 2009, and I hope to have the good fortune to complete my quest.[44]

---

[44] Kuriaki has continued his attempts on Hunter. When we went to press with this book, he was returning from his eighth solo trip on that mountain. Despite two summit attempts, he was turned around by icy conditions and high winds.—Editor

ICE AND ASHES:
A YOUNG SLED DRIVER TAKES ON A MORAL IMPERATIVE

Blair Braverman

2011

This story arrived "over the transom," as editors used to say, in 2010, after the stories had been picked for the next issue. Blair Braverman was then a student at Bates College in Maine. Soon after we decided to fit this piece into the journal, Braverman began graduate work at the University of Iowa, where in 2014 she earned her master of fine arts degree from the nonfiction program. She now lives in northern Wisconsin. Her work has appeared in Orion, The Best Women's Travel Writing, Waging Nonviolence, *and elsewhere. She races sled dogs. Her first book about the Norwegian Arctic is expected to be published in 2015 by Ecco/HarperCollins.*

THE SUMMER I TURNED EIGHTEEN, I LIVED ON A GLACIER. It was a broad, slanted finger of snow, a home I shared with 200 huskies and a dozen people. From above, the camp was smudges on the white, pressed against the base of a black mountain: canvas tents, ordered doghouses, trails that stretched into the fields beyond. I was working as a dogsled guide in Alaska, leading tourists through a wilderness nicknamed "the moon": Juneau's ice field, which covers an area the size of Connecticut with ice up to a mile deep. Each morning I would pull myself from my sleeping bag, slip on my raincoat and boots, and step from my tent into the pale light of the northern summer, the glacier luminous beneath me in the rising sun.

After chores—feeding the dogs, cleaning trails—a distant purr would echo over the mountains, and a line of helicopters would grow in the sky until they were right above us, the air throbbing with the beat of their rotors. I waited by the sled while the birds landed, the handlebar jerking under my hand as the dogs jumped in excitement, and for one hour I would escort passengers on a tour, skimming across the ice field in gentle silence. Over the summer, I gave almost 700 tours, so that the season's runs melt into a single memory; of these, one alone stands out.

On that tour, I had a single passenger, an older woman with a southern accent and a creased face. As we left the kennel she told me her story: how she and her husband had always longed to visit Alaska's glaciers; how they had finally made it up, last year, only to be forced down in a sudden storm; how he had fallen ill—cancer—and passed away that winter. I listened, kicking snow with one foot as we slid along the trail.

"I'm sorry to hear that," I said.

She smiled. "Don't be. I'm glad to be here today."

Two miles in, I paused to give my dogs a rest, a chance to bite snow and cool down. When the sled stopped, the woman pulled something from the folds of her coat: a sandwich bag filled with earthy powder. She pressed it to her heart for a moment, then leaned over the side of the sled basket, scooping at the snow with her free hand. Hurriedly, she emptied the ashes into the hole, patted a handful of snow on top, and returned both hands to her lap like an attentive child. Her papery skin stretched tight across the knuckles of her clasped hands.

"Are the dogs ready yet?" she asked. "Let's keep going."

For the rest of the run, neither of us spoke. I doubt I could have. When the tour ended, I touched the woman's hand, then watched as she climbed into a helicopter and lifted into the sky. I wondered if I wasn't the only one watching her go.

Throughout the evening, I was troubled. I realized that the next morning, when we cleaned the trails, the ashes would be collected with the other dirt, then packed into a barrel and flown to the Juneau sewage treatment center. This, after the woman had come such a long way. I went to my boss and told him of a plan I was forming, but he only shook his head. "This isn't your

The mile-thick glacier near Juneau, Alaska—home to sled dogs, a few people, and occasional tourists—became something more for a pensive tourist who rode with Blair Braverman in her sled.

responsibility," he said. "It would be much too dangerous. One dead body is enough for today—we don't want you hurt, too."

That night as I tried to sleep, the day's events whirled and eddied in my thoughts. He's right, I told myself. It's not my responsibility. But the longer I lay awake, the more I was certain of what had to be done. And so in the young hours of the morning, deeply uneasy, I stepped from my tent.

We kept three snowmobiles in camp and I started the smallest, wincing as its engine cut the night's silence. After a few minutes' driving, I found the ashes, a gray-brown patch that seemed to pulse against the white trail. What had seemed so simple in the tent—to dig up the ashes and move them—seemed, suddenly, very difficult. And no one was allowed beyond the outermost path, which was where I planned to go; it was the only place where the ashes wouldn't be disturbed.

I closed my eyes and took a slow breath, feeling my lungs expand and cool with the night air, and as I exhaled, I reached down and dug my naked hands into the snow. The ashes were buried more deeply than I had expected, and I pulled them up in handfuls, gathering a dirty mound. My fingers stiffened with the cold and I breathed on them, trying to ignore the dark crescents jammed under my nails, trying to forget that they were part of a human body.

When I could move my hands again I began packing the pile together, carefully pressing the growing snowball into a perfect sphere, stained gray like frozen smoke. Then, lifting the ball to my chest, I stepped off the trail. Out here, crevasses waited, blue and veiled under the surface, plunging like cracks to the center of the earth, and I walked cautiously, expecting to fall through with every step. When the burn of the snow in my palms forced me to stop, I looked back. I could no longer see the trail or the snowmobile; only my footprints broke the billowing expanse, a dotted line shrinking into the horizon.

I crouched down and placed the ball on the snow, wondering, reflecting. A man lives his life, falls in love and marries, and dies, only to be carried by a stranger across a barren glacier in the Alaskan wilderness. His ashes would melt into the ice with the next rainfall, then creep downhill for a decade or more before calving into the sea in great white boulders. It struck me that I had never before felt this alone, here on an empty ice field under dark moun-

Blair Braverman with ice-encrusted face.

tains, with the burden of leaving a man behind. It was as if I were packing part of myself into the snowball, as if I would emerge less than whole.

It seemed disrespectful not to provide some sort of ceremony, and I felt a sudden anger at the man's wife, his nameless loved ones, for leaving me—a stranger!—with the tremendous responsibility of the final goodbye. What could I possibly say that could do justice to an entire life lived, that could show compassion, kindness, understanding? I knew nothing, nothing at all about the man in my hands. I bit my lip until it ached, trying to think clearly. And then, cautiously, I began to speak.

"I never met you," I said, "but I think you were probably a good man. You were probably just like any of us, good sometimes but not always, just trying to be a better person. I bet you did things you were proud of and things you regretted, and you learned from your mistakes. There are people today whose lives are better because you were part of them. If you have kids, I'm sure they love you very much. I know your wife does." I swallowed. "She's in Juneau right now, thinking you're where she left you, and maybe that brings her peace."

I stood long in the clouded moonlight, thinking. I thought about what makes us human, our shared truths, our deepest hopes, the peace that comes from understanding that we are not alone. In the distance, a soft howl rose and fell, trailing off so gradually that I couldn't tell when it ended, and after a moment I turned. As I walked toward the trail I felt the weight of tears on my cheeks, but when I reached up to brush them away, it was only snowflakes.

FRANKENSTEIN CLIFF AND THE BLACK DOG: A FRIGHTENING HIKE BEATS BACK A MAN'S SENSE OF GLOOM

Christopher Johnson

2013

This story takes us onto a popular and sometimes precarious cliffside route near Crawford Notch in New Hampshire's White Mountains. Many people of all abilities attempt to climb Frankenstein Cliff each year, but for history writer and editor Christopher Johnson, the trek brought him face-to-face with a dark time in his life, which he called (after Winston Churchill) his black dog. The 1980 adventure, told many years later, shows how even the lower mountains can push a man's personal limits. This essay marked a movement for Johnson into more personal essays for the journal, for which he has written many fine history articles. Johnson and his wife, Barbara, now live in Evanston, Illinois. Matthew, their son who took the lead in this story, lives with his family in Denver, where he handles marketing for a tree service. Johnson, a former teacher and book editor, now writes full-time. His books include This Grand and Magnificent Place *(University of New Hampshire Press, 2006) and (with David Govatski)* Forests for the People *(Island Press, 2013).*

*A*S I GAZED FOR THE FIRST TIME UPON CRAWFORD NOTCH, a mountain pass of sublime beauty that winds through the heart of New

Hampshire's White Mountains, I remember thinking, "This vista should be touching me more." It was July 1986, and my wife, Barbara, and two children, Matthew and Emily, and I had driven north from Boston to visit Crawford Notch, the Old Man of the Mountain, and the countless other extraordinary sights that our friends and neighbors had urged upon us flatlanders, who had only recently relocated from the Midwest to New England.

From our campsite in North Conway, which was crammed full of retail outlets and shopping malls, we had driven north on US 302, which rolls through the middle of the notch. As we entered the southern fringes of the valley, the mountains rose to the east and west like exuberant eruptions of wild earth. On the west side of the notch, endless forests carpeted the dizzying heights of Mounts Willey, Field, Willard, and Avalon. The east side of the valley, bounded by Mounts Crawford, Jackson, and Pierce, presented a stark contrast because those mountains were fairly denuded of trees but were dotted with enormous boulders, as if a god had tossed granite eggs from heaven that had broken into a thousand pieces. Along the base of the eastern wall, the Saco River tumbled over and around myriad clots of granite, and as the water leaped, it caught snatches of sun and gleamed like diamonds. As I slowly drove north, the road curved through mountains that overlapped one another like a series of green velvet curtains. We turned around and immediately drove back through the valley, and as we reached the southern edge of the notch, I pulled over onto the shoulder of US 302, and we all got out of the car and drank in the sight. Directly facing us was a massive headwall which, I would later learn from my newly purchased *White Mountain Guide*, was named Frankenstein Cliff.

I ordinarily was moved and would even be overwhelmed by such extraordinary vistas, but now, as we stood and gazed upon the elegant curvatures of the mountains and the towering cliff that faced us, I felt completely removed from the sight. The others were oohing and ahhing, and I just felt like shrugging my shoulders. The fact is that at the age of 39, I was in the throes of depression—what Winston Churchill referred to so vividly and appropriately as his black dog. I was just beginning to realize that something was not quite right, that my reaction as I stared at Crawford Notch was different from what it would have been in the past. Now I felt flat, I felt nothing. I put the best face I could on the black dog, and as we stood there on the shoulder of US 302 and the others exclaimed upon the splendor of the mountainscape, I joined in. But my heart was unmoved, stone-cold. It was as if all feeling had been squeezed out of me.

We returned to our campsite and cooked our dinner of franks and beans, and as the others chattered about the day, I sat silently in the tent. Matthew particularly had been impressed by the cliff, and he looked it up in the *White Mountain Guide*. An avid consumer of information even at age twelve, he told us that the headwall was Frankenstein Cliff and that it had been named after Godfrey Frankenstein, a German artist who had moved with his family to America in 1831 and had embarked upon a successful career painting landscapes of Niagara Falls, the White Mountains, and other sites in the East's unspoiled wilderness of the nineteenth century. Then he said, "I want to climb it."

"The cliff itself?"

"No, Dad," he said, with the impatience of a preadolescent teaching something to his father. "There's a trail that goes alongside the cliff."

I looked at the guide, and the path started just off US 302, slithered west to Arethusa Falls (at 176 feet, the highest single waterfall in New Hampshire), ascended behind the west ridge of the cliff, reached the overlook that we had seen from the road, and descended along the east ridge of the cliff, completing a loop back at US 302. Barbara and I decided that the climb would probably be a little much for Emily, who was only nine, but Barbara and Emily would drop Matthew and me off at the trailhead and go canoeing down the Saco River. It was all settled.

We turned off the battery-powered camp light and settled into our sleeping bags for the evening. I lay there in the dark. I should have been thrilled at the prospects of a climb like the one that Matthew and I had planned . . . but I felt nothing. As I listened to the cackle of the crickets, I felt an overwhelming sense of helplessness, which had been gathering for at least a year. I didn't know what it was. I came from a family that was reticent in expressing emotions, and I had inherited (or learned) that trait. It was difficult for me to reach out to others, and as I had grown toward middle age, I felt it harder than ever to reveal myself. In my work at a publishing house in Boston, I had mastered all the social graces and was known and valued as a good team player. But in spite of all that, I felt isolated. And I had the inchoate but persistent sense that some spirit was straining to burst forth from inside me. Haunted by these thoughts, I slowly drifted into a restless sleep.

All four of us awoke early, cooked eggs and bacon over our propane stove, stuffed our backpacks with lunches, and filled our canteens to the brim. I tried to rally myself. Barbara and Emily dropped Matthew and me off at the trailhead. We agreed that they would pick us up in four hours, which according to the *White Mountain Guide* would leave plenty of time for the hike. We started west on the trail toward Arethusa Falls. I was groggy from my poor night's sleep and felt the dour mood on me like a boulder that had been added to my backpack. I kept my eyes on the ground, not taking note of the forest that surrounded us. I must have been moving slowly because Matthew, full of energy, ran ahead of me.

Barbara and I had known since he was a young child that we had a character on our hands. He was energetic, outgoing, could be aggressive, could be given to moods. He adored baseball and loved U2 and the anthemic themes that rang from the band members' soaring blends of voice and guitar. And he was intense. If he made an out with men on base, he felt deeply that he had let the team down. Now, on the trail to Arethusa Falls, he ran ahead of me and then waited restlessly for me. Meanwhile, I felt as if I were wading through sludge. "Dad," he finally said, "you're walking like an old man." From beneath my gray cloud, I smiled. I liked it when he kidded me.

In an hour, we reached the falls and watched the resplendent water dance over rocks and tumble down to form an iridescent emerald pool. We both took off our hiking boots and woolen socks and lowered our feet into the pool. The water was frigid at first, but after a couple of minutes I felt the waters caressing my feet, soothing them sensuously, as if a masseuse were working out the kinks. Cooling our feet in the water felt like a ritual, an ablution. We gobbled our peanut butter and jelly sandwiches and drank the cool water from our canteens. I looked closely at Matthew's face. It was almond shaped, and he had uncommonly long eyelashes for a boy. His lips were full, and he had Barbara's nut-brown skin. I was struck by how much he resembled her family.

He waded into the green water of the pool, joining two other boys about his age who had also ventured into the water. The water reached almost to the bottom of his shorts, and he started splashing water with two other boys. I envied them the carefree ways of youth—and my mood darkened further. Where, I wondered, had my sense of isolation come from? I didn't know. I couldn't point to any event that had awakened the black dog. Instead, over the past year, I had slipped bit by bit into a gray dullness. Externally, every-

Christopher Johnson broke through a deep depression the day his son dragged him to see this view on Frankenstein Cliff, above Crawford Notch in New Hampshire's White Mountains.

thing seemed fine. My career was going reasonably well, the children were getting good grades, we had a nice home, etc., etc.

Yet at the edges of my life, I felt a fear that I could not define or get a handle on. It was like a fear of exposure. I somehow felt ashamed of revealing myself. As a kid, I'd had this goofy sense of humor and had been quick to laugh, but that had disappeared. Barbara and I had had our children early, and I had felt deeply the weight of responsibility. We'd had no money, and I had poured myself into work. I'd grown quieter. I would sit in my living room chair and watch sports for hours on end. Barbara was the one who had said we should head north for vacation, that I needed a break from the grind. She asked me what was the matter, and I just shrugged her off. "Nothing. Nothing at all." I knew she was worried about me.

I was lost in these thoughts when Matthew came up and shook my shoulder and disturbed the cloud that hovered over me. "Let's get going, Dad!" he said. "We still have a long way to go to the top of the cliff."

I forced a smile. It was as if he were taking charge of the hike. "Lead on, buddy," I said. We rolled up our lunch bags, deposited them in our backpacks, dried off our feet, put our socks and boots back on, and resumed our climb. The trail led northeast and ascended more seriously, more assiduously, entering a series of switchbacks that followed the west fringe of the cliff toward the granite shelf overlooking Crawford Notch. As the trail grew steeper, I began to lag, stopping more frequently to catch my breath. Matthew ran ahead of me, and we started playing a sort of game of tag in which he would forge ahead for a couple hundred yards and then sit on his haunches and wait for me. I approached him, and he barked, "Get the lead out, Johnson!" It was a perfect imitation of his Babe Ruth League coach that summer. "When the going gets tough, the tough get going," he bellowed, mouthing one of the endless stream of clichés that had rolled off the coach's tongue. I grinned, and Matthew laughed. I loved the way his face lit up and his eyes sparkled when he laughed, and I thought to myself that he was a pretty neat kid. For the first time in a long time, I felt completely immersed in the moment.

After a little more than a half-mile of strenuous climbing, we reached the granite overlook, the crown of Frankenstein Cliff. I bent down and planted my hands on my knees to catch my breath. Then I looked out at the scene that unfolded before us. The mountains, the land, the forest emanated a sublime energy that, despite my mood, I could feel. Matthew and I sat down side by side on a boulder about ten feet from the edge of the cliff and looked south at the thousands of trees that populated the valley like soldiers. The sky that day was as crystal blue as ice and glowed with a clarity that made visible the mountains of the Sandwich Range far to the south. I wondered what caves and waterfalls were hidden in the corners and folds of this extraordinary landscape. I loved the way in which the forest-encrusted walls of the notch swept down to meet at the bottom of the valley. A hawk circled in the air perhaps one hundred feet in front of us, riding the invisible currents of air and then plunging like a dive-bomber toward the floor of the valley. The sight made my heart palpitate. I noticed an ancient pine to the left of the boulder we were sitting on. It was gnarled and bent by the winds that had swept through the White Mountains for eons. The hold of that pine on its granite perch seemed tenuous, but still it clung to its tiny patch of earth. Across the valley, shadows were beginning to crawl across the tops of the mountains, as if an invisible hand were pouring ink over the landscape.

We left the boulder and, on our bellies, crept close to the edge of the cliff and stared down. It was a sheer drop, and I felt a strange mixture of vertigo and euphoria. I looked at Matthew, who was transfixed by the sight. The black dog had momentarily disappeared, and I felt a reconnection between Matthew and me. "How does it make you feel?" I asked him.

"Like that hawk," he said.

Perfect answer. Free and soaring and unconnected to the ground. Silence surrounded us. "Close your eyes," I said. He listened to me. He shut his eyes, and his face was that of an angel. "What do you hear?" I asked.

He didn't say anything right away. Then he said, "I hear the wind."

"What does it sound like?"

"Like a breath whistling through the trees."

"What else do you hear?"

"I hear birds calling. And I hear kind of a chirrup."

"That's a squirrel. What else do you hear?"

He listened. "I hear the trees."

"What do they sound like?"

"They sound like they're talking."

"What are they saying?"

"It's like they're murmuring, but I can't tell what they're saying."

"Nobody can," I said. "They speak, but we can no longer understand what they're saying."

Still he had his eyes closed. He was so at peace. He opened his eyes and said, "That was cool."

We got up and dusted ourselves off. I put my hand on his shoulder and gave it a bit of a squeeze. He looked at me. "Are you all right, Dad?"

I smiled back and said, "I'm fine."

The trail continued on, and we started to descend, heading east and south of the cliff. As we resumed hiking, I felt that nature and this vigorous, unique son of mine were beginning to crack something open for me. I was feeling more connected. The descent was perilously steep in parts, and my boots slid on the gravel-laden trail, which had narrowed like the neck of a duck. Matthew, however, was as sure-footed as a mountain goat and had no trouble descending the narrow path. I looked down, and the valley loomed below us. If we had slipped, we would definitely have rolled down that mountain until a convenient tree or boulder stopped us. We rounded a corner, and the trail had a gap of about six feet. "Crap!" I seethed.

I tried venturing across the gap, hoping that I could get enough of a foothold to balance my way across the cleft to the continuation of the trail. I put my right foot forward, but it slipped. "Damn!" I raged. "I don't want to turn around and hike all the way back."

I looked at Matthew, and he had a defiant gleam in his eye. "I'm not hiking all the way back," he said. He took three steps back.

"What are you going to do?"

"I'm going to jump across," he said, with the uninhibited confidence of youth.

"Wait!" I said. I had a short length of rope in my backpack, and I tied it around his waist. That way, if he lost his balance, I could at least haul him back to the spot where we were stranded. He took a deep breath and ran toward the gap. I thought he would jump, but he didn't. Instead, he veered above the gap, up the side of the valley, letting centrifugal force carry him above the break in the trail. In two breathtaking seconds, he was back on the trail and on the other side of the gap, and he was grinning madly with delight.

"Now, Dad, you gotta do it." I was extremely leery, but I knew I had to do it. He unhitched the rope around his waist and threw the end to me across the gap. "Tie it around yourself, Dad," he said, taking charge. That little piece of rope gave new meaning to the word pathetic. It didn't look as if it could hold a flea. "Back up and get a running start," he ordered. He was the father talking to me, the son. I retreated, took a deep breath, and scampered up the side of the valley, above the gap. But I was losing momentum, feeling myself start to plunge down the side of the valley. "Grab me, Dad!" he yelled. He reached out his hand, and in the crazy way in which senses sharpen during a crisis, I noticed how almond-tan his hand was. He clasped me and yanked me onto the narrow ledge that he was standing on. I stood next to him, breathing hard and trembling. And then we both laughed. We laughed uproariously. I put my arms around him and wrapped him in a tight bear hug.

With the exhilaration born of danger, we careered our way forward, descending the trail that wound downward. It remained gravelly, and we grabbed the branches and trunks of trees lining the trail to steady ourselves. At times, we skidded down on the gravel as if we were on skateboards. As we slipped down the side of the mountain, Matthew at times extended his hand to steady me. I didn't really need it, but I deeply appreciated his trying to help his old man.

By now it was late afternoon, and as the sun declined, the giant balsams and spruces cast enormous shadows across the trail, and the air around us was absolutely silent and still. I felt, for once, firmly planted in the here and now. I had stopped thinking about the future, about where I ought to be in my career and my life, about my disappointed expectations. I was acutely aware that not a leaf stirred as the shadows of dusk crept across the mountain. We neared the bottom, and the trail took us beneath Frankenstein Trestle. I felt a renewed interest in what we were encountering on this hike, and Matthew and I stopped to study this striking bridge, which supported railroad tracks with steel girders angling out like spiderwebs and extending to the floor of the canyon, where the girders were secured by concrete abutments. Later I read that the trestle had been built in 1892—an astonishing relic of the Industrial Revolution that is still used to transport tourists north from North Conway for the 30-mile sojourn through Crawford Notch.

After another half a mile, we had finished our hike. We returned to the parking lot. For three hours, we had been in a separate world, and together we had negotiated our way down that gravelly path from Frankenstein Cliff. We were closer to each other than we had been in a very long time. I tried to say what I was feeling to him, but I could not. The emotion was there, but the words wouldn't come. Barbara and Emily soon arrived, and as we wended our way south on US 302 back to North Conway, Matthew fell asleep. His long lashes blanketed those brown eyes, just as they had when he had been a baby. He slept the deep sleep of an angel, and Barbara kept the car steady through the gathering dusk as we wound our way out of the mountains.

This day had redeemed me. The black dog had temporarily disappeared, and I felt alive from having shared the experience of a beautiful place with a son who was brimming with the possibilities of life. The green pool at Arethusa Falls, the pine clinging to the granite cliff, the hawk riding the up-currents, the soaring mountainscape—all had touched a place in me that had been buried for too long. To be sure, my black dog would reappear, and ultimately I would require the skills and insight of a professional to make the beast disappear with only an occasional growl. But on that day spent with Matthew, I had learned that the black dog was malleable. I had learned that it could be tamed.

FURTHER READING

This very selective list represents the avalanche of climbing and adventure books and periodicals that remain in print—including some favorites of the editor—proving yet again the allure of the writing of those who venture to the edges of their capabilities.

Periodicals

Alpinist

A fine large-format magazine founded in 2002 in Jackson, Wyoming, this quarterly is now published by Height of Land Publications out of Jeffersonville, Vermont.

American Alpine Journal

Established in 1929, this is the official publication of the American Alpine Club. Before 1929, *Appalachia* served in that capacity for the AAC.

Appalachia

The source publication for this book, founded in 1876. A complete index through 2012 is available online and in print.

Canadian Alpine Journal

The annual journal of the Alpine Club of Canada has been in print since 1907.

Books

Fletcher, Colin. *The Man Who Walked Through Time*. New York: Vintage, 1989.

> Some believe Fletcher reignited the 1970s backpacking movement with this 1968 classic. His narrative of a 200-mile hike through the Grand Canyon lays out the psychological journey of any backcountry immersion.

Howe, Nicholas. *Not Without Peril*. Boston: Appalachian Mountain Club Books, 2009.

> First published in 2000, this book collects stories of accidents in the Presidential Range in the White Mountains of New Hampshire. The tenth anniversary edition features a foreword by hiker, climber, AMC leader, and former *Appalachia* Accidents editor Mohammed Ellozy.

Herzog, Maurice. *Annapurna*. Guilford, Connecticut: Lyons Press, 1997.

> Originally published in 1952, Herzog's story of the French team that summited Annapurna in 1950 remains controversial and intriguing.

Krakauer, Jon. *Into Thin Air*. New York: Anchor, 1999.

> Krakauer is that rare combination of climber and crack reporter. His narrative of the deaths on Mount Everest in 1996 explores the dangers of blind ambition.

Roberts, David. *Deborah: A Wilderness Narrative*. Seattle: The Mountaineers, 1991.

Roberts, David. *On the Ridge Between Life and Death: A Climbing Life Reexamined*. New York: Simon and Schuster, Reprint edition, 2006.

Roberts, David, *The Mountain of My Fear*. Seattle: The Mountaineers, 1991.

Ridgeway, Rick. *The Last Step*. Seattle: The Mountaineers, 1999.
 The latest edition of this 1979 narrative captures especially well the tensions that strained friendships and marriages during the first American ascent of K2.

Simpson, Joe. *Touching the Void*. New York: HarperPerennial, Revised edition, 2004.

Underhill, Miriam. *Give Me the Hills*. New York: Dodd, Mead, 1971.
 A memoir of a groundbreaking climbing life by a former editor of *Appalachia*.

Waterman, Guy, and Waterman, Laura. *Forest and Crag: A History of Hiking, Trail Blazing, and Adventure in the Northeast Mountains*. Boston: Appalachian Mountain Club Books, 2003; Green Mountain Club e-book edition, 2011.
 The Watermans, both accomplished climbers, spent a decade researching this comprehensive history of exploration of the mountains of the American Northeast.

Waterman, Jonathan. *Surviving Denali: A Study of Accidents on Mount McKinley*. Golden, Colorado: American Alpine Club Press, 1991.

ACKNOWLEDGMENTS AND CREDITS

The Appalachian Mountain Club extends its thanks to the staff, volunteers, and community members who aided in the making of this book. Special thanks go to AMC Archivist Becky Fullerton and AMC Books intern Casey Curran. Additional thanks for contributions to specific articles may be found below. Credits are given by article, then page number.

Foreword

Image: xiii, courtesy Appalachian Mountain Club Library & Archives

Introduction

Images: xvii and xviii, courtesy Appalachian Mountain Club Library & Archives

A Climb through Tuckerman Ravine

Image: 3, courtesy Appalachian Mountain Club Library & Archives

A Climb on Mount Adams in Winter

Image: 11, courtesy Appalachian Mountain Club Library & Archives

The First Ascent of a Glacier in Colorado

Image: 22, courtesy Appalachian Mountain Club Library & Archives

The Casualty on Mount Lefroy

Images: 27 and 30, courtesy Appalachian Mountain Club Library & Archives

A Winter Ascent through the Great Gulf (Mount Washington)

Images: 36 and 38, courtesy Appalachian Mountain Club Library & Archives

Snowbound in September

Image: 45, courtesy Appalachian Mountain Club Library & Archives

Over Ice and Snow on the Equator: An Ascent of Kilimanjaro

Image: 60, © istock/Jon_Johnnidis

The Attack on Crillon

Image: 73, © Bradford Washburn, courtesy DecaneasArchive.com
Special thanks to Betsy Washburn Cabot.

The Bietschhorn in a Thunderstorm

Image: 87, courtesy Appalachian Mountain Club Library & Archives.

The K2 Expedition of 1939

Images: 93 and 97, courtesy Appalachian Mountain Club Library & Archives, Christine L. Reid Collection

On Arizona's San Francisco Peaks

Image: 109, courtesy Northern Arizona University, Cline Library, Gale Burak Collection, NAU. PH.2006.11.15.18

Manless Ascent of Devils Tower

Image: 117, courtesy Jan Conn.
Special thanks to Daryl Stisser of Sylvan Rocks Climbing School.

Free Fall on the Dent Blanche

Image: 124, courtesy Charles Levin and the Levin Family

Climbing the Four Thousand Footers in Winter

Image: 132, courtesy Appalachian Mountain Club Library & Archives

Lost on Mount Crescent
> Images: 146 and 148, courtesy Appalachian Mountain Club Library & Archives

Avalanche!
> Text © Robert D. Hall Jr.
> Image: 153, © Robert D. Hall Jr.
> Special thanks to Mr. Hall for his donation of the image in this book to the Appalachian Mountain Club Library & Archives.

Thelay Sagar: Paradise and Disillusionment
> Text © Jonathan Waterman
> Image: 164, © Jonathan Waterman

Like Hay in the Wind: Tragedy on Mount Washington
> Text © Douglass Teschner, et al.
> Images: 176, courtesy Appalachian Mountain Club Library & Archives; 180, © Tom Murri; 191, courtesy Appalachian Mountain Club Library & Archives

Paine and Suffering in Patagonia
> Text © Todd Swain
> Image: 196, © Todd Swain

A Leg Up: One Person's Accident
> Text © Doug Mayer
> Image: 201, © Jonathan Kannair, "Doug Mayer, on the Quay, Mount Adams, 1993"

Trailing Dreams: Magic Along the Appalachian Trail
> Text © Elizabeth McGowan
> Image: 212, © Elizabeth McGowan

Remembering Rick
> Text © Michael Lanza
> Image: 217, © Wikimedia Commons/Hadrianopolis

Japanese Caribou: Alone in the Alaska Range—In Winter
    Text © Masatoshi Kuriaki
    Image: 226, Masatoshi Kuriaki

Ice and Ashes: A Young Sled Driver Takes on a Moral Imperative
    Text © Blair Braverman
    Images: 233 and 234, © Blair Braverman

Frankenstein Cliff and the Black Dog: A Frightening Hike Beats Back a Man's Sense of Gloom
    Text © Christopher Johnson
    Image: 214, © Jerry and Marcy Monkman, EcoPhotography.com

INDEX

ABOUT THE EDITOR

Christine Woodside has been the editor of *Appalachia* journal since fall 2005. The defining ordeal that qualified her for this work was probably her thru-hike of the Appalachian Trail in a single season. She has climbed all of the 4,000-footers of the White Mountains, many of them multiple times, and she continues to backpack and run on trails so that she can keep up with the journal's contributors. Most of her writing is about people's clashes with the environment. She was born in Philadelphia and grew up in New Jersey but has lived most of her adult life in the lower Connecticut River Valley. She welcomes contact from writers and readers. Visit her at chriswoodside.com.

ABOUT *APPALACHIA*

Since 1876, the Appalachian Mountain Club's journal *Appalachia* has published stories about mountain adventures, ecology, and conservation. Its dedicated committee members analyze accidents in the Northeastern mountains, publish poems by established and new writers, recount international mountaineering expeditions, review outdoor-related books, and much more. Preview the current issue, order back issues, browse the archives, and review submission guidelines at outdoors.org/appalachia.

APPALACHIAN MOUNTAIN CLUB

At AMC, connecting you to the freedom and exhilaration of the outdoors is our calling. We help people of all ages and abilities to explore and develop a deep appreciation of the natural world.

AMC helps you get outdoors on your own, with family and friends, and through activities close to home and beyond. With chapters from Maine to Washington, D.C., including groups in Boston, New York City, and Philadelphia, you can enjoy activities like hiking, paddling, cycling, and skiing, and learn new outdoor skills. We offer advice, guidebooks, maps, and unique lodges and huts to inspire your next outing. You will also have the opportunity to support conservation advocacy and research, youth programming, and caring for 1,800 miles of trails.

We invite you to join us in the outdoors.

YOUR CONNECTION TO THE OUTDOORS

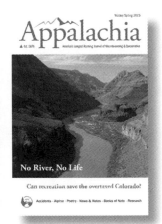
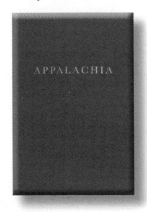